Every Inch of the Way

My Bike Ride around the World

By Tom Bruce

First published in the UK by Tom Bruce in May 2013

3rd Edition published in May 2014

"*Every Inch of the Way is a great page turning adventure, and is as close as you can get to adventure without actually saddling up and pedalling yourself into the unknown. It takes real magic to turn a great adventure into a great book. For one thing, most people can't relate to the mind-set of the long distance cyclist, and I found myself laughing along to Tom's thoughts and observations, wondering if they were in - jokes, shared by those who had seen the world at the speed of a bike, for example his relationship with Serbia's stray dogs! But his anecdotes have a great balance of the cultures and places, as opposed to just inward reflections, so I am sure would be enjoyed by anyone with an interest in travel and human experience. A lovely story, written from the heart.*"

Mark Beaumont (around the world record breaking cyclist and adventurer)

"*A challenge that tested Tom to his limit, but in return gave him more than he could ever have imagined.*"

Bear Grylls

Firstly to Laura, thanks for waiting,

Secondly to Mum and Dad, thanks for supporting me,

Thirdly to Phil and Harry, thanks for coming along for the ride,

Finally to my new friends on the road, I couldn't have done it without you.

Contents

Motivation

I have written this book to share my story. It's not a book full of descriptions about beautiful places, and it doesn't have any clever metaphors; it's just my story. It tells the story of an ordinary person spending nine months experiencing the world from the saddle of a bike.

When I contacted magazines and newspapers to try to raise awareness for the charity I chose to support through undertaking my ride, SOS Children's Villages, I received the following response:

"Did you have any accidents or try to break any records, what's your unique selling point?"

There is no unique selling point; the only way that my adventure was unique is that I pedalled around the world in just nine and a half months, and had time to see the places I travelled through. I wrote this book to show you that anybody can achieve something extraordinary in a relatively short period of time. I didn't want to try to break a record or attempt to gain fame by doing something crazy, like riding in fancy dress or towing a piano. It was simply to travel. The only rule I set myself was that I had to get around the world using only a bike, every inch of the way.

Why? *Why not?*

So here's my story, it will be great to have you along for the ride…

A bit about me

I have always liked adventure. Apparently I've always loved cycling too. At the age of three, I ditched the stabilisers on my first bike. It wasn't planned. My poor mother stood watching me whizz downhill in a London park as the stabilisers snapped and fell off. I didn't fall off though and wasn't scared in the slightest. I was a natural and went onto spend a great deal of my childhood riding bikes. One birthday, I was given a cheap full suspension bike from Halfords and was hooked. I used to ride it over jumps in the local quarry, which it wasn't good enough to do, and as a result it kept breaking. Not having any money, I learned how to fix it myself, and by the time I was fifteen had learned much about bike maintenance.

My first bike tour was the coast to coast across England, completed with my friend Jonny after our GCSEs. I tackled a few other short trips in Scotland at university in Edinburgh, but my first and only major bike tour before this adventure was a trans-Alpine off-road ride from Munich to Lake Garda and back. On this trip, I fell in love with bike touring. The freedom and ease of day-to-day life opened my eyes to a new way to travel. The whole ride only cost around two hundred pounds for two weeks on the road. I was living in Munich at the time so I cycled from my front door to Italy. The seed was sewn on that ride, although I didn't know it at the time.

I started dreaming about a much larger bike tour. At first I planned a tour of Europe, and then my imagination got carried away. I thought about cycling into Asia; *so what about across Asia? Is that even possible?* After some research I decided that it was. Other people had done it. If I could cross Europe and Asia, then what the hell. *Why not cycle the world?*

In 2009, I made the decision to attempt a cycle ride around the world, and by 2010 the idea had consumed me. I finished university, got a job to save some money, and planned to begin the tour in early 2011. My boss almost managed to persuade me to postpone the ride with an attractive contract offer. I decided to concentrate on my career for a year, then to begin the ride in 2012.

One day I suddenly changed my mind. The company that I was working for was going downhill and I couldn't wait any longer. I quit my job, and planned to set off and to cycle around the world with a start date just six weeks away in mid-March. As a result, I wouldn't say my preparation was brilliant. I didn't have long to buy kit, plan my route and arrange a visa for Azerbaijan, the first country that I'd need one for. My kit was a mismatch between high quality, lightweight equipment and cheap, functional, heavy stuff. I hadn't really decided what I was taking until I packed my panniers the day before I set off. My kit didn't really fit in properly and there was no room to pack food anywhere. I left with a plastic bag of food liberated from my parents' fridge tied onto my rear rack. My sleeping bag arrived the day before I left and my passport was still in the Azerbaijan embassy in London. I hoped to be able to pick it up on the way.

Training didn't really happen. With very little time I didn't get a chance to test all my kit before leaving. Everything was last minute. My mum often calls me '*lastminute.tom*', and I guess she has a point! I did manage to commute to work on my bike and was riding around two hundred miles a week for the last few weeks before setting off. This wasn't quite the eighty-five miles per day that I would be aiming for, but was probably a help.

One thing that I was confident about was the bike, which I had custom built during the last few months before my start date. It was brilliant; I couldn't have put together a better machine. It was built to last; weight wasn't a consideration, with heavy duty mountain bike wheels, cranks, handlebars and a steel jump bike fork. I was kindly given a steel bike frame by Sanderson Cycles and was provided with a fantastic fourteen-speed internally geared hub from Rohloff. Other stuff donated to my cause included: an Olympus camera, a ferry crossing from Sea France, and an ultrasonic dog deterrent from a company called "Dazer".

Here's what I wrote in my diary five days before setting off:

"Only five days to go and the last minute nerves have set in. It's only recently dawned on me what I'm trying to do. It's very easy to say I'm going to cycle around the world, planning is fun and you get to buy a load of gadgets and gear. Actually doing it is going to be another story. Leaving is going to be the hardest bit, then it should be amazing, although I'm worried that I'll spend most of the next year absolutely shattered!"

Preparations finished with a small leaving do with family and friends. It was lovely to see everyone and great that they came to see me off. I didn't enjoy it though; nervous and dreading saying goodbye to Laura, my girlfriend of six years, not knowing when I would see her again, although hoping that she would be able to come out to see me at some point over the next couple of months, whilst I was still fairly close to home. Laura had been a wonderful partner up to that point and we both planned to be together for many years to come. I was under no illusions that this would be easy for us, but Laura had supported me in the decision to undertake this adventure. I can't thank her enough for letting me go, and for waiting for me to return.

My bags were packed, and everything was ready (or as ready as it ever would be). I had a few days in the UK before I reached France so this gave me some time to make sure I had all I would need. The final diary entry before I left was: "*I'm terrified and I feel like I'm on a runaway train. I've set myself a massive target and have told everyone I know what I'm going to do. Everyone said "You'll be great, you'll definitely make it". People have sponsored my charity, SOS Children's Villages. I couldn't back out even if I wanted to. All I can say to anyone planning something like this is be one hundred percent sure you want to do it! There's no way out now…"*

PART 1: EUROPE

From my home in Peckforton, Cheshire, to Istanbul, Turkey

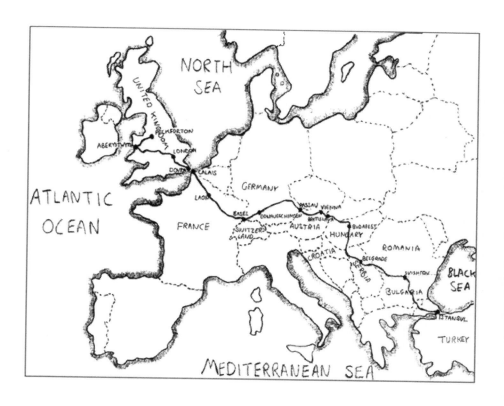

1. Leaving home for a new life

All our dreams can come true, if we have the courage to pursue them
- Walt Disney

I set off. It came around so quickly. One day I was making final preparations, the next I was saying goodbye to family, friends and Laura. Leaving was horrible, but I hoped that everything would become easier after taking that first plunge. The hardest part was saying goodbye to Laura. I cycled out of my front garden, watched by my family and the friends who'd come to my leaving party, then the two miles along the road to Laura's house. I felt numb, dreading what I had to do. After a very difficult and sad conversation and a final hug, I got on my bike and rode off without looking back. Ideally, she would come and visit me somewhere on the route, but we had nothing planned because my schedule was too unpredictable. It was horrible to part in that way. I told myself it would be fine once I got going, but felt the tears welling up behind my sunglasses.

Around the corner, my Dad was waiting (on his bike) to help ease me through the first twenty miles. We chatted about what lay ahead for me, cycling at a slow pace. I felt much more cheerful as we arrived at a local pub, where we had a meal with my Mum, Nan, Uncle Mike and Cousin Phil. I don't remember what I ate. Unusually for me my thoughts weren't on food. After a final farewell I set off alone. Once on my bike, I realised I had no idea which way to go because my map wasn't detailed enough to include the small village that we were in. I wished that I'd had a few more weeks to prepare. If so, maybe I wouldn't be attempting to cross Europe using a cheap, large-scale road atlas. If I could find my way to the River Danube, it should be fairly straightforward, I thought. *The second biggest river in Europe should be pretty easy to follow!* I waited to wave my family off at the junction by the pub. Too proud to let them know that I was already lost, I gave them a false thumbs up and they drove off. I suddenly felt very alone.

With no useful map, I resorted to asking directions for the first of many times over the next nine and a half months; *"Which way to Wrexham?"*

The passer-by indicated the way by pointing down the country road. I was off again, turning my pedals until dusk. *The first few hundred rotations of millions.* As it got dark, I stopped to look for my first campsite, uneasy and unsure of where to pitch my tent. I had wild-camped before, but usually in mountains or forests, far away from populated areas. Twenty miles from my home, the choice was between a farmer's field and an enclosed area around a shed which had *'High Voltage'* written on it. The field was waterlogged and the shed with the electric equipment in it was buzzing loudly. It took me forty-five minutes to decide that neither would do. I couldn't spend as long as this to find a place to sleep every night. It was almost pitch black, so I decided to cycle down a track off the main road. It looked like it led to some large houses a mile or so away, but there wouldn't be much traffic. A small sheltered wood looked suitable, so I pushed my bike into it, unloaded my panniers and erected my tent for the first time on a flat patch of land. It was easy to pitch and I didn't have to cook after eating in the pub, so went straight to bed. My sleeping bag was very warm, even though it was freezing outside, which was encouraging. I fell asleep with all sorts of thoughts going through my head; feeling lonely, upset and terrified, but also excited and sure that I'd made the right decision in leaving my job and the people I love to pursue my dream.

My first morning on the road was mercifully sunny. I woke up in the little copse and looked at my surroundings. My tent was pitched in a dip next to a small pond and was surrounded by trees, almost invisible to the rest of the world. I had picked a dark green tent so it would be well camouflaged. Beyond the copse were fields covered in a morning frost that the low sun had not yet melted. It was a beautiful day and I thought that it had been a good choice for my first campsite of the trip.

That morning, the riding was lovely as I progressed through North Wales, crossing the River Dee at Bangor-Upon-Dee on a single track stone bridge built in 1660 next to the village church, built three hundred years earlier. There used to be a monastery here, until the 1200 monks were slaughtered in the Battle of Chester. Shortly after crossing the bridge, I got my first puncture. My cost-saving measures included not replacing my cheap, half worn out tyres before leaving. I hoped that they would last a while before being replaced with some tougher ones for Asia further down the road. Because of the way my bike was set up, a rear puncture was a time-consuming problem. I had to unload the panniers from my rear rack in order to take the wheel off because the axle held on the rack. The frame I'd been given didn't have pannier rack attachments, so I'd had to improvise. Once the puncture had been tracked down and fixed, the rack had to be re-attached, panniers clipped on, tent balanced on top and the bungee re-attached to hold it on.

I followed a canal towpath through the same Welsh towns that I'd visited the previous year on a canal boat holiday. Bizarrely, there was a field full of bison, which would have looked more at home on a North American plain than a wet field in North Wales. I passed the spectacular Pontcysyllte Aqueduct, which carries the Llangollen Canal over the River Dee valley on huge arches. It is still the longest and highest aqueduct in Britain despite being over two hundred years old and is a world heritage site. I was absolutely starving by lunchtime and bought half a pannier full of high calorie food from a small shop in Llangollen. It's a charming town, with the white water of the River Dee rushing under an ancient stone bridge in the centre. Next to the bridge is a railway station, where a steam engine sat belching smoke into the country air. Sitting on a bench, admiring my surroundings and planning my afternoon route, I decided to cycle on the main road to Bala and then take a smaller back road through the hills rather than the busy A494. I had time to spare since and didn't have to be in London for over a week.

Climbing and descending through rolling Welsh hills, I thought about what lay ahead. All my gear appeared to be working and I seemed to be adapting well to my new life. Sunlight filtered through the clouds in bright rays, lighting up different sections of the landscape and projecting cloud outlines onto the hillside. Patches of green grass, brown heather and grey rock outcrops painted a perfect picture as I reached the top of a pass. I whizzed down the other side on my first long descent, and was very pleased with the Shimano SLX hydraulic disc brakes that I had decided to fit. Difficult to maintain maybe, but I could always count on reliable stopping power. I had packed some spare parts and thought that I would be able to work out how to fix them, should it become necessary.

I was keen to meet local people everywhere I went, including somewhere so close to home. In a sparsely populated area like this, people are different village-to-village. In a local pub, over a pint of bitter, I chatted to some people who asked where I was going. I said Aberystwyth, which was half a day's ride away. It was easier; I didn't want to steal the limelight by telling them I was planning to cycle around the world. I wanted to hear their stories and they were impressed enough that I was cycling to Aberystwyth anyway. Beer tastes so much better after a day of exercise.

The next day I reached the coast at Aberystwyth. I bought some fishing equipment; a line, a weight and some hooks, planning to improvise a homemade rod; imagining catching fat salmon and cooking them over a campfire by the side of the Danube in one of my many long evenings off.

During the first couple of days of my trip, I had been heading west to the coast. This was the only time I cycled west on the whole tour. As I was planning to cycle all the way around the world, it seemed that I should start from the coast. I took the necessary photographs at Aberystwyth, with the sea in the background, and felt a bit stupid for bothering with the diversion. Something told me it was the right thing to do on this trip and if there was somewhere I wanted to go, I would go there. These next nine months would give me the greatest freedom of my life, and I didn't want to be tied down by sticking rigidly to any plans. My trip would have one purpose, to make it around the world using a bike and only a bike. Other than that there were no rules.

I cycled away from the coast, heading east for the first time. If I kept the sun on my right and cycled for nine months, I might just end up on the other side of the ocean that I'd just left. I examined my useless map, kept in a see-through plastic case attached to my handlebar bag. There seemed to be a shortcut through the mountains. Eager to experience more beautiful Welsh scenery, I decided to take the small road that was marked as a country lane on the map. Unfortunately, the tarmac ran out after about five miles and it turned into an old drover's road that degraded into a bumpy track into a wood. My map had failed me again. I knocked on the house at the end of the tarmac and the guy who lived there said the track would take me to where I wanted to go:

"Turn left at the first junction, right at the second, and it's about ten miles to the main road."

It was an okay track, gravelly, but quite easy to cycle along. In the world of mountain biking, we would call a track like this 'double-track', because there are two parallel tracks separated by a grassy centre. This is as opposed to 'single-track', which I don't think I need to define for you! This particular track was a good test of my fully laden bike's off-road capabilities, without being too challenging. The seemingly easy

4

directions weren't that simple however. I ended up having to guess which way to go on three or four forest track junctions following a southwest (ish) bearing on my compass. I had no idea if I was going the right way, but I had to keep going or turn back for at least a forty-mile detour. *This would not be the first time someone's directions would let me down...*

Forcing myself to continue over the stony surface I rounded a corner and didn't regret my decision to come this way. The scenery was spectacular; rolling hills with mountains in the distance and green fields below the thickly covered pine-forested slopes. I looked around and thought how beautiful the UK was; not enough people appreciate the British countryside. How would this compare with the rest of the world?

I climbed and climbed; a total of 1,000 metres as the road undulated up and down and up and down. I had fitted a pretty fancy speedometer, which could count total height gain as well as altitude and temperature, so be prepared to be bored by statistics throughout this book! I had to rely on my sense of direction here, making educated guesses at each junction, looking at the landscape and guessing where the track probably went. It didn't let me down. After a brilliant twenty-mile off-road ride ending in a great descent, I reached tarmac again. The road greeted me with a twenty-five percent incline followed by a steep descent to another pub. I thought that I could get used to finishing each day like this. I watched my football team, Man United, beat Marseille in the Champions League. It was a bit odd, returning to the normality and simplicity of watching a game of football in this situation. I switched off any worries about leaving home and the unknown that lay ahead, thoroughly enjoying the match with the other Man United fans that are almost always present in pubs. During the game, I spoke to a guy about my adventure, telling him my full plans this time. He was really interested and said he'd love to do a bike tour. I told him he should, since almost anybody can go cycle touring; all you need is a bike and the courage to leave your home. Even a weekend trip on a bike with a tent enables you forget everything else and escape the hectic schedule of the real world. I cycled out of the small village in the dark and pitched the tent at the first opportunity; in a farmer's field by a small river. I was already much more confident about wild camping, and made the decision to camp there as soon as I saw it.

Dreary weather arrived on the fourth day and my tiredness brought back worries. *'Why are you doing this?' 'What if you fail?' 'Is this really what you want?'* Keeping mentally strong is vital when riding a bike all day. Without any motivation, I only managed sixty miles along boring main roads. To make things worse, my chain snapped. It was easy to fix, but I wished I'd fitted a new one before I left, not knowing how long this one would last and resolving to buy another at the first opportunity. I gave up on the day's ride at five o'clock, with a determination to make up for it the next day. I scoffed about 2,000 calories in preparation and got an early night. My mood didn't improve when I checked emails on my phone and found out that my Iranian visa had been refused. I arranged that the 'agency', which was attempting to secure it (be aware of commercial agencies offering visa administration services), would put in an appeal on my behalf. Much more annoying though was the Azerbaijan embassy's email. It read:

"We are pleased to inform you that your visa is available for collection from tomorrow, Thursday 18th March. Please note that we are closed for our national holiday from 21st - 25th March."

Argghhhh! I was in Wales and had to get to London by the morning after next. That was a very long way to cycle in one day; impossible on a heavily loaded mountain bike? The Azerbaijan embassy hadn't informed me of this when I'd gone there the weekend before last. They had said I could pick it up the following week. Now I was stuck, and would have to delay crossing the channel by a week until after the Azerbaijan national holiday. Thanks for the notice; thrown in at the deep end!

I woke up before sunrise feeling refreshed, having decided to get as close to London as possible to keep the inevitable train fare as low as I could. Based on my previous daily mileages, it seemed impossible that I would make the 130 miles to my Nan's house in Letchworth, forty miles north of London. Deciding to give it a go, I headed in that direction on main roads. I planned that if I could make it, I would stay in Letchworth and get a train into London in the morning. With a target, motivation, and a lot of energy, I powered through the miles, completing fifty by lunchtime. I ate lunch in around ten minutes before getting back on the bike. After a gruelling afternoon, I arrived at Nan's at half ten absolutely shattered. I don't remember much of the day except that I went through Stratford-Upon-Avon, which is where Shakespeare comes from, and that Milton Keynes has a lot of roundabouts. I was in the zone and put my head down to get the miles done. It was good to know that I was capable of a big day when it was needed. Maybe I have another gear when absolutely necessary. This proved to be very important later on in the trip. The 133-mile day turned out to be the longest day of the whole bike ride.

A bath and some fantastic food cooked by my French Nan helped my recovery that evening. Nan needed to go to London too, to get a visa for Kenya, where my Aunt Lucy and Uncle Jonathan live. I left my bike in Letchworth the next morning and we took a train into London very early. The Azerbaijan embassy was shambolic. There was a huge queue outside the door when I arrived, half an hour before the embassy opened. I was told that visa collections weren't possible until after eleven o'clock and to come back then. I considered going to the nearby Iranian embassy to see if I could get a visa there, but reasoned that it would be impossible to do so in less than a week at best, so would be a waste of time. I would think about the Iranian visa further down the road. Instead I found an upmarket Kensington café and bought an espresso (the cheapest thing on the menu). The previous morning I had woken in a damp tent in Wales but was now in one of the wealthiest postcodes in the country!

Returning to the embassy at half past ten, I waited in line for over two hours, and picked up my visa fifteen minutes before the embassy shut for the week, at one in the afternoon. One more person was allowed in after me, and then they turned everyone else away! People protested angrily. With a completely emotionless face, the ambassador helpfully advised them to come back a week on Monday. This was a bit too close for comfort but I was delighted when I got back on the train to Letchworth. I had crossed my first bureaucratic hurdle and the first country that I would need a visa for was now open to me. My mammoth previous day's ride had been successful and I could chill out. I didn't have to be in Dover until the 22nd of March for my ferry crossing, so planned to have the weekend off in London.

That evening I ditched some non-essential kit: a spare torch, second thermals, most of my underwear, some T-shirts and my backup phone. I had over-packed and now was carrying the bare minimum, except for five books, which I considered necessities. I had a lot of spare parts too, which were vital for the more isolated parts of the trip that lay ahead. My gear was roughly sorted into four panniers and a handlebar bag. One rear pannier contained my stove, pans, and everything else I needed for camping, along with all my maps wrapped in a carrier bag. The other had spare parts, tools and electrical items, like chargers and spare batteries. The rear panniers were not completely waterproof so I packed everything that needed to stay dry in plastic bags. My front panniers were around the same size as the rear ones, but were waterproof. I kept my clothes and sleeping bag in the left front pannier. In the right were books and essential things that I needed throughout the day; my raincoat, high visibility waistcoat, puncture repair stuff, my diary, bike lock and food. In the handlebar bag, that unclips easily to take into shops, were my camera, maps, phone, wallet and all other valuables. My tent and sleeping mat were wrapped in a waterproof survival bag and attached to my rear rack by bungees. Two water bottles and a petrol bottle were on holders on my frame. I kept a solar powered light, solar charger, speedometer and GPS on my handlebars.

The rest of my journey through England was much more chilled out, and a very important few days which allowed me to adjust to my new life. It started with a forty-mile morning ride from Letchworth to London, where I went to my Aunt Claire and Uncle Dave's for lunch. I cycled in past the new Olympic stadium, which stood imperiously over the canal towpath that led me into the city, ready for the London Olympics in 2012. I'd be home by then. It seemed too far away to imagine. In the afternoon, I watched England lose to Ireland in the Six Nations with some mates from Edinburgh, where I went to University; a terrible performance. The evening turned into a big night out in Shoreditch, which wasn't great physical preparation for the bike ride to Dover, but it was a good way of saying goodbye! I was hung-over and very tired the next day when I returned to Claire and Dave's house. We had a huge Sunday roast for Dave's birthday, then I left London on Monday morning.

Crossing the Thames proved to be more of a challenge than I was expecting. The lift in the Greenwich foot tunnel was broken and I wasn't going to carry my fully loaded bike down and up hundreds of steps. I thought that London had loads of bridges over the Thames, but apparently none of them are anywhere near Greenwich, so backtracking was necessary to take a ferry over the river. I'd spoken to my Mum at the weekend and she'd reminded me to buy some decent rear lights. I did so at a bike shop south of the river, whose staff advised me of a good route out of London, avoiding busy roads. Eventually I left the urban sprawl of London and entered the peaceful countryside of Kent.

Kent is a beautiful county. I love the old buildings with their steep tiled roofs, set in dreamy villages separated by fields and woodland. After seventy-five very pleasant and easy miles in one and a half days, I reached Dover and the ferry in good time. It was fun cycling through the car check-in booths and explaining to a large and boisterous lady that what I was planning didn't mean I was completely crazy (although I wasn't too sure myself). I had to go through security and my heart sank when the operator pointed at the bag scanning machine, thinking that I'd have to unload my panniers, and put them through. In the end, the operator just put my Camelbak (water carrying backpack) through and asked me to empty my pockets. I was asked a couple of security questions:

"Do you have any knives?". "No."

 "Do you have any explosives?". "No."

I rode off remembering my Swiss army knife and bottle of petrol for my stove in my luggage. I waited in car lane 122 and was eventually called onto the ferry. I managed to ride up the very steep ramp onto the ferry (every inch of the way and all that) and locked up the bike, christened 'Sandy' after the frame manufacturer Sanderson, who had given it to me for free. I left my bike and kit in the car parking area and walked up onto the deck to wave goodbye to the White Cliffs of Dover. I wouldn't be seeing England again for a long time. It was an emotional moment, but really exciting. *This is where the adventure really starts,* I thought. As I imagined what was ahead of me the hairs on my neck stood up in anticipation. I had been planning and dreaming about this for so long, and now I was living my dream.

2. The adventure begins

Life is like riding a bicycle. To keep your balance you must keep moving
- Albert Einstein

Looking back on the trip, this was one of the most dramatic border crossings. France was instantly completely different. Most land borders merge together with language, traditions and culture changing gradually between the countries on either side. The narrow channel separating England from France eliminates this, which made for an instant contrast when I got out of the ferry and into Calais. I'd cycled from Cheshire to France!

Calais isn't just a huge port, as I'd originally thought; it has a lovely town centre full of local shops. I stocked up on French cakes in a patisserie and *'chipolatas maison'* in a boucherie, then cycled fifty miles until dusk and found my first (distinctly average) wild-campsite on mainland Europe. I pitched my tent just off the side of a main road, hidden from view by a steep verge, and then planned my route for the next few days as I sat on the grassy bank. My tactic was to look ahead to a point in the trip not too far away. The distance of 14,000 miles to the East Coast of America seemed impossible. It would be very difficult to persuade my legs to keep moving if the journey wasn't broken down into smaller distances and I decided never to plan much more than a week or two into the future. This broke down the unimaginable distance into manageable chunks. My next target was the source of the Danube in Germany, Donaueschingen.

In the morning, my kit was damp with condensation, so I hung my sleeping bag and tent over the fence on the roadside to dry while I had breakfast. Trying to keep kit dry became one of my daily challenges and whenever I stopped for a break, I would hang my sleeping bag somewhere to battle the dampness, which came with its own unique and rather unpleasant smell! Rolling hills kept the riding interesting that day; I much preferred to be going up and down than along a flat road. My route through the rolling countryside took me through the ancient town of Saint-Omer, with its cobbled streets and picturesque main square. My phone beeped; it was a text from Dad, who would be driving past me in a few hours, on the way to work in Geneva. I sped to our arranged meeting point in Thérouanne, where Dad treated me to a coffee and cake in a pretty café while we discussed the trip so far. We arranged to cycle together again in a few days' time and closer to Geneva. I finished my *'pain au chocolat'*, and Dad left. Alone again, I continued until having a break in Arras, a gorgeous, typically French town. It has an historic central square, the *'Grande Place'*, surrounded by restored seventeenth century mansions and the town's cathedral. Parisian style tall and thin terraced houses with shutters and balconies peer down on a rabbit warren of alleys and winding streets surrounding the square. Arras was almost completely destroyed during World War One, but was rebuilt in the same style and has retained its character. I relaxed on the square, eating a snack and absorbed the atmosphere.

Unfortunately, I was struggling on the mileage front and only managing around seventy miles a day. This needed to improve if I was going to reach Azerbaijan in time for my visa start date. Eighty-five miles was my daily target in Europe and I wanted to reach Asia as quickly as possible. This was partly because I wanted to spend more time exploring there, but mainly because Europe is much more expensive. In a bid to speed things up, I cycled along a dual carriageway for an hour or so. At a roundabout, gendarmes (French police) were waiting for me. I had seen a police car on the other carriageway and they'd obviously informed some colleagues that I was coming. They made it clear that I wasn't allowed on the road (which I already knew due to the large and obvious no cycling signs) but feigned ignorance: "Je suis Anglais, je ne comprends pas".

Once they realised that I was English, they were very helpful in directing me down country lanes to my next destination. I was grateful that they'd let me off when I played the naïve young Englishman card, one which I would use many more times during my trip.

Northwest France has fairly dull scenery, which didn't change much. The area that I cycled through was mainly agricultural. There were large flat areas of farmland, broken up by quaint but often derelict villages, with the odd ancient and beautiful town centre to brighten things up. The roads were great, and it was easy to find back roads to ride along, with superb quality surfaces and almost no traffic. Each night I camped in woods off the side of roads, keeping out of the way. Unfortunately, people didn't seem to understand what I was doing or why and just thought of me as a bit odd, so I didn't get much help in finding places to sleep. My campsite cuisine became more adventurous, with improvised, one-pot cooking. Menu options included sausage ratatouille and cassoulet, both accompanied by small bottles of red wine. Aldi turned out to be a lifesaver in Europe, since there were stores all the way through the continent that were all very cheap. Whenever I came across one, I stopped to stock up on high-calorie snacks. The delicious cakes at the patisseries also made a great way of boosting the calorie count to the 6,000 calories per day needed to stay healthy. I was living cheaply, but wasn't prepared to eat badly for nine months. A little bit of thought and effort livened up camp cooking enormously. I decided to have a go at cooking at least one dish from each country, using my camping stove.

The highlight of this area of France was definitely the larger towns and cities. Although near impossible to navigate due to the maze of pretty, cobbled streets, the town centres are always beautiful and often accompanied by giant, ornately decorated cathedrals. My favourite was the monster gothic cathedral in Laon, perched on the hill in the ancient old town. It reminded me of Notre-Dame in Paris. I could see it looming ahead of me for miles, perched on its hilltop, growing slowly bigger with every pedal stroke. I climbed up the steep winding streets, getting lost in the maze that is the old town. On reaching the cathedral, the enormity of its inside was what really struck me. It seemed a mile up to the ornate ceiling and another mile to the gold decorated altar. After looking around the cathedral for as long as I was happy to leave my gear unattended outside, I cycled down the other side of the hill and found a quiet place to pitch my tent, in woodland at the top of a steep bank on the roadside. I checked the spoke tensions in my back wheel and was annoyed to find some very loose ones. I tightened the loose spokes and tried to balance the slightly buckled wheel.

I woke early the next day, wanting to get my mileage up. It was misty, and the roads deserted as I passed through '*Parc naturel régional de la Montagne de Reims*'. It was eerily quiet at seven in the morning, but it was beautiful cycling territory as I traversed the wooded hillsides. On a long hill climb my hamstrings starting feeling very tight and, despite stretching them out a number of times, I couldn't stop the pain. I was worried about injuring myself and lowered my saddle to change my leg position. It seemed to work. On the other side of the climb was the region of Champagne, where I passed painlessly through many famous vineyards in beautiful sunshine, including Moet and Chandon.

I reached Châlons-en-Champagne, a city with another spectacular cathedral that I remembered from an earlier visit with my family. All of the drainpipes had large gargoyles sticking out of the walls where they meet the gutters. I would be camping again that night, so continued on my lonely way. Canal towpaths took me out of the city and easy flat miles passed under my wheels. The weather was sunny and hot as I cycled along the canal. Because of the heat, I was forced to strip down to only lycra shorts for the first time. This was sacrilege, coming from a mountain bike background, where baggy shorts are a must. It would take me many more days of cycling in lycra to become comfortable wearing it, but I found it to be a fantastic material to wear, when riding day after day in hot climates.

At the next village, a lady in a patisserie must have thought I looked hungry because she gave me a free pain au chocolat after I bought my first one. The manager in a tourist information office in Joinville then let me use his computer while pouring me cup after cup of coffee, which he wouldn't let me pay for. The French were showing their friendly hospitality and I really appreciated it. When you are travelling alone, help from a stranger means so much. I left the tourist information office and climbed 600 metres on a caffeine high, before descending into a dense woodland. At a pretty clearing by a stream I pitched my tent in the pouring rain, which had started in the early evening. My speedo read ninety-six miles for that day. It increased my confidence in my ambitious distance targets. Feeling pleased with myself, I had a wash in the stream and cooked four '*steak haché*' on my stove.

Heading towards Switzerland, the scenery improved as I climbed through a forest park; however at the top of a pass I had run out of water. Perfectly on cue, a passing car pulled over and the driver gave me a bottle through the window before speeding off. While celebrating this act of kindness and quenching a thirst, my back tyre blew up for some reason. I had to take everything off the rear rack, remove the wheel and put a new inner tube in. This area was very remote and I went for hours without seeing a house. The hills and forests were pretty, but the grey weather didn't do much for my spirits.

At the end of that day, I descended to a small village and tried to talk with some locals in a café. I bought an espresso, but failed on the communication front; feeling that I was viewed more as a spectacle rather than a person. They weren't prepared to make the effort to bridge our language barrier. I asked for somewhere to pitch my tent, using a mixture of terrible French and sign language, but they said they didn't know of anywhere. I left and found a wood down the road, feeling glum. To make things worse, it rained again that evening.

I had an unintentionally early start the next day, wondered why it was so dark when I surfaced but found out later that the clocks had changed and the time on my phone had automatically updated itself. My alarm had gone off at the same time so I'd lost an hour's sleep. Time didn't mean much to me anymore, as I had no schedule and no commitments. I woke up around sunrise, ate when I was hungry, cycled all day and stopped at sunset but still set alarms if I was camping somewhere where I might be found. In such cases I rose before sunrise, so as not to get into trouble for wild camping, which is generally not allowed in the UK (minus Scotland) and France, as well as many other countries. It is, however, tolerated by most people, provided no trace is left and you pack up and leave at dawn.

I had managed to keep track of time enough to know that today was the day that Dad and I planned to meet up again, something I had been looking forward to greatly. He called as I left the campsite and we arranged to meet on the road; planning to park in the town of Lure and cycle towards me until our paths crossed, then turn around and we'd cycle together back to Lure. As I cycled onto a main road, a van pulled over. The side came down and there were rows of cakes and bread. *A mobile Boulangerie!* The van had stopped especially for me; there was no one else around. I was delighted and still hungry, so I had a second breakfast of a croissant and orange juice, while explaining to the lady who served me that I was heading to Switzerland on my bike, a distance that seemed impossible to her.

It was Sunday and nothing was open. Nobody was about and the villages where like a series of abandoned ghost towns. I continued on my way until St-Loup, where I saw a familiar face cycling down the other side of the road towards me. Dad joined me for an afternoon of cycling though pine forests, to the town of Lure, where we destroyed an all-you-can-eat (a lot more than usual) Chinese buffet in the only open hotel in the town. It was great to see him again, but when he left this time I knew that I wouldn't see anyone I knew for months, so it was another very difficult farewell. I stayed in the hotel that night and washed my clothes in the bathroom sink, before heading to bed, exhausted. My body was feeling the strain, in particular my knees were aching and I was worried having previously had tendonitis so decided to have a lie in the next day and a late start.

The final two days in France started off with a long climb over picturesque wooded hills to the west of Belfort, followed by fast descent into the city, passing industrial estates and an airport on the way, following signs to the *'Centre Ville'*. I had my final French coffee on the main square and admired my surroundings. It's an impressive place and the architecture of the buildings makes it clear that it is a border town, with both French and German influences. The huge red fortress looming over the city used to be located in between France and the Prussian empire. It survived a siege for 103 days in 1870 until the French were ordered to leave and surrender the city to the Germans.

Savouring the bitter taste of the excellent strong black coffee, I reflected on my time in France. Apart from the worries about being alone and missing home, I had enjoyed it immensely. I don't think my route took me through the most beautiful parts of the country, but there had been some great highlights, in particular the ancient town centres. One of the great things about cycle touring is that you end up in some places that you would never visit otherwise and these experiences are often the best.

The Rhone-Rhine canal guided me to Switzerland, where I headed to Basel and visited two places that France had lacked: a decent bike shop and a clean public toilet with soap and toilet roll provided. I locked myself into the toilet for a proper wash. People were speaking German, the buildings were different, and the tram system looked typically efficient. The vast River Rhine flowed through the city, separating Switzerland from Germany to the east, and France from Germany to the north. I was on the corner of three countries. Basel seemed lovely and is a place that I'd like to re-visit one day. Like the rest of Switzerland though, it's not cheap.

After stocking up on very expensive food supplies, I left Basel following the Rhine past some large factories and cranes loading the enormous barges in Basel's river port. The river took me into the countryside and through some pretty Swiss towns perched on the southern riverbank. The multi-coloured buildings were built right on the edge of the river, with steep roofs and painted shutters. I crossed into Germany over an old footbridge and swapped my remaining Swiss francs for euros with a passer-by who gave me an excellent exchange rate. People made me feel very welcome straight away with waves and '*hallos*'. Maybe it's because I can speak more German than French (which isn't saying much), but I felt more at home here.

I continued to follow the well-surfaced and signposted cycle lanes along the other side of the Rhine for a few more miles until I reached the bottom of the Schwarzwald (Black Forest). The road led me up a narrow gorge through a thick pine forest, following a fast-flowing river. This was my first major climb and I really got into it, finding my rhythm and timing my breathing with the pedal strokes. It was a test and I passed. It wasn't a huge ascent compared to some of the mountains that lay ahead, but it was pretty significant and the effort was more than worth it for the scenery. That evening I reached the top, happy that I was capable of dragging my heavy load up mountains. My campsite that night was on top of a very cold and snowy mountain at over 1,000 metres. As I ate my food looking around at the wonderful night time scene with moonlit, silhouetted mountain tops rising from pine forests, I appreciated my freedom and felt very fortunate to be in this moment. I was free here, away from the conveyor belt of a nine to five job. I was seeing the world and loving it; imagining what lay ahead; Asia would be amazing.

The bike was performing brilliantly and I was delighted with how I was coping. It had been far from easy so far but my body was adapting to the daily physical challenge of riding long distances every day.

3. The mighty Danube

Far from the Black Forest you hurry to the sea, giving your blessing to everything.
- Johann Strauss: The Blue Danube

I appreciated the altitude gained by my late night climbing of the previous day as the next morning started under a blanket of snow. My road wound down the slopes of the Black Forest, through snowflake dusted pine trees. A short ride across the plain at the bottom of the forest took me to the source of the River Danube at Donaueshingen. The Danube would guide me through the next seven countries so I was looking forward to following signposted bike paths and not having to worry about navigation for a few weeks. As I approached the river it surprised me that it was so small. The Donau (the German name for the Danube) begins where its two source tributaries join (the Brigach and Berg). It begins as a small river, which then disappears just a few miles along its journey to the Black Sea at a sinkhole, before resurfacing further downstream. The Danube would grow to be massive, but for now my guide was narrow and fast flowing.

The Donau Radweg is an excellent way to cross Europe. It is a long-distance cycle route that runs from the source of the Danube and ends at its estuary on the Black Sea. As I had hoped, it was well signposted and mostly on good tracks or country lanes. Some of the cycling was off-road, which kept the riding interesting. The first day's ride took me through a tight valley with high cliffs on either side. Castles were perched on the cliff tops and many of the towns contained ancient monasteries. The villages in this part of Germany are picturesque; clean and well-kept, with pretty paintings on the side of the buildings and quaint little shops. All of the towns I passed through had inviting guesthouses and restaurants, which I would love to return one day with some money and good company. I camped by the river on my first day by the Danube and had a wash in the cold water.

The first full day of rain tested my panniers' waterproofness (or lack of), and by mid-afternoon I was thoroughly miserable, leaving the beautiful valley in the morning to cycle along a fairly dull plain and sheltering under a bridge to eat lunch. Thankfully, a friendly chap who was on his way home from work cycled up alongside me and offered to guide me to the next town, where he lived. The cycle path had left the river for the time being and the route was not as clear, so it was good to have a guide. We had a chat, as well as my faltering German would allow. I managed to explain what I was doing and asked him a few things about himself. Unfortunately I didn't ask his name. I made a mental note to do so in the future. Riding with my new companion passed the time more quickly, and having company for the first time in over a week, helping me to forget about being cold, wet and miserable. I waved goodbye to him on the edge of Ulm and carried on to explore the city.

Ulm has a picturesque city centre with a gigantic cathedral. In the old town centre are a great many traditional restaurants, sat in black and white Tudor-like buildings by the Danube. The river flow is diverted down a series of artificial channels between the old buildings. I assumed that there must have once been a reason for this; perhaps for sewage or maybe water wheels. Now, it made for a lovely old centre to the town, almost like a small German Venice. The cathedral, Ulm Munster, is the tallest in the world and until 1901, was the world's tallest building. It is a different style from the French cathedrals, much darker in colour and more imposing, but not as pretty, with one towering gothic spire. I treated myself to a kebab that night. Unfortunately my budget wouldn't stretch to the much more inviting restaurants around the Danube, in the centre of the city. I am a big fan of German food. The simplicity of a big hunk of meat, some potato based side dish and a pile of cabbage is perfection for me. I have had my fair share of German food having lived in Munich for half a year during a work placement. I couldn't blow my money here though; it was more important to budget with Asia in mind, where it would be more important to have enough for the odd luxury now and again.

My ever-present guide, the Donau, led me through the cities of Ingolstadt, Regensburg and Passau, as well as numerous small towns and villages. The German towns have a very different style from those I had passed through in France, but are equally beautiful. The Germans obviously love their cycling too, and at the weekend the Radweg was completely packed with cyclists, a lot of them on long tours. I visited a few ancient abbeys, with ornately decorated baroque churches, but more importantly their own home-brewed beer. Many old abbeys, or *'Klosters'* in German, brew beer on site in the same way that they did centuries ago, and it is always delicious. The highlight was Weltenberger Kloster, the oldest monastery brewery in the world, which has been in operation since 1050 AD. It was the best beer that I have ever tasted. I sat in the sunshine in the packed courtyard, savouring it and enjoying the ancient surroundings. I watched my bike leaning against the wall while sitting drinking my beer and considered how far it had already taken me but how much further it had to go. What an amazing machine, I thought; it's opening the world for me.

After Ulm I was rarely alone, having started making an effort to cycle with other people on the Radweg. First was a companion called Christian who grew up in communist East Germany. I think he must have been in his forties. He pulled up alongside me and I was impressed by his pace, having to put extra effort in to keep up. We cycled together all afternoon, until he had to stop at his planned campsite. Speaking to him was really interesting, as he told me about his childhood and the fall of the Berlin Wall. He had grown up in a Soviet tower block and couldn't speak English because he had been taught Russian at school instead. He recounted how different things were after the wall came down, mainly the vastly improved choice of food available. He was a child during most of the Soviet days and so missed the daily paranoia and worries that adults would have had to deal with. Food was something that a child could remember though. Incidentally, I had a bit of a surprise that night with my choice of food. Not having read the bottle properly in Aldi earlier, I had bought tomato ketchup instead of pasta sauce. It made for a pretty disgusting dinner of pasta and ketchup as I camped in a wood by the river.

I woke up tired the next day and had a bad morning, trying to motivate myself to put some miles in. The day improved after lunch, when I met another cyclist called Michael riding along the Radweg. He was training for a bike tour and was sponsored by a bike company. He had cycled in thirty-five countries and had been to a lot of the places I was planning to go; Mongolia sounded incredible. He gave me some good advice other than telling me that I would get kidnapped if I took the Pamir Highway in Tajikistan. In my head the Pamir Highway would be the highlight of my trip, having heard nothing but good things about it from other travellers. He lit up a cigarette as we chatted. *'Not great training for a sponsored cyclist,'* I thought.

Despite feeling down and having a slow start in the morning, I was surprised when I looked at my speedo at the end of the day. I had been achieving my eighty-five mile target most days now but had ridden eighty miles that day without really pushing hard. I was pleased that my fitness was improving. The Radweg was a much faster path than the roads of England and France, which also helped me to get the miles done. There was no navigation to worry about and the lack of hills meant my average speed had risen. The days were getting longer too, so I had more hours of daylight to cycle.

After a good night's sleep, my mind was back in business and this was the first morning that I didn't have one ache or pain. During the first couple of weeks, I had awoken in the night with cramp in my legs having to curl up into a ball then very slowly extend my legs to stop the pain. This was a thing of the past now though. I got straight into my rhythm leaving the campsite in the morning and passing the confluence with the River Isar, which flows from the Alps through Munich until it reaches the Danube. Munich had been a fantastic base to explore the Alps during my work placement. I remembered a boat trip on the River Isar, further upstream. A group of us took a cheap blow-up rubber dingy to a town fifteen miles up the Isar called Wolfratshausen, letting the river current take us home via a few excellent riverside beer gardens and some pretty serious rapids. One time we hit a log, the dingy punctured and started deflating so we mended one hole with a puncture repair kit and took it in turns to continuously blow it up for the next five miles back to Munich. The Isar bike track also provides the fastest way by bike into the Alps from the city and I'd cycled along it to Austria a couple of times with my friend Shaun.

Another day's ride along a perfect riverside cycle path took me to Passau, the border town where three large rivers meet: the Inn, the Ilz and the Danube. In actual fact, the Inn is larger than the Danube at the confluence, so I wondered why it was called the Danube and not the Inn downstream. I liked the local beer adverts, *'Passau; three rivers, one beer'*. There was nowhere to camp outside Passau and I was forced to haul my bike up a steep forested bank until I found a relatively flat spot. This would be my last night in Germany, which had been a superb country to ride through. I had met the friendliest people so far and the Radweg had increased my daily mileage considerably. I was starting to think I might just be able to get enough miles completed each day to get around the world by Christmas.

My first day in Austria was along more tracks that were flat as a pancake beside the now much larger river. It started raining heavily just before lunch, and shortly afterwards I discovered that I had been following the wrong side of the Danube for about five miles. I hit a dead-end and was forced to turn around. There was supposed to be a ferry across the river but the rain must have put the boat captain off, or maybe he'd stopped for lunch. I couldn't find him in any case so backtracked the five miles to cross the river at a bridge and continue on the other side. When you're cycling and have a target and time schedule in mind, there is nothing more demoralising than retracing your pedal strokes, particularly in the pouring rain. Finally, back at the bridge, I met another cyclist called Julius; a German who was on his way to Istanbul by bike. He was planning to meet his girlfriend in Vienna in a few days so we decided to cycle together until then, it would be great to have some company. The wrong turning had meant that I had a companion and I probably wouldn't have met him otherwise.

We passed through Linz and met another cyclist, Nino from Switzerland eating lunch outside an Aldi supermarket. Nino joined our party and was to become a good friend for the next six weeks. We continued together all afternoon, chatting and sharing our plans for the weeks ahead. I was delighted to hear that Nino was also on a long distance tour and was on the way to Southeast Asia. That night, our group of three had a memorable evening wild camping in a wood, with a few beers and some excellent pasta. Comparing my two new companions was interesting. Julius had an old Dutch touring bike with only five gears. It was a quick bike, probably easier to ride than Nino's and mine on the flat. I thought that he might struggle when he had to cross the mountains in Serbia and Bulgaria though. Nino was the exact opposite and had, like me, custom made his touring bike. Unlike me, however, he'd spent a lot more time preparing and had four immaculate Ortlieb panniers and an Ortlieb waterproof roll-bag on top of the back rack. He had an iPad to write his blog, a water filter and a lot of other expensive-looking kit. I was jealous of his '*Schwalbe Marathon Plus Tour*' tyres, which were bombproof and never got a puncture. I decided that I would get some when my cheap ones wore out.

Riding into Vienna was great. The three of us rode in formation, taking it in turns to take over at the front; Tour-de-France peloton style to minimise wind resistance. No one wanted to be the slowest; it was great to be in the slipstream but hard work when it was my turn to take over at the front. I had never appreciated how much difference cycling in formation makes. As we continued along the Radweg I was amazed to see free tool stations; red metal boxes, with all the tools you might need to fix your bike provided on the end of long chains. The path led us into the city centre, avoiding all busy roads, at which point Julius left Nino and me to go and meet his girlfriend. I was very jealous, thinking how long it had been, and how long it might be until I saw Laura again. Nino and I continued onwards and quickly found a hostel and bike shop. We spent the afternoon servicing the bikes; a few adjustments were needed. I bought some handlebar tape for comfort and a cheap spare mountain bike tyre (which was to come in useful later in the trip). It was great to sleep in a bed that night, although the snoring backpacker from New York kept me awake.

We had a brief look around the tourist sites in the morning, but I had been to Vienna before and neither of us could afford to stay long, so we didn't spend much time there. It is an impressive place and very beautiful, with its large palaces and open parks, but I wasn't here to see tourist sites. I wanted adventure, and to be out of my comfort zone; Eastern Europe was waiting...

On the way out of Vienna I noticed that my cranks were wobbling a bit, so I went to a bike shop to get them tightened. It was an easy problem to fix, but required a special tool, which was too heavy for me to include as part of my kit. All in all, I was impressed with the lack of maintenance that my bike had required. This was very encouraging as the bike had to be completely reliable during the remote stretches of the unknown lands that lay ahead. A serious mechanical failure in the desert could be catastrophic.

We left the city in the early afternoon for Bratislava and Slovakia, chatting as we went. Nino was a great person to travel with, very easy going and good to talk to. He was very appreciative of what was going on around him, very observant, and great with other people. We decided that we would ride together, at least until we reached Istanbul. One advantage of cycling with an equally matched rider is that the petty competition to not be the slowest really helps to get the miles done.

Leaving Vienna was tricky because the Danube is divided into about ten channels and they all have to be crossed. It was difficult to navigate the maze of bridges and tracks. More than once we had to backtrack a few miles because the path we were cycling along simply stopped as two river channels joined up. To make things more interesting, nude bathers populated some of the channels. Nino's official Donau Radweg map, despite the occasional setbacks, kept us on route and was significantly better than my road atlas that was now a lot thinner than when I started. After crossing a page, I ripped it out to save weight. I had spent a few hours at the beginning of the trip ripping out all of the pages of Europe that I wouldn't need. There was still a surprising percentage of the atlas left after completing my purge!

After a morning's ride on a well surfaced track through pretty countryside on a flat floodplain, we reached the Slovakian border, which seemed a long way from home. Slovakia sounds much further away than Austria for some reason. I had passed through Austria quickly, on a very flat route, which was a bit strange in such a mountainous country. It was an easy place to travel and felt very safe, but I was hungry for the unknown that lay ahead.

4. Across the Iron Curtain

From Stettin in the Baltic to Trieste in the Adriatic, an iron curtain has descended across the Continent. Behind that line lie all the capitals of the ancient states of Central and Eastern Europe. Warsaw, Berlin, Prague, Vienna, Budapest, Belgrade, Bucharest and Sofia.
- Winston Churchill, 1946

The wind was behind us as we crossed into Slovakia and we half rode, half were blown to Bratislava, which we had a few hours to explore. This was the second of four capital cities that the Danube would take us through; more than any other river in the world. Bratislava was a fantastic contrast to the spotlessly clean German and Austrian cities, and it felt much more real. The people approached us to ask what we were doing and were amazingly helpful and friendly. We had a beer at a restaurant on the main square and looked around the cobbled streets. I loved the city's relaxed atmosphere. From the bridge over the Danube we could see huge Soviet tower blocks in the northern outskirts of the city. I imagined growing up in one of those apartment blocks during communist times and felt very lucky to have had such a privileged childhood. There was an excellent view of the famous tenth century Bratislava castle from the bridge, which was an imperious sight; cubic in shape, with four corner towers, standing proudly over a beautiful Danube sunset. We camped on the outskirts of the city in thick undergrowth, keeping quiet so that the many dog walkers and roller skaters who passed on the river trail just ten metres away from our tents didn't spot us.

We had entered the former Eastern Bloc. To think that the influence of the Soviet Union spread from here to the other side of Asia is mind-boggling. I read about the history of the Soviet Union that night and imagined what it must have been like for people like Christian (whom I met in Germany), to have grown up under the oppression of a leader who lived thousands of miles away and wasn't even from their country. I would see so much of the vast Soviet legacy as I travelled east and the thought excited me. I thought about how easily my crossing from Western to Eastern Europe had been, and that just over two decades ago (within my lifetime) it was an impenetrable barrier for those in the Eastern Bloc. Again I felt very fortunate.

Slovakia was treating us well. The next day, an even stronger tailwind was behind us and we had covered ninety miles by six o'clock. It was great to explore the small Slovakian towns and to try new foods in the small village shops. A lot of the shops were low on useful supplies but had a vast array of vodkas, all of which were very cheap. One bottle was cheaper than the mineral water that the shop was selling! Much of the food was imported from Russia and Cyrillic text was common on the packaging. Almost everyone we met in Slovakia spoke Russian as well as Slovak and most people spoke at least basic English. The roads were noticeably worse and the Danube (now the Donaj) bike track was almost non-existent. Navigation was still simple enough, as the Donaj was easy to follow and Nino's map was proving very useful.

We reached a giant reservoir, being blown along by a gale-force tailwind, which was creating four foot high waves that broke over the artificial banks, spraying us as we passed. Halfway along the reservoir we met a German lady; at a guess she was in her seventies, riding a bike with far more gear attached than I had and almost as quickly. She was clearly incredibly fit and was soon telling us stories of places she had been. She didn't have a home and lived on her bike, but it didn't seem as though she was forced to do so; it was choice to live that way because she said she had money. On her bike rack, she carried a large tent and two sleeping bags to make it look like she had company every night for security. I pondered her lifestyle for a few hours after we left her and thought it must be very lonely. Although I was very much enjoying cycle touring, she was a permanent cyclist living in a bubble on her own, away from society and the 'real' world. I wondered what she had left behind. That lifestyle definitely wasn't for me; I want a family and a career one day, and felt that it would be very difficult to return to normality after such a long time on the road. She probably never wanted to return though.

We camped in a wood near the Hungarian border and I had a swim in the river. It was (obviously) freezing because it was April. I felt obliged to swim in the Danube having camped next to it for a few weeks!. We sat down to cook. Nino is a vegetarian, so we usually cooked separately as I like to have meat in every meal if possible. I had goulash and potatoes that night; he had pasta. As we were cooking dinner, a car pulled up and two people got out. We were paranoid that they had seen us come into the wood earlier and wanted to rob us so we kept quiet and hid in the trees. They didn't see us though and they drove off fifteen minutes later. I reckon they were collecting firewood or maybe dumping something in the wood. We were very jumpy, and looking back I think we were still nervous about wild camping. It was good to have a certain amount of misgivings towards sleeping rough in a strange country, but as you will read, this attitude significantly relaxed as I grew into the trip.

Slovakia is not a large country and we were through it in a couple of days. We reached the river again, and an iron bridge that would take us into Hungary. As we approached my seventh country, we were greeted by its largest cathedral, sitting on a hill above the *'Danube Bend'.* It is an enormous square building, with a large green dome between two tall side towers: quite an introduction to a new country.

We crossed the river into Esztergom; the former capital of Hungary. There were lots of other pretty towns on the way into Budapest, including the artists' colony of Szentendre, with its pretty narrow streets and central square full of people painting pictures on every corner. The riding was great, away from the traffic, and the weather was hot and sunny. The bike path itself sometimes deteriorated to the point that it was almost not possible to ride, but dodging the potholes and bumps kept things interesting.

Over the last couple of days, I had been anticipating reaching the city that I was looking forward to visiting most in the European leg of the trip: Budapest. We rode into the Hungarian capital at around mid-afternoon. It must be one of the most beautiful cities in the world. We rode past the imperious parliament building, with its huge purple dome staring down on the river below. We were on the Buda side of the city, on the East side of the Danube, looking over to the parliament on the West side; Pest. Budapest used to be two cities, until they were combined in 1873. We saw the grand castle, the striking cathedral (St Stephen's Basilica) and the Matthias Church with its multi-coloured tiled roof.

The Austro-Hungarians built the parliament building to be larger than the Houses of Parliament in London, which it beat by a couple of metres. Now it's been beaten again by the much larger Bucharest Parliament building in Romania. It is the joint-tallest building in Budapest, along with St Stephens Basilica and no other building is allowed to be constructed taller in order to preserve the city's character. After looking around the city and finding the cheapest hostel we could, we headed out to a traditional restaurant to sample some Hungarian food. I had delicious butternut squash and beef stew. The atmosphere on the Budapest streets was electric. All around were outdoor restaurants and bars, full of young people on nights out. On the way back to our hostel we passed the beautiful Opera House, and a very well dressed crowd were making their way onto the street, buzzing after the concert they had just watched.

We left early the next morning as our respective budgeting meant we couldn't stay in the city any longer. I noticed that all of the shops were open despite it being Sunday. Eastern Europeans are clearly more lax about the Sabbath than the French, Germans and Austrians. All of that day, we followed the Danube through pretty, green and flat countryside, but it wasn't particularly interesting cycling. The river was very wide now, with large cruise ships and barges making their way both up and down the river. The local people approached us when we stopped, and although interaction was limited they were always friendly and wore a smile. As we cycled, Nino and I chatted about our plans after Istanbul and we thought we would probably go our separate ways. Unless I could get an Iranian visa, I planned to ride along the Black Sea coast in the north and Nino wanted to take a more southerly route. As the sun lowered in the sky and we watched the shadows cast by our bikes lengthen, we crossed a bridge and set up camp on an island in the Danube, which was home to a herd of wild boar. Judging by the hideouts and the shotgun pellets lying around in the woods they were shot for sport.

The next morning, back on the road, we met Andreas and Johanna, a friendly German couple who were planning to cycle to Australia over the next three years. They were in no rush and didn't really have a schedule. We left them on a forested riverbank, eating lunch and reading a German newspaper. While I thought that maybe it would be nice to have a bit more spare time, they had a huge amount of heavy photography kit with them, which I was glad wasn't on the back of my bike. Before we knew it, the flat flood plain came to an end and so too had Hungary. It had been a beautiful country to cycle through, particularly in the towns and cities, and the people had been very welcoming.

At the Croatian border post we spoke to the female guard, who couldn't believe what we were doing, screaming something like *"Sheista"*, which I imagine is an exclamation of some kind. The man at passport checkpoint didn't look remotely interested but flamboyantly gave us a stamp in our passports, holding his stamp like a trophy. The first sign of arrogance in officials that became increasingly frustrating on every land border as we travelled east. Keeping on the right side of these guards could be the difference between being let though a border with no issues or being held for hours.

We spent our first night in Croatia in a park next to a football pitch, and fell asleep with the sounds of children kicking a ball around. In Croatia, all of the towns, even the little villages have immaculately kept football pitches. This was the first time I had ever wild-camped in a public place in plain view of people, but it was absolutely fine. We decided to stay in the park because throughout Croatia there are signs in fields; a red triangle with a skull inside. *Landmines.* Croatia has the largest landmine problem in Europe and hundreds of people have been killed and many more injured. It wasn't worth the risk of camping off the beaten track here.

Croatia was more expensive than Hungary, more like Austria when it came to grocery shopping. It only took one day to cycle through the country to Serbia. The countryside we saw was not particularly interesting and many of the towns were derelict. It wasn't a fair representation of the country, which is very beautiful nearer the richer areas on the coast. We passed through the city of Osijeck, which was pleasant, with its open parks and modern tram system. Nearing the Serbian border, we saw an old water tower in the town of Vukovar. It was a wreck, with large holes in the tank, but a large Croatian flag was flying on top of it. It seemed strange that they had left it standing, much stranger that they were proudly flying the Croatian flag above this ruin. I did some research and it turned out that it had been left as a war memorial. During the Serbian attack on Vukovar in 1991, the water tower was one of the most frequent targets of enemy artillery. It was hit more than 600 times and today it is left as a symbol of victory and new life; it was a striking memorial.

In the evening, we asked permission to pitch our tents under some beach huts on the side of the Danube. The beach belonged to a hotel and they were more than happy to let us stay on their grounds for free. The staff were very friendly and let us use the toilet for a wash. They even had the Champion's League quarter final on; I watched Man Utd beat Chelsea two goals to one.

Slovakia, Croatia and Hungary were great to ride through, with some really pretty parts, but also some poorer areas, with derelict buildings and rubbish everywhere. From then on, I expected countries to become poorer, but the people that I met as I travelled east were very friendly, interested in what we were doing and eager to help. All the villages and towns seemed to have a great community spirit. I did not know what to expect in Serbia the following day.

5. Friendlier and friendlier

Turn your face into the sun and let the shadows fall behind you
- Maori proverb (written on a bike path sign on the bank of the Danube)

Crossing the border into Serbia felt more serious than the other border crossings. We cycled through a few hundred metres of no-man's land, approaching the tiny, ramshackle hut that was the border post. Annoyingly, the Croatian border guard had stamped my exit stamp on a different page from the entry stamp. My passport was already pretty full and I was worried that I might run out of pages by the time I reached the other side of Asia. The Serbian guards looked at us suspiciously and checked our passports meticulously. As soon as we crossed the border it was clear that Serbia was significantly poorer than Croatia. The roads were in terrible condition and many of the buildings were ruined. It looked as though many people were living in the ground floor of two storey houses and leaving the upper floor to fall into disrepair, with boarded up windows and missing roof tiles. Another shock was the ferocious dogs. They chased us, barking and growling as we approached them, which caused the hairs on the back of my neck to stand up and adrenaline to shoot through my body, raising my alertness. To begin with we tried racing away from then as fast as we could. This just wound them up and made them more ferocious as they chased us. We found that stopping was better and they usually left us alone when we turned round and faced them. I tried out my dog 'Dazer' which I'd kindly been donated. It scares them off by releasing an ultrasonic noise and it worked brilliantly. I saw one dog that looked completely crazed, like the dogs in zombie films. It was slobbering and running after us. I have never seen an animal with rabies but this dog looked like it had it.

All in all the entrance into Serbia was a bit intimidating, but after settling into the country I very quickly began to love it. The people here were so welcoming. Every time we stopped, people approached us. On the first day it was raining, so we sheltered under a garage forecourt and the guys who worked there invited us in for a coffee. By the end of the first day I noticed that I was getting fitter too. The last couple of days had been over eighty-five miles and I felt fresh at the end of both of them. Eighty-five miles felt like an easy distance and a few weeks earlier it had been a real struggle. Getting up in the morning was easier and I was really starting to enjoy myself. Cycling with Nino seemed to add more of a schedule to the day too and helped me settle into a rhythm as we crossed Europe together.

We cycled past Novi Sad and on to Belgrade. I found neither city attractive, but Belgrade turned out to be fantastic. Concrete Soviet-style tower blocks dominated the skyline as we entered Serbia's capital city. The outskirts were patrolled by packs of stray dogs and the Dazer came in handy again. We cycled in along the riverside bike trail and saw expensive-looking floating restaurants, bars and nightclubs on the Danube. The place was buzzing with character along the main street in the city centre. We stopped to ask a guy for directions and he couldn't have been more helpful. His name was Dragan and he showed us a cheap place to eat that evening. He said if we waited a couple of hours we could stay at his house, but he was busy until then. We wanted to accept but were too tired and the lure of a shower in a cheap hostel was too much. Also, we knew there could be a fine of one hundred euros when exiting the country unless you have a card proving the use of official accommodation in Serbia. Instead, we arranged to meet Dragan at the restaurant he had shown us, where he ordered traditional Serbian dishes and the best local beer. I had juicy pork rolled in cabbage, which was delicious.

We shared stories that evening. It turned out Dragan was a bike fanatic; he owns seven and showed us his Hercules (from Birmingham). It is sixty years old and still going strong. He is an author of short stories and he sent me one that had been translated into English. The next morning we met Dragan again and he showed us around the new orthodox temple in Belgrade. I say new, it has actually been under construction since 1935. Lack of money and the various Balkan and European wars have repeatedly stalled its construction, but they've recently finished the outside. The inside will take another ten to fifteen years because there aren't many people who have the skill to paint the frescos on the walls in the traditional way. We cycled out of Belgrade with Dragan on his Hercules. He left us near the edge of the city and pointed the way out, adding that he was very tempted just to ride off with us. He was yet another amazingly open and friendly person, and they seemed to be becoming more common as we travelled east.

I didn't enjoy the rest of the day. It was raining heavily and we spent most of the time on a main road, cycling up and down hills through rubbish tips. We reached a village in the evening and asked around if there was anywhere we could put our tents up. No one could help, instead suggesting a hotel we could stay at. Our tight budgets meant that this wasn't an option, so we searched for about an hour for a place to sleep, finally following a track alongside a railway where we found a small wood to pitch the tents in. Once we had stopped, I cheered up. We had some pasta to cook and Dragan had given us a bottle of red wine from his family's vineyard. We spent a pleasant evening discussing our experiences in Serbia and drinking Dragan's wine. The rain finally stopped.

More dogs were scattered by my brilliant ultrasonic dog deterrent in the morning. It was great fun taking out my frustration on them, and I rather nastily used it on a couple of dogs that weren't coming for us. I was developing a hatred for Serbian dogs, perhaps driven by the knowledge that most of them would have loved to sink their teeth into my legs if they got the chance. We cycled through friendly villages, where people waved and shouted greetings at us. I noticed that a lot of people drove Yugos. They are rebranded Fiats and were the cars that everybody had under the communist Yugoslav government. They look like the drawing of a car by a young child; very square. They must be pretty good though because there are thousands still running but were manufactured in the seventies and eighties. We entered another village and a small boy on a full size racing bike followed us, shouting loudly and overtaking us, dropping back then overtaking us again. It was a poor but very close community, more like those

I have experienced in India or Africa than Europe, or at least what my preconception of Europe is.

The villages passed behind our wheels and the scenery became spectacular as we entered the beautiful *'Ðerdap National Park'* on the border with Romania. The river had turned into a huge lake at the widest point on its journey to the Black Sea. It leaves the lake through the narrow Kazan Gorge, with towering cliffs and a wooded valley on either side. We explored an expansive stone castle on the lake shore, which was built by the Hungarians when they ruled this land. A huge face of the much-loved King, Decabalus (a name which means 'strong as ten men'), the last King of the Kingdom of Dacia, was carved into the rock face on the Romanian side of the river. The road wove up and down the sides of a spectacular gorge and was excellent quality, with long climbs followed by smooth, flowing descents.

A park warden joined us while we had our lunch and proudly told us about his job. He showed us his motorbike, which was about thirty years old. He had spent most of his life riding around the trails in the national park; *not a bad job*, I thought. After lunch, a wonderful afternoon ride led us to a campsite on the riverbank that was closed for the off-season. There were stunning views of the river, which was so wide that the other side was almost too far away to see. They had left the toilets open and the water and electricity on, so we enjoyed a night of relative luxury. I tried my fishing gear to no avail; *those salmon were still waiting to be caught...* The fisherman in Aberystwyth had told me that sweetcorn sprayed in WD40 is good bait. I tied the line onto my bike and lobbed the hook out into the river. Either my method was rubbish, or the bait was. I left the line out overnight, but the corn was still there in the morning.

The next day we cycled out of the national park and arrived at one of the Iron Gates, which has a road over to Romania across the top of it. The Iron Gates are a series of large hydroelectric power plants and dams. Their construction began in 1964 and they were built to tame the river. Before this the fast flowing water and rapids in the gorge were a notorious obstacle to ships navigating the Danube. We used the impressive engineering project as our route into Romania and said a fond farewell to Serbia, cycling past the very long queue of cars at customs and assuring the border guards that *"No, we haven't bought any cigarettes"* and that they didn't need to check our bags!

Entering Romania was quite surprising. From what I had heard, I was expecting it to be poorer than Serbia but the roads were better and there was a lot less rubbish around. The dogs were also less vicious. That first day we cycled through the quiet city of Drobeta-Turnu Severin and got some Romanian money at a bank before finding a place to camp. We stayed on an 'official' campsite called *'Smile',* but it didn't really have anywhere to put the tents. We were allowed to pitch them next to an empty swimming pool and closed outside bar, and we told the lady we couldn't afford more than three Euros each. That was fine by her.

I immediately fell in love with Romania. The people were even friendlier than the Serbians and there was never a dull moment. Whether it was being chased by a dog, kids wanting high fives as we passed, old ladies huddling together unashamedly staring, adults smiling and waving, shouts of *"hola", "what's your name", "salut"*, we were never bored. We cycled out of a town and the tarmac road turned into tiny track, on which horses and carts were more common than cars. I stopped to think; *I had come from England, to a tiny track in a forest in Romania on a bike.*

At the next town we went to buy some bread at the bakers and the guy who ran the shop spoke Italian. Nino speaks six languages and Italian is one of them, so we were able to communicate with him. It turned out that the man had worked in Italy and, judging by his Mercedes, made quite a lot of money there. He took us back to his restaurant for a 'real Italian coffee'. It was delicious, and so was the house wine he gave us (it was eleven in the morning). His name was Stefan and he looked like a vampire, with curly grey hair, large front teeth and spectacular sideburns. I thought this was fitting for a Romanian. He must have told someone to prepare some food for us because two plates came out of nowhere with fish and spicy rice. Apparently it was a traditional meal eaten the weekend before Easter (which it was). Everyone was partying that day for a national festival so Stefan opened the whisky. We refused because we still had around fifty miles to cycle, but he had some and then topped up our glasses with wine. We looked out over the river towards Serbia. He was very suspicious of the people on the other side and not very complimentary about them. He still referred to Serbia as Yugoslavia and obviously thought that it was a dangerous place to cycle through. He told us that we would be much safer in friendly Romania but that we would probably be robbed in Bulgaria. This suspicion of people in neighbouring countries was present all over the world.

We left him back at his bakery and he gave us a cake for the road. Slightly wobbly because of the wine, we cycled on through village after village, constantly being watched by the inhabitants, most of whom seemed to spend the whole day outside on the road; the women gossiping, the men drinking beer and the kids playing in the street. That evening, we reached a beautiful camping spot in a field. It was just off the road, down in a valley, with a stunning view of rolling fields stretching out to the sunset on the horizon. We made a fire next to a stream and watched the sun sink from the sky as it turned orange. At dusk some shepherds brought their animals to drink from the stream. Although slightly surprised, they waved to gesture we were welcome and let us get on with cooking our dinner.

Romania carried on in the same wonderful way for the next couple of days. One night, we finished at a farm. There was no need to ask permission to camp there. From my experience of Romania, it is okay to assume that you can pitch a tent on a farmer's field. At about six o'clock the farmer saw us putting up our tents. He came over and, using a book with pictures called *'Point It'* (a very useful leaving present from Laura) we managed to communicate with him. He told us that he had to go home but was coming back with wine. An hour later he returned with a bottle of wine that he said that he had made from grapes grown on the farm, and some pork fat sprinkled with chilli powder. The pork was delicious and very filling. I wasn't hungry at all the next day. He had also brought a radio with flashing disco lights. We listened to some Romanian pop music, which in my humble opinion wasn't great, simply an average singer accompanied by an accordion and a fiddle. The disco lights were funny though. They sensed the beat of the song somehow and flashed in time with it.

The farmer's name was Petre and he told us that he earned 2,500 euros per year working as an electrician after paying fifty percent tax. Most of the food that he made on his farm went to feeding his family. He also recently crashed his car when drunk and had lost his licence, which unfortunately seemed to be a common problem in Romania. He used my '*Point It*' book and sign language, to communicate to us that animals lived on the farm and warned us that there were snakes, tics, and (we think he said) jackals about. We assured him that we would be careful, waving as he left. He was another unbelievably friendly person, and an example of Romanian hospitality.

In the morning, we continued along a good road with a slight headwind. It was difficult to find bread in the poorly stocked village shops but there was still no lack of vodka on the shelves. It really was incredibly cheap. We refused the kind offer from a drunk guy to sit down on the side of the road with him and share his vodka and coke. At lunchtime we stopped in a park, which was a mistake. Within minutes we were surrounded by an audience of children and teenagers. We scoffed some food and kept a close eye on our stuff before making a swift getaway. At the village shop, we experienced our only bad moment in Romania. We bought some food from a supermarket and Nino left his chocolate milkshake on the side whilst packing food into his panniers. A gypsy child came up and stole it and ran off. I went and retrieved it, but he had opened and started drinking it. I couldn't believe he'd done it with both of us watching and his parents there too. They didn't seem to mind in the slightest. Having heard Romanians complaining about gypsies, it seems that they cause huge crime problems in that country.

We left Romania on a ferry, crossing the River Danube for the last time. I was sad to leave Romania, a country I had loved without having any knowledge or expectations before entering. Bulgaria was up next, another country that I had never been to and knew nothing about.

I was loving this form of travel. Usually holidays are researched and planned to make the most of the short break from the nine to five. This was indefinite. I didn't have to rush and I was visiting real places that no one I know had been to, and most of which I would never return to. This is adventure.

6. Goodbye to the river and the end of Europe

Whenever I see an adult on a bicycle, I have hope for the human race.
- H.G. Wells

We cycled out of Shivstov, the town where we crossed the Danube for the last time. Our route took us along a country road through some pretty, grassy hills. As we climbed one of the larger hills, the road moved away from the River Danube, the river I had followed through most of Europe. It had been a perfect guide, making navigation easy and my route almost flat (with a few notable exceptions). The Danube had taken me through seven countries, four capital cities, hundreds of quaint villages and incredible natural scenery; I met such hospitable people and enjoyed the cycling on the bike trail immensely. When cycling next to the river, I was always in a better mood than when away from it. When our route took us away from the river for an afternoon or a whole day I always wanted to be back on the riverbank. My one regret was that my pitiful attempt at fishing didn't bring the huge grilled salmon that I had imagined. I was in great spirits that day, because Laura had contacted me, saying that she could come to Turkey to meet me in a few weeks' time. I just needed to work out where I would be at the time and she'd book her flights.

It was a surprise to discover that Bulgarians use the Cyrillic alphabet and that it was invented there in the Tenth Century. I had always assumed it was Russian in origin. It made the road signs difficult to read, although I picked up on the similarities between some of the letters and managed to work out what most words said after a day or two's practice.

We climbed the hills to the south of the river. After the biggest pass of the trip so far, we descended to a very busy and dangerous road. Dodging crazy lorry drivers, we cycled to the old capital of Bulgaria, Veliko Tarnovo. It is an impressive place, perched on cliffs above a river gorge. We found our way through a complicated motorway junction involving crossing three lanes of fast-moving traffic, then headed for the Balkan Mountains.

The climb out of Veliko Tarnovo was beautiful but very hot. A small country road wound up the mountains to a 700 metre high pass, followed by a superb descent with views over an endless plain. There were almost no houses in sight, and a meandering river ran through the centre of the plain, with herds of cattle dotted on the riverbanks. We reached a gigantic lake surrounded by lush fields. The sun was shining on the deep blue water and a green island poked out of the middle; it felt so remote. I was very tempted to stop early and put up my tent, but it was only midday and we had to push on to Turkey. We wanted to arrive in Istanbul before the following Monday, so that we would have a full week to get all of the visas we needed. We had three and half days to do 280 miles so we needed to push on.

Another pass took us over the mountains onto another, less beautiful plain, across which we could see a number of large power plants. We found a place to pitch the tents by another lake, next to a vineyard after asking a guy called Pedro if we could camp by his caravan, where he lived with his three dogs. He seemed surprised that we'd asked and shrugged to say '*Of course you can*'! Pedro came over with coffee as we put up the tents, followed by homemade grape liquor that wasn't particularly nice but warmed the cockles. I got my hipflask out and shared some Talisker whisky that I'd brought from home. He loved it. The look on his face showed amazement that something could taste so good. Pedro told us that the town that we had cycled through earlier was where the famous Bulgarian footballer Dimitar Berbatov was born and that he got married two miles down the road from his caravan. It turned out that neither of these boasts was true, Berbatov isn't married and he was born on the other side of the country in Blagoevgrad. I think his girlfriend may have come from that town. This wasn't the first boast about Berbatov in Bulgaria; he is a national hero.

Pedro's dogs kept me awake all night. I used my Dazer to scare them off because of the constant barking, but they kept coming back. I only got a couple of hours sleep and was absolutely shattered when Pedro came over in the morning with coffee for us. He seemed amazed that we could take our tents down and put them into bags on our bike. He made a circular motion with his hands which seemed to indicate he was enjoying himself and was impressed. We cycled across the rest of the plain and over another mountain range before descending to the Turkish border. It was Nino's birthday so I bought him a huge bag full of biscuits with the last of my Bulgarian money, then we crossed into Turkey.

We cycled past an enormous queue of lorries waiting at the border. I had to show my passport six times for some reason and spend fifteen euros on a Turkish Visa. This wasn't necessary for Nino, whose Swiss passport is much better to travel on than mine. My Iranian visa still hadn't come through, so I had nearly given up on that route now. It was looking like I'd have to bypass Iran by taking the Caspian Sea ferry to Turkmenistan, or Kazakhstan from Azerbaijan. On the bright side, I would be cycling through the Caucasus, a region that I was very excited about visiting. I have a friend who was working in Georgia too and it would be great to meet up if possible.

Finally across the border, we were into Turkey, which felt a million miles away from home. Two more days hard cycling and then a week off in Istanbul was not bad motivation to keep going. My body was feeling the strain and waking up at six o'clock every morning to cycle all day was becoming difficult. I needed a break. My bike was struggling too. The once perfectly smooth drivetrain was loud and squeaky and it needed a clean and chain replacement. The rear wheel was also buckled, from one of the Serbian potholes no doubt, and needed to be straightened. I thought I could make it to Istanbul before fixing it though.

We crossed the border to a Muslim call to prayer. For some reason I was expecting European Turkey to be an extension of Eastern Europe, with more churches than mosques, but it definitely wasn't. We were in a completely different culture and so close to Asia. We managed a few more miles that evening and made it to Erdirne, a lively city with a large and spectacular byzantine mosque. We bumped into the Erdirne bicycle club, who were very interested in our ride. While we talked, a young guy brought us tea without us asking and said *"Welcome to Turkey"*.

The novelty of a heavily laden touring bike encourages people to approach you. On foot, I don't think we would have had as much help or met as many people who wanted to share their culture with us. Thankfully, the sharing usually came in the form of food or drink.

A guy from the bike club went to fetch his bike, and he led us to a quiet campsite where the owner let us stay for free, and brought us fruit juice and mineral water. There were toilets and showers, but neither of us could be bothered to wash. We had a great evening sitting outside, listening to the noises around us: Turkish singing, drumming by the nearby river, birds calling and the far off traffic in Erdirne, heading towards Istanbul. We discussed our adventures in Europe and what lay ahead. I fell asleep with the drumming in my ears and a smile on my face.

The next morning, Joachim, the security guard at the campsite, saw us eating yogurt and muesli for breakfast and pulled a disgusted face. Five minutes later he brought a bowl of bread, cheese, olives, cucumber and tomatoes and cups of coffee: *a great start to the day.*

The road from Erdirne to Istanbul wasn't beautiful; a wide dual carriageway but with a generous space on the side of the road to cycle in so it was safe enough. The road surface had just been re-laid so we made good progress in the morning despite the constant climbing up rolling hills. We passed through many large towns, which were built along the main road, and were given tea at most by Turkish men with huge moustaches and even bigger smiles. Various people interrogated us every time we stopped. It seemed that we fascinated the locals even more than they did us. Some schoolgirls thought we must be famous so took our photos and asked for our autographs. By the evening, we arrived in Çorlu, having battled against a headwind all afternoon. After unsuccessfully asking for accommodation at a truckers' park, we tried a BP garage and they let us camp on some grass between the forecourt and some JCBs. We were offered a shower in the bathroom but I was too lazy again. I hadn't had one for a few days, but we'd be in Istanbul tomorrow. A wash could wait; sleep was more important.

The last day of European riding started with a coffee, bought for us by one of the pump attendants who had been working all night. He spent his hard earned cash on the coffee to give to two complete strangers; the Turkish people were so generous. We rode along the same dual carriageway all morning and arrived on the outskirts of Istanbul by lunchtime. As we rounded a corner, I saw a blue glow ahead. *We had made it to the Mediterranean.* Twenty-five miles of manic urban sprawl separated us from the Bosphorus and Asia.

We entered Istanbul on a terrifying motorway on Easter Sunday, thinking that it might be a bit quieter than usual, but no. I supposed that Easter isn't really celebrated in Turkey, as there weren't many Christians. After crossing four lanes full of crazy Turkish drivers moving at about seventy miles an hour, negotiating junctions and trying to stay alive, we arrived at a bridge into the main city. Looking back on it, riding into Istanbul was a stupid thing to do. It was incredibly dangerous. My goal of cycling around the world on an unbroken chain was less important than my life. We both made it into the city in one piece though. I felt stupid and irresponsible to have taken that risk.

We followed the sea around a headland on a bike path, and in the distance the towers of the Blue Mosque appeared. Asia was in sight over the Bosphorus and we were so close. Then a nail went through my tyre. I examined my back wheel and found two broken spokes. We were so close, but I now had to repair a wheel and fix a puncture. *So close but yet so far.*

The maintenance took about an hour, during which Nino was typically helpful and patient. Eventually it was fixed and my newly straightened wheel seemed okay. We set off to Sultanahmet, the area around the Blue Mosque. As we rounded a bay on the coast, I saw the towering minarets of the mosque and started believing that I'd made it. *Europe was almost over.* A few weeks of riding a bike had taken me across a continent. Istanbul was waiting and I couldn't wait to have a decent break from the daily physical effort. We found a hostel with some space and booked a night there. The next morning I would be in an embassy. That night I had to decide which visas I needed and what route I would take across Asia.

7. A well-deserved break

If the earth was a single state, Istanbul would be its capital
- Napoleon Bonaparte

Asia was waiting for me over the Bosphorus and Europe was behind my wheels. All I had to do before I could continue was get to some visas but that meant making some difficult decisions. How should I get through Central Asia? The only places I specifically wanted to go to were Samarkand in Uzbekistan and the Pamir Highway in Tajikistan and Kyrgyzstan. It looked like I wouldn't be able to get an Iranian visa so would either have to take the ferry across the Caspian Sea or fly over it. I wanted to travel over land the whole way if possible so a flight was a last resort. I considered the following options:

1. Try to get visas for Iran and Turkmenistan in Istanbul, then cycle through Iran to Turkmenistan, from which I would cross into South Uzbekistan. I could get more visas in Tehran if I went that way (my original plan).

2. Get a Turkmenistan visa in Istanbul and take the Caspian Sea ferry from Baku, Azerbaijan, to Turkmenbashi, Turkmenistan. I would need about eight days to cross Turkmenistan from the port though. I wouldn't get a visa for more than five days due to the communist government not allowing tourists to travel freely in the country, so I would have to take a train part of the way. This would ruin my 'every inch of the way' philosophy.

3. Get a Kazakhstan visa in Istanbul and take the Caspian Sea ferry from Baku to Aktau, Kazakhstan. I had heard that the ferry only left once a week and that this route would involve crossing the desert around the Aral Sea in the middle of nowhere, which would be tough in the forty-plus degrees heat. I wasn't sure it had been done before by bike or if it was even possible. Apparently, the roads were absolutely dreadful. I could either cross the border and cycle through the desert to Uzbekistan on an almost non-existent road south of the Aral Sea, or go to the north and cross into West Uzbekistan near Tashkent, which would mean travelling through the empty Kazakh Steppe and seeing nothing but sand, shrubs and camels for a few weeks.

After researching on the internet for hours, I decided on option three. It wasn't really a choice in the end. I probably wouldn't get an Iranian visa with my British passport without having to jump through a million hoops and spend a lot of money. The Turkmenistan visa would take ten to fourteen days and was not guaranteed anyway. Only option three was left, presenting the only possibility to succeed in crossing the whole of Asia by bike. I planned to cross the border at Beyneu and cycle though the barren Karalkalpakstan desert through Northeast Uzbekistan on the south side of the Aral Sea. I couldn't face thousands of miles in the Kazakh Steppe, which was the only other option. The choice that I made was going to be a seriously remote crossing on a dirt track, but from my research it looked like people had cycled at least part of the route before so I thought it would be possible and planned to give it a go and to hope that nothing went wrong. It was intimidating though. That desert is a very large space full of nothing and it would be very easy to meet someone on one of those empty roads who wanted to rob me. The hot temperatures were a worry too, but I thought I could deal with that as long as I could get enough water. I needed a break now, so tried not to think that far ahead. I would just get the visas that would open that path to me and stop worrying about it.

A week off in Istanbul sounded like it would be relaxing and a chance to rest and prepare for the next leg. It wasn't... I had to get three visas, which took up the majority of the first five days and the following Monday. I had to go to each embassy three times and I was delayed by disorganisation and their random opening hours. I went to the Uzbek embassy first because it had a reputation as the most difficult one. Nino and I arrived early, went to the desk and were told we needed to fill in a form online then print it off. We ran to an internet café, got the required form and ran back just before the embassy closed for the morning. We photocopied our passports and left them to 'process' the visa. It would take five days apparently so we would get them back on Friday. We met a Dutch guy named Paul at the embassy, who said he had got his in one day, so we went back on the Wednesday. Nino paid an express fee to get his quickly; I couldn't afford it. Nino hung around to pick it up on Wednesday afternoon but it wasn't ready; he would get it on the Friday morning, I'd get mine on the Friday afternoon.

The Kyrgyzstan visa was a bit easier and the embassy did pretty much what they said they would. The ambassador was a pretty woman, who looked like she had an enjoyable life. She dressed well and seemed to be on the phone to a friend about a night out the previous evening. On each of the three days that we went to the embassy, she didn't manage to open it on time. We waited for over an hour on two of the occasions for the door to open. On the plus side, she arranged that we could pick our visas up on Thursday rather than the Friday as this would have clashed with the Uzbek embassy pick-up. That was two visas sorted.

The final visa was for Kazakhstan. It seemed so easy on paper and was apparently the simplest to get. I went to the embassy on Tuesday morning and was told to return the following Monday morning to pick it up. I planned to get the visa first thing, and then leave Istanbul in the afternoon. I went to the embassy the following Monday and it was closed for a national holiday. I returned on Tuesday to pick the visa up. The ambassador was very apologetic. All in all it wasn't a bad effort though. I'd managed to get three visas in eight days and my path to the other side of Uzbekistan was open. I would get Tajik, Russian, Mongolian, and Chinese visas in Tashkent, the capital city of Uzbekistan. After a lot of time, frustration, 190 dollars, and a lot of patience I was clear for my onward travel.

The rest of the first five days in Istanbul were spent fixing the bike and ordering parts to be brought from home. Laura had arranged to meet me in Eastern Turkey in a couple of weeks' time. I couldn't wait to see her and felt massively guilty asking her to fill her baggage allowance with bike parts. Spare time in the day was spent planning the next leg to Baku, Azerbaijan, which looked very exciting. This was my next mental milestone and I wasn't thinking about the desert crossing after it. I also improved my bike with an air horn, which was a lot louder than the bell that I had. People should hear me coming now!

After one night in a hostel run by a drunk, we moved to a much better one recommended by Paul, the cyclist we'd met at the Uzbekistan embassy. At Sinbad Hostel we met two more cyclists, Gordon and Theo. Paul is Dutch and cycling to Southeast Asia, Gordon is from the Isle of Wight, and was off to India having cycled through Europe. Theo is French and was travelling west. He had just cycled through Turkey so had some good advice for my onward travel. It was good to have a group to spend time with and discuss experiences.

By the weekend I was getting frustrated that I hadn't had much time to look around Istanbul. Nino's family arrived on Friday night to spend the weekend with him and very kindly put me up in the same hotel that they were staying in and bought me some delicious meals. On our first evening there, we put the TV on to find out that the Americans had killed Osama Bin Laden. I wondered if this would affect how people treated me in the Muslim world. I doubted it would, but perhaps animosity towards the West would increase slightly amongst certain groups. The UK often seems to be grouped together with America in people's minds.

I visited all the sights with Nino's family; the Blue Mosque, the Aya Sofya, the Grand Bazaar, Topkafi Palace and others. It was a lovely weekend and I was overwhelmed by their generosity. I would never have been able to afford to see all the sights without their kindness. The hotel was an almost ridiculous luxury in comparison to my life over the previous weeks (particularly the breakfast buffet, which I made the most of!) and the company was great.

On Tuesday I finally had my visas and was ready to go. I left the others, including Nino, whom I had cycled with since Austria. He had become a good friend and I was sure that we would stay in touch. Such a lot had happened since meeting him all that time ago in the supermarket car park in Austria. As a leaving gift, Nino had given me a squeaking giraffe that attached to my bike. He had a camel on his, which entertained kids all the way through Europe, and the addition of the giraffe would be great for this purpose in Asia. I christened it Nino.

I was delighted that Laura was going to fly to Turkey to meet me in two weeks. We planned to meet in the city of Trabzon on the other side of the country. I had a long way to go to arrive there on time and was anticipating a difficult couple of weeks. The Black Sea road is very hilly. As for Istanbul, it's one of the best cities in the world.

Where else in the world is there such a mix of cultures, history, geography, food, religions and nature than Europe? Each country had been wonderful to cycle through and Europe as a whole eased me into my adventure. Ahead lay the real unknown. I would be out of my comfort zone from now on. I couldn't wait…

Photographs of Europe

Leaving family and friends behind

The drover's road near Aberystwyth

Goodbye to England

French tarts and coffee with my Dad

On the Donau Radweg with Nino (behind) and Julius (at the front)

Sandy in front of the Hungarian Parliament Building in Budapest

37

Sandy and a shop in Serbia

From left to right, Nino, Dragan and me in Belgrade

The roads in Serbia weren't quite finished!

Camping by the Danube

Decabalus, the last King of the Kingdom of Dacia, carved into the Danube Gorge

Romanian horses and carts were a common sight

Drinking grape liquor with Pedro in Bulgaria - spot the caravan!

Istanbul at last!

PART 2: TURKEY, THE CAUCASUS AND CENTRAL ASIA

From Istanbul to China

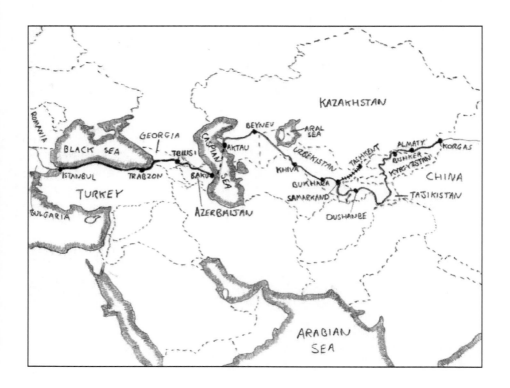

8. Cup of tea?

There is no trouble so great or grave that cannot be much diminished by a nice cup of tea.

- Bernard-Paul Heroux (Basque Philosopher)

I finally left Istanbul on Tuesday the third of May with three visas and a route through Central Asia planned. If all went to plan, after cycling through Turkey, Georgia and Azerbaijan, getting a ferry to Kazakhstan, then crossing the desert to Uzbekistan, I would pick up visas for onward travel in Tashkent. It was difficult to navigate on the way out of Istanbul but rewarding when I reached the boat that would take me across the Bosphorus. I wheeled my bike on board and stood by the window, watching Europe get smaller and Asia get bigger. It felt like a big step when I wheeled my bike onto the shores of the Asian side of the city. I was finally in my second continent!

It felt good to be alone again, travelling at my own pace. Nino had been fantastic company and had really helped ease me into the ride, but I was ready to experience Turkey alone. Solo travel forces you to spend time with local people, and as a result you experience the culture more completely. There's nowhere to hide when you're alone. It is more difficult but also more rewarding. I was delighted to be out of Istanbul. Although it was a lovely place to be trapped, I had been there for ten days and wanted to be out on the road again. I rode hard for the first couple of days, only stopping when offered tea (which was quite often). At almost every town a jolly looking, overweight, smiling, smartly dressed, moustached and very friendly gentleman waved me over. The weather was appalling so I appreciated the shelter of the tea stops to get out of the rain. I had to sleep in a wet sleeping bag for most of the first week. It was warm when wet, but it smelt awful and the dampness was very uncomfortable. Unfortunately there wasn't much I could do about this but managed to sleep so long as I didn't move around too much. The parts of the sleeping bag I wasn't touching got cold quickly.

A special part of the Turkish camping experience is the Muslim call to prayer, which you can hear all over the country. It echoes around the mountains from different mosques, each one with a slightly different call. Every Muazzin who sings the prayer call has his own unique sound, ranging from beautiful, soulful singing, to out of tune abuse of the eardrums. It made me feel very far from home. It also woke me up every morning at about five o'clock, when the first call to prayer was sounded. At this time of day, I wasn't quite as happy to hear it, but at least it got me moving early.

My first night in Asia was spent in a remote wood by a dual carriageway. I had lost my confidence in wild camping for some reason, so hid my tent well in a lot of undergrowth. I was worried again; perhaps because I was in a new continent, or because I was camping alone for the first time in over a month. In either case, I was cautious at my campsite for the first time since Western Europe.

Over the next couple of days the riding got more remote and the road passed through beautiful countryside. I rode over a mountain range between Istanbul and the Black

Sea. The closer I got to the coast, the more beautiful the scenery became. Most of my time was spent climbing on a road that wove up and down the hills. It takes significantly longer to climb on a bike than descend, so a high percentage of my time was spent fighting gravity. Due to this, I was struggling to reach my sixty-mile daily target. My old eighty-five mile target was now a bit ambitious so I'd lowered it to the minimum distance that would get me to Trabzon on time. The rain persisted and I was constantly wet, battling to keep my kit dry, as I had done in Western Europe, by airing it during the short periods when the rain stopped.

It was more difficult to find campsites in this part of Turkey because there was no flat land anywhere. The road was almost always cut into the side of the mountains and anywhere that was flat had a town built on top of it. I often tried to stop at the top of a hill to have an easy start the next day. It also meant a campsite with a good view. One memorable campsite had taken a while to find because the only flat land available was halfway down a steep slope. It was a bank built up against a huge tree with drops on either side of it and there was just enough room for my tent on it. After a good night's sleep, I woke up on my precipice and packed up my tent, pushed my bike back up the bank then zoomed down the other side of the hill. At the bottom, I was delighted to be invited into a café for a free second breakfast, while the owner's daughter practised her English with me.

Unfortunately the day got worse from then. My gear shifter locked up and wouldn't change gear. I took it off and changed gear with a spanner directly on my Rohloff internally geared hub, then had to get off the bike every time a gear change was needed. I was riding single speed most of the time and tried progressing like this for a while, wanting to reach a campsite in the evening to fix the problem there. It started raining heavily again though, so I pulled into a bus stop to try to sort it out. I had to remove the cables, oil them, cut off the frayed cable ends, clean out the outer cable covers and put it all back together again. The maintenance worked, but it meant that by lunchtime I had only ridden seven miles and was getting worried about reaching Trabzon in time to meet Laura.

I was plagued by mechanical problems all the way to Trabzon. My tyres were wearing out and the sidewalls collapsed on both. I used the spare tyre that I'd bought in Vienna, but had to bodge the other one with gaffer tape and a tea towel, which supported the sidewall and allowed me to limp to Trabzon. I also got about ten punctures and two inner tube blowouts. One of these was at a garage with an audience of five local men. They found it hilarious that the stupid English cyclist had overinflated his tyre and blown it up using the air compressor. I hadn't, it was a dodgy tube, but they wouldn't let me put more than twenty PSI in the next one (this is a pretty flat tyre; it's supposed to have between forty and sixty in it). Other problems included the front pannier rack bolt coming loose, a disc brake pad failing, my light holder snapping and another broken spoke in the back wheel. All these things needed fixing as I went along and my full toolkit was getting tested.

A couple of days after Istanbul, I reached the Black Sea. The road between Amasra and Sinop on the coast is absolutely stunning, with raised viewpoints looking out to the sea to the north and forested mountain slopes to the south. The rain stopped and I finally had a few days of good weather, being able to unpack my tent and sleeping bag at lunchtime to dry them in the sun. Despite its beauty, the road was really hard work. It was so steep, with over twenty percent inclines in some places. The hills were constant too; the road either climbed or descended steeply, with no flat sections. On my heavily loaded bike, it was a really tough few days; the hardest part of the ride so far, but also one of the best.

The wildlife in Northern Turkey was varied and wonderful. On one quiet corner of a closed road, I came across two tortoises walking along in front of me. The one in front was quite large, and was followed by a smaller one; presumably they were a mother and child. The mother watched me out the corner of its eye, and as I approached it retreated into its shell. The smaller one didn't know what to do so it repeatedly bashed into the mother's shell making a loud banging noise. Then it climbed on top of the mother. I rode off and looked back to see them disappear into the bushes on the other side of the road. Birds of prey swooped through the hills and followed the cliff edges and lizards scampered on the rocks. I saw a couple of snakes sunning themselves on the side of the road. One memorable night I pitched my tent in a beautiful orchard with fruit trees planted in diagonal lines. I was eating my dinner, sat on the lush green grass when a deer galloped past at full speed, being chased by another just a few metres from me.

A few days along the Black Sea coast and I arrived at a junction with a closed road. There were road works on my planned route ahead and a detour had been set up, which would involve a monster climb and an extra fifteen miles of riding. A guy at the bottom said that I would make it past the road works at the top of the hill on my bike. I had to choose between a longer climb and fifteen extra miles, or fifteen beautiful miles with sea views on an empty road, but the possibility of having to turn back and having to do the detour anyway. Ever the optimist I decided to take the closed road. It was a good decision to begin with. No traffic meant I could drift all over the road and enjoy being completely alone. The views were even better than before. I climbed and climbed, approaching the top of the hill. Looking back, I could see that I had ascended a long way, climbing for around an hour. Turning back now would be seriously demoralising. It would also dent my chances of arriving in Trabzon in time to meet Laura. *I had to get past the road works.*

As I rounded the corner at the top of the hill, my heart sank. A landslide had come over the road and it was a boulder field. There were diggers moving large rocks and I very much doubted that I would be allowed through. One of the workers came over and I managed to persuade him to let me. It was a two hundred-metre walk over very difficult terrain consisting of large rocks, with a bike weighing about the same as a person. I started over the rocks and was managing okay as the road worker waved me on. I strained my muscles, lifting my bike over the boulders and struggling to place one foot in front of the other. To my horror, the JCB above me started moving again, drilling the rocks. The guy who had let me through started panicking; he'd obviously not told the driver I was there. A landslide started above me! I picked up my bike and ran as fast as I could out of the way. Large rocks came crashing down and landed where I'd been moments before. Thankfully, I had escaped them. I was getting yelled at by the driver, who had finally seen me, but I managed to indicate that I'd been told it was safe to come across. The disgraced worker who'd waved me forwards helped carry my bike the rest of the way. I rode off a bit shaken up but glad to have missed the detour and during the next seven miles along my beautiful private road, reflecting that although I had almost been crushed by falling rocks, I had found time to rescue my bike!

My route along the Black Sea continued in a spectacular but difficult way for the next few days. The hospitality there was second to none and helped me to carry on when I was shattered. One evening, I was waved over by a guy in smart car. A well-dressed businessman wound his window down and started talking to me. He was an engineer who worked in Turkmenistan for an oil company, but was back in his native Turkey to visit his family. I followed him to a campsite that he recommended and he bought me dinner. The campsite owner wouldn't take any money from me for the night's accommodation and when I started pitching my tent he took me to a dormitory and gave me a bed for the night, which I shared with the on-site kitchen staff. More kindness from total strangers; again it seemed that the further east I went, the friendlier people got. I hoped the trend would continue.

I climbed and descended for the whole of the next day, finishing on a long steep climb into the mountains, moving away from the Black Sea for the first time in a week and now in remote, wild countryside. The villages here looked poorer than those on the Black Sea coast. I pitched my tent in a wood at the top of the climb, but didn't sleep well at all. I had been writing my diary (as I did at this point every evening) and was about to go to sleep when something outside the tent growled. I knew that wolves live in Eastern Turkey and I was worried that there was one outside. It was probably more likely to be a stray dog, but it sounded big, so this wasn't a comfort. I imagined it could smell my food. I decided not to use the Dazer on it because I didn't want to annoy it, kept very quiet and turned my off my torch, listening to the snuffling and the footsteps. Eventually, and thankfully, it left, but I was nervous for the rest of the night. I would never find out what had been growling outside, metres from where I lay.

The next morning I had three punctures to fix. My tyres were almost worn out and had picked up thorns from the campsite bushes. I was really tired that day, but finally reached the end of the hills on the Black Sea Coast at Sinop; the last town on that stretch of coastline. Sinop is named after a Greek lady, *Sinope*, who according to legend died a virgin. Zeus had become amorous towards her and granted one wish in an attempt to seduce her. Sinope knew what he was up to however and wished that she could live the rest of her life as a virgin. Zeus reluctantly kept his promise.

I took a shortcut inland over some large mountains as an alternative to the much longer but flatter route around the Sinop peninsula. This was Turkey, remote and real. The villages were pretty, with people sitting on the side of the road, watching the world go by. Each village was full of little shops, including grocers, blacksmiths, tool shops, butchers, bakers, tea shops and many more. There were often people welding up cars or agricultural vehicles in makeshift garages on the roadside. As I reached one of the more dishevelled looking villages, a large dog started running at me. It caught up with me and sank its teeth into one of my front panniers. I stopped and went to hit it and it scarpered. Its owner looked very embarrassed and apologised. My pannier had teeth marks in it; *the rain would be able to get in now.*

After sleeping in the mountains, I descended to the coast early the next day. Beyond Sinop the coastline has been completely destroyed in favour of a dual carriageway. It must have been beautiful at one time, but now tunnels and sea defences have replaced the beaches and villages. It is quick and easy to ride on however, and has a large, safe hard shoulder so progress was swift. I stopped at five o'clock that day, having completed my target of sixty miles and in need of an early night and rest. I asked permission to camp in a farmer's field on the edge of the city of Samsun, then pushed the bike up a steep bank and found a flat piece of land to pitch my tent.

That night, I found another broken spoke in the back wheel. I dismantled my hub to get access to the eyelet where the spoke attaches to the hub. When it was in pieces, it started raining so I moved into my tent. A small cog dropped out of the hub but I didn't realise until the next morning after reassembling the bike and pushing it back down the steep bank. Panic built inside me when I discovered the cog was missing. I raced back up the bank and searched frantically for it. After a long time, I luckily found the small cog lying in the long grass. It was a miracle to find it, and if I hadn't managed I would have been stuck. No one in Turkey sells Rohloff components, and ordering one would have taken a long time. If I had been delayed by this, my visas for Central Asia would have started to run out before I'd even reached the countries. I would have had to hitch a lift to meet up with Laura in time too. A *very lucky escape.*

The next couple of days were uneventful, cycling along a dual carriageway and passing through a number of large towns, which were not particularly memorable. One of the nights, I slept in an old ruined house on a beach. On the final morning, the day before Laura arrived, I set off with the expectation of reaching Trabzon later that day. After an hour or two of quiet cycling, I cycled past a Croatian guy called Josep, who was riding a bike through a tunnel:

"Where are you going?" he shouted. *"China,"* I replied. *"I'm going to India!"*

This took me by surprise. I had assumed that he was local because all he had on the bike was a small backpack and the bike was very basic and in poor condition. The brakes barely worked and it only had one gear, so he had to push uphill on even the slightest inclines.

"Why are you going to India?" I asked. *"I'm telepathic, I was contacted through telepathy by an Indian Buddhist monk who lives in the Himalayas. I've left everything I own behind and I'm going to go and live a spiritual existence there."*

"Have you been to India before?"

"No, but I think it will be a much more considerate place than Europe, people will be much nicer to me there."

I had been lucky enough to visit India before, meeting Laura while she was there on her medical elective, then my brother came out and we travelled around the country for a fortnight. It was a fascinating place and the people were very friendly, but *'considerate'* is not a word that I would use to describe it. We received an annoying amount of attention. Personally I would have done a recce before leaving my home, everything I have and my family. Then again I'm not telepathic…

"Yes, my mind is twenty percent more powerful than normal people. I've left everything I own behind, I don't want material possessions." he continued.

It turned out that he didn't have a map and had left his glasses at home because they were included in his list of material possessions. He didn't have a tent so he slept in bushes or if he was lucky, in mosques. He told me he pretended to be a Muslim to get permission to sleep in them. With no glasses or map, he couldn't see very much and had no way of navigating. I gave him a spare map that I'd been given at a petrol station but he couldn't really read it without the glasses. I thought he was going to struggle crossing the Iranian deserts and the mountains of Pakistan. I shouldn't have been sceptical. Maybe he would make it.

We cycled together into Trabzon. As soon as we arrived, Josep and I were offered lunch in a restaurant for free. Josep gratefully accepted an old pair of glasses belonging to the owner that were luckily the right prescription. Maybe he decided that the 'no material possessions' thing was a bit over the top when it came down to his eyesight? We talked about football with the locals, *the international language*. Trabzonspor were second in the Turkish League with two games to play and they had a chance of winning the title. It was a position they hadn't occupied since their glory years in the eighties and the population of the small city was very excited about the season's penultimate match that afternoon. I looked into getting a ticket but unfortunately they were sold out. Josep and I ate until we were stuffed, then he cycled off towards Iran. I cycled to the hotel that Laura had booked for us, very excited about seeing her.

There were processions in Trabzon, and vans with a blaring loudspeaker. The whole place was covered in pictures of the prime minister. He was standing for his third consecutive re-election and was obviously very popular. It was a humorous election campaign for an outsider to witness; way over the top, with colourful buses covered in posters thundering past. Speaker systems blared out music and campaign slogans through poor quality sound systems on the bus roofs. The whine changed pitch as the loudspeakers drove past and it sounded awful. In such a noisy country though, I assume the loudest election campaign is deemed to be the best.

I spent the afternoon trying to make myself look and smell vaguely respectable, and removed my beard so that Laura would recognise me. I caught up on my diary and wrote down a list of mechanical problems that I'd had so far. Here it is:

1. One snapped chain (Wales)
2. One broken disc brake pad (Austria)
3. Three broken spokes (Turkey)
4. One worn out chain (Romania)
5. One shredded tyre (Turkey – replaced with spare tyre from Vienna)
6. Another damaged tyre (Turkey – split repaired with a tea towel)
7. One lost (and found) cog from hub (Turkey)
8. Lost front rack bolt (Bulgaria – replaced with spare)
9. Worn disc pads front and rear (Turkey)
10. Gear shifter locked (Turkey)
11. Broken light holder (Turkey)
12. Twelve punctures

My bike was tired. I had experienced a lot of mechanical problems in Turkey but Laura was bringing some spare parts so I would service the bike before getting going again. In the evening, I managed to barter a cheap lift from the hotel porter to the airport and picked Laura up at half one in the morning. I think she was pretty much the only girl on the flight. Trabzon isn't exactly on the tourist trail, although it's definitely worth a visit if you happen to be passing through. I saw Laura coming through security a mile off; there weren't many blondes in Turkey! It was so great to see her after two months and I was ready for a week off with her.

We spent the next day relaxing and using the hotel pool and beach. The following day we moved to a cheaper hotel in central Trabzon and stayed there for the rest of Laura's visit. We visited the spectacular 'Sumela Monastery' in the nearby mountains, which was built into a cliff face. There was a lovely old church in Trabzon, the 'Aya Sofya', with frescos painted all over the walls. We also visited a grand villa that was given to Ataturk (although he only ever stayed there for one night).

Other highlights included the culinary specialties, such as brain, tongue and 'grieved runover'. God knows what the last one is. Our two favourite places were a great fish restaurant, and a bakery where Laura became a bit of a celebrity. We went there twice. The first time we had flat bread covered in minced lamb, which was tasty but very filling. Laura only managed to eat a bit of it. The woman there loved Laura's fringe and kept hugging her, called her beautiful, making sure that she was looked after. When she went to the toilet the lady announced it to the whole (mainly male) restaurant and got someone to take her there. Pretty embarrassing! Unfortunately, I didn't get the same treatment. The second time we went, Laura was made a special small cheese bread pizza because the lady remembered her small appetite. It was good to be out of the limelight though. On the bike I attracted curiosity every time I stopped and was constantly surrounded by a crowd in every town. I was very happy to let Laura have some of that attention but I'm not so sure she was though.

Laura got her degree results whilst we were there and found out that she had qualified as a doctor, so we went to celebrate. We couldn't find any wine in Trabzon, so I took the new Dr Mulcahy out for a beer in a bar full of students. We sat down and someone at the next table shared their birthday cake with us. I couldn't imagine that happening in England. It was a lovely week, but too soon it came to an end and I was taking Laura back to the airport. It was very hard to see her go. I didn't know how long it would be until I saw her again, a few months at the very least.

I cycled through the rest of Turkey as quickly as I could feeling lonely, constantly close to tears. Having been looking forward to seeing Laura for so long it was terrible to be alone again. My morale had been great before Laura had come but now it was shattered. It had been a difficult week because although we were having a lovely time together, we both knew it was limited time and in a few days Laura would be moving back to start a job as a foundation doctor and I would be alone again. Laura was still being very supportive but I could see what a difficult position I'd put her and us in. While feeling very guilty about this, I knew that in the grand scheme of things, nine months is not a long time and that I would regret it for ever if I pulled out of this trip now.

I also had the worry of the desert crossing in Kazakhstan coming ever closer. It didn't help that the last part of the Black Sea coast is ugly, with uninspiring towns. I followed the coastal road towards Georgia and passed through a series of tunnels, in which cycling is not allowed. I got shouted at over a loud speaker system on a few occasions but ignored it and pushed on. It rained constantly for two days. On the first lunchtime three staring kids joined me, when I really wanted to be alone. They sat really close and just looked at me. I ignored them, just not being in the mood. All in all, I was looking forward to leaving Turkey. I had been there for almost two months and was very much looking forward to Georgia, having heard great things and planned to meet up with a friend from university, Henry. He was teaching English in Gori, Stalin's birth town. It would be great to have the company of a friend, and maybe it would help take my mind off missing Laura.

Eventually I reached the border, very much ready for a change. Turkey had been a very different experience. The country is beautiful and full of wonderful people. I had been in Turkey for much longer than any other country so far, and had really got to know it. I left Turkey with a feel for what life is like there, and on the whole I'd say most people have a very good quality of life.

9. Churches, wine, friends and fools

I may not have gone where I intended to go, but I think I have ended up where I intended to be.
- Douglas Adams

I changed the rest of my Turkish Lira into Georgian Lari in a dodgy looking shop window then crossed a pretty chaotic border into Georgia at the town of Sarp. It took a long time because the officials thought my passport was a fake. There were creases around the photo that made it look like it might have been replaced. My passport was looking more and more tatty every day, and this reaction was worrying for future border crossings. After discussing it for about half an hour, I got out my driving license and showed them that. It swayed them and they finally believed that I wasn't trying to enter their country illegally. I cycled into my thirteenth country, which turned out to be paradise.

I liked Georgia straight away; it had more character than Eastern Turkey. The road wasn't a groomed dual carriageway, but a smaller bumpy road that hadn't destroyed the scenery. There were waterfalls, statues, a Roman castle and ancient churches. I reflected that I preferred churches to mosques and wouldn't miss the Turkish morning call to prayer before sunrise. I was in the former Soviet Union for the first time and was reminded of this when I got to Batumi, a city dominated by concrete tower blocks. In the evening I reached the village of Makihjauri, where I was offered a cheap bed in someone's outhouse. I had a shower, which was heated by a home-made wood-burning boiler, and was then invited round to the home of a guy called Mareb, who could speak English and loved heavy metal music. We spent a great evening drinking coffee then beer, accompanied by chocolate and cake. Then the Georgian cognac and Russian vodka came out. We watched videos of Iron Maiden on Mareb's wide screen TV. Two of his friends arrived and they told me about their old jobs. They all used to work on Soviet cargo ships so have travelled to many countries. We discussed Stalin, and compared life today to life during the communist years. Mareb was an intelligent guy and had done well for himself in recent years. He now drives a Chevrolet imported from America, instead of a Lada, which is the most common car in the former Soviet Union. He didn't like Stalin or his methods, but took an admirably diplomatic view on the subject. He could see that life for much of the population of Georgia was better under Stalin. This was the first of many discussions I had about Stalin and communism; a subject that is still at the front of people's minds in Georgia. I left the three of them at about half past midnight, feeling a bit tipsy. They were all very drunk, having been drinking vodka for at least three hours.

The next day I woke up at nine o'clock with my first hangover for months. There was monsoon-like rain outside, so I used it as an excuse to have a lie in, and got going at around midday waving goodbye to my new friends as I left for the countryside. As I rode through Georgia I fell in love with its beautiful scenery, perfect weather, kind people and delicious food and decided not to rush through the country, which is small, and to make the most of my time there. I rode about sixty miles per day at a leisurely pace and stopped every time I was offered tea, food, wine or beer. Georgia is a varied country, with the Caucasus Mountains in the north, the beaches in the west and pretty, ancient towns surrounded by forested mountains. Even the ugly Soviet tower blocks seem to look better here. The Georgians somehow managed to build wonderful old churches perched on the most spectacular mountain peaks, which improve the already beautiful scenery. I visited a few of the churches, and the interiors are decorated with ancient frescos and gold leaf.

I cycled along a small lane, which followed a river valley up and the over a pass in the hills. At the top of the pass there was a wonderful view. Looking back down towards the Black Sea there were corrugated iron roofed houses dotting the hillsides. The houses are set in generously sized plots of land and have small personal vineyards in the gardens. I got occasional strange looks when passing some of the small villages; people couldn't quite believe what I was doing. The people here are very old-fashioned, and it seemed that life hadn't changed much over the last few decades. The clothes, houses, culture and way of life seemed very dated compared to the countries I'd been to so far. I passed a village at dusk and found a beautiful place to pitch my tent on a hillside field overlooking a river valley. That evening I lay outside eating my dinner, drinking tea and admiring the valley. It was a special place.

Despite all the other highlights, the best thing about Georgia was being invited into people's homes. My first night spent in a Georgian's house was in a small village with a history teacher called Jarji from the local school. His wife was a fantastic chef and she cooked us a huge meal with pork, cheese, fish, salad, bread and homemade sauces. He even cracked open his expensive champagne, although I drank the homemade wine. An American guy called Sean joined us and told me about life in the village. He was spending a year there teaching English and living with a local family. Sean told me that it is a great honour in Georgia to have a guest. A British cyclist attempting to circumnavigate the world was the ultimate honour, so they had really pulled out all the stops for the meal. Sean continued recounting memories of the recent winter. There was a lot of snow and the village was isolated because the road was closed. This wasn't a problem for the inhabitants because every household grows grapes and makes their own wine, which is stockpiled for such situations. Life carried on pretty much as normal with a lot of eating and drinking. It was difficult for Sean though who couldn't leave the village during this period.

In the morning before I had reached Jarji's, I had left my camping spot early, not wanting to be found camping in the field. The small back road was enjoyable to cycle along, with tough climbs followed by rapid descents. Although I had to dodge a few potholes, the surface was pretty good on the whole. I passed the old capital city, Kutaisi. Because of the permafrost in many parts of the northern reaches of the former Soviet Union, it is difficult to excavate the ground. Although Georgia doesn't have permafrost itself, its plumbing systems were built in the same way; above ground level. Kutaisi's water pipes were on display, painted a bright yellow colour. They skirt the roadside, and smaller branch pipes run off to each individual house. At every drive and side road, the pipes arch up over the road to allow a car to pass underneath them. I wove my way along a river floodplain then followed another pretty river valley, looking for a place to sleep for the night. I asked a guy who was leaning over his garden fence if I could camp in his field and he agreed. His neighbour wandered past and told me he would be honoured if I would stay in his house that night; I accepted and had that memorable evening with Jarji and his wife.

Jarji, like many Georgian men, was red faced and overweight but incredibly hospitable and content with life. In the morning, breakfast was interesting. I got woken up at half past six because Jarji wanted to have breakfast with me. Breakfast turned out to be some sweets, a cup of coffee and some Cointreau! I managed to get away with only having one shot, despite his protests. My host however downed three full glasses before going off to school to teach primary school kids. A lot of alcohol is consumed in Georgia. This is fun if you are just passing through, but the Georgian people look considerably older for their age, in comparison to people in the West. They smoke a great deal too and their general health is poor. My friend, Henry, who is also teaching English in Georgia, told me a story when I met up with him a few days later. One of the other English teachers at his school went on a run around the local village. He put his shorts on and ran down the road then someone spotted him. The observer went to get his mates and he soon had a large audience of Georgian men howling with laughter at him. Not only was he wearing shorts (this is not done in Georgia) he had gone on a run; not a normal activity in their eyes.

I walked around the garden, was given a tour of Jarji's vineyard, and then set off for another brilliant day. I cycled five miles further up the river valley and was annoyed to find that the tunnel at the top of the valley was shut for roadworks. This added a long climb over a pass, although as I reached the top, my annoyance turned into admiration for the country once again when I got my first view of the Caucasus Mountains. The snow-capped peaks on the horizon were a spectacular view. I whizzed down the road on the other side, into the town of Surami where I explored two churches, although I was chucked out of the first one by a nun, who was outraged that I was wearing shorts. Kviratskhoveli Church is a beautiful building. It is white, angular and symmetric on the outside with a central tower and a red roof. The hexagonal inside is covered in ancient, slightly faded frescos. Gnarled trees stood at the entrance to form an arch and had two cast iron bells hanging from them. This design is typical of a Georgian Orthodox church, one of the oldest forms of Christianity, which was founded in the fourth century. Most Georgians are Orthodox Christians.

The second church is a beautiful Armenian building. It is also grandly decorated inside, with tapestries, gold ornaments and frescos. As I left the church a woman saw me unlocking my bike and invited me to her house for lunch. It was another beautiful home, with grand carved ceilings, fitted dark wood cabinets and plates and other ornaments on display. Before I knew what was happening, six courses appeared on the table in front of me; sausages, salad, bread, homemade jam, cheese, fish, pork and homemade corn bread. I stayed for about an hour, and on leaving they gave me a present; a terracotta donkey carrying two large barrels. You pour wine into the barrels and drink out of the mouth. It was heavy but a unique gift, which I couldn't possibly refuse. I would post it home. They invited me to stay for the night, but I had planned to meet my friend Henry that evening, so had to push on.

A few miles along a flat road brought me to Gori; Stalin's hometown. I met Henry in front of the town hall and we went to a restaurant to celebrate. I was his first visitor since he came to Georgia a couple of months ago and was as talkative as I was. The problem with having short term friends, however nice they are, is that you don't have any shared memories. It was great to talk about our time at university and tell stories about our mutual friends. We caught up over a blow-out meal and a bottle of Georgian wine, which cost about the equivalent of five pounds each. After the meal we were invited to join a table of middle aged local men for a proper Georgian piss-up. I was impressed with how much Georgian Henry had picked up in seven weeks; he could understand most of what was being said.

Henry was concerned that I didn't have anywhere to stay. It would be difficult for me to stay with the family who were looking after him due to lack of space. He suggested leaving to get a hotel. I wasn't worried and was sure, based on my previous experiences in Georgia, that one of the guys on the table would give me a bed for the night. Sure enough, we spoke to a lawyer called Zaza, who offered me a place to stay in Gori for as long as I wanted. I gratefully took him up on the offer and he gave me the guest bedroom, with antique ornaments including a gold clock and a beautiful king size four poster bed covered in gold sheets. We were brought yet more drinks by Zaza's son when we got to his house, a special bottle of Jack Daniels. I managed to escape the whisky, but Zaza and his friend Merab drank half the bottle.

The next morning, when I left Zaza's house, he was sleeping on the sofa. I would return to his house in the evening. My bike was safely locked in his garden; he had assured me the previous night that it would be safe there. Henry and I met at the Stalin museum, which is very interesting, but a bit surreal. There is no mention of Stalin's appalling treatment of his own people and he's portrayed as a God. I had discussed Stalin with the group the previous night and they had proved again that there is a split view in Georgia about Stalin. Some people still love him because when he was in power they had a job and a car, stability, and plenty of food for their families. He was a simple man from a poor family, who became one of the most powerful men on the planet, and led a superpower for twelve years. They were able to ignore the twenty million people he killed (many of whom were Georgian) because they had a good life under Stalin's regime. Now unemployment is Georgia is high and the country is stuck in a rut, not really going anywhere. This didn't happen under Stalin. There are however a large number of people, like Zaza, who detest Stalin, believing him to be a barbaric power-mad mass murderer.

The museum included: his death mask in a shrine-like burial chamber, his outfits, letters to and from Hitler, photos, a statue of him, and a train carriage which Stalin used to travel to the Yalta conference during the Second World War. Stalin's childhood home is also at the museum, which is its original location. The rest of the neighbourhood was knocked down and a temple built over his house so that it now also resembles a shrine. Looking back at the museum, I found it disgusting that Stalin is portrayed in such a favourable way. There was no mention of the gulag, the Ukrainian famine, the assassinations, or any other of Stalin's war crimes and appalling treatment of the Soviet people. In the visitor's book was an entry from an American couple:

"You (meaning Georgia) are trying to move forwards and want to be accepted around the world as an open and accepting nation. How do you expect the rest of the world to respect you and believe you want to put the past behind you if you continue to support this barbaric oppressive regime." This sums up my thoughts about the museum pretty well.

I had another evening with Zaza, and this time his son, who spoke reasonable English. We discussed Georgia all evening. Zaza had welcomed me because I'm British. He sees Brits and Americans as 'on Georgia's side'. Recent violence between Russia and Georgia included the invasion of Gori in 2008. The Russians occupied the city for a single day and eleven civilians were killed. The UK and America spoke out against Russia, and the Georgians remember this. Zaza also explained Georgian society, which has a lot of emphasis on respecting the older generation, who are viewed as heads of their families. Society in Georgia is old-fashioned in the way that women are viewed, as they seem to do all the cooking and housework while the men entertain visitors. Oddly, men are expected to be sexually experienced before marriage, while women are supposed to be virgins on their wedding day. Clearly this doesn't quite add up. Zaza explained to me that this is where the Ukrainian prostitutes came in and promptly offered to pay for their services for me. I explained that I had a girlfriend, but this didn't seem to register as a problem. He offered again and I politely declined. In the UK, that would have been outrageous behaviour, but in Georgia it wasn't. Zaza was a very kind man and a great host and was acting in an acceptable way in the country that was home to him. I think that these dated societal norms may be preventing Georgia from developing in comparison with the countries around it.

With much to think about, I left Zaza's and cycled towards Tbilisi. I wanted to stop at Mtsketa on the way, which is an ancient city, founded prior to 1,000 BC. It became the capital of the old Georgian Kingdom of Iberia between the third and fifth centuries AD. It is a world heritage site and the spiritual home of the country, containing the headquarters of the Georgian church. It is a stunningly beautiful place; an old city on a river bend, with two large cathedrals, a ruined castle and two monasteries, including one perched on a hilltop. In the afternoon I looked around the cathedrals and went to camp in the city's park. I was invited to pitch my tent there by the warden, Annis. A spontaneous party erupted as Annis' friends arrived, inevitably involving large amounts of Russian Vodka. I cooked rice and vegetables for everyone on my stove, which interested them as it runs on petrol. I played music from my phone. They loved Pink

Floyd and Bob Dylan. The party was still going strong at midnight when Annis started a fire and cooked massive lamb kebabs.

The next morning I was hungover again, as were many other Georgians most mornings! I cycled the twenty miles to the capital city, Tbilisi, where I met up with Henry again in front of the parliament building with its unique egg shaped glass dome. Tbilisi is beautiful, with its large collection of ancient churches on its many hills, and a bustling old town full of restaurants and bars with heaps of character. We had a banquet in one of the restaurants spending less than ten pounds each. The Kura River weaves through the middle and there's a magical atmosphere. It became one of my favourite cities in the world and is still very cheap as it's not on the mainstream tourist trail yet. I watched Man Utd unfortunately get annihilated by Barcelona in the Champions League Final, but other than that we had a fantastic time.

I woke up in our hostel feeling quite ill to find two more broken spokes in my rear wheel, which had to be fixed before continuing. As I climbed up the hill a few miles outside the city, nature called. I had to use a public toilet on the side of the road. It was dirty, smelled awful and was, disturbingly, fully communal. Thankfully I was alone, it would have been rather embarrassing to have an audience. The illness was taking it out of me, so after just fifty-six miles I found a place to camp, feeling very down. I could probably have stayed in someone's house again but I needed a night off the booze. I went to bed early and opened a letter that Laura had given me, instructing me to open it when I was feeling sad; it cheered me up considerably.

The last part of Georgia was quieter but still lovely. I crossed some forested mountains, entered the wine growing region of the country and passed a pretty walled town in the hills called Sinaghi, with its ancient fortress and delightful restaurants and shops. Leaving the small town, I rode down a cobbled road, underneath an arch in the wall then onto a long descent to a very hot, swampy river floodplain. Every group of people I passed flicked their throats, gleefully waving a bottle of vodka at me. The slightly threatening throat flicking action meant they wanted to drink vodka with me. *A lot of vodka*. I'd had enough vodka for one lifetime so I waved at them, pretending not to understand what they wanted.

There were snakes on the road as I crossed the plain to the base of the Caucasus Mountains and the Azerbaijan border. Georgia was the most incredible country and I'd thoroughly recommend going there soon if you get the opportunity. Ryanair are possibly going to start flying there and I can't help thinking that the inclusion of Brits on stag dos on the streets of Tbilisi won't improve the atmosphere much. I hadn't originally planned to come to Georgia but did so because without an Iranian visa it was my only pathway east. It's the best country I've ever been to.

Azerbaijan started off very hot and with swarms of mosquitoes desperate to suck my blood. I got a lot of attention at the border, and then again, at the first town. Feeling shattered and really wanting to have a relaxing evening and an early night, as I passed a house I heard more people shouting after me and beckoning me over. I decided to see what they wanted. Straight away they offered me a place to sleep and dinner so I accepted and enjoyed another Georgian meal on my first night in Azerbaijan. It was delicious; pork, cheese, fish and bread. We had a couple of beers, but thankfully I managed to keep my vodka glass empty. Unlike the Turks, the Azerbaijanis didn't seem to pay much attention to the strict Islamic no drinking rule. An incredibly drunk guy drove off and came back with three girls. They went into an outhouse. An hour later he drove them away again. I didn't ask what they were doing there.

I slept in the front room with the father (called Islam) and his son. It was really hot in the room and the window was shut to keep out the mosquitoes. Islam also left the TV on all night, so I didn't get much sleep. I thought that I would definitely camp the following night. I got going early in the morning and cycled along quiet and scenic country roads. I say roads, but they were really just stony tracks, skirting the edge of the Caucuses Mountain foothills, sometimes passing through forests, sometimes, stony and sandy plains. At one point I had to ford a large river because the bridge had collapsed, but luckily it was pretty shallow. It was slow progress but immensely enjoyable and beautiful. I stopped for yet another free cup of tea that, thankfully, I didn't have to drink with sugar. After all of the sweet tea that I had been given in Turkey and Georgia, I felt at severe risk of developing diabetes! The tea drinking party also forced a shish kebab on me, which would have been welcome if I hadn't just had a massive lunch. I enjoyed it anyway although regretted eating it slightly when I was almost too full to move in the afternoon. The temperature reached thirty-two degrees, the hottest it had been so far, it was muggy and I was tired.

At Saka, I climbed a long hill to try and find an ancient Khan's Palace. It took about an hour and was a difficult climb. I was reluctant to take the diversion but the guidebook said it was worth a visit, an opportunity not to be missed. When I arrived, the palace looked a bit disappointing, so I didn't pay to go in. I rode back down the hill and asked a shepherd if I could camp on his land. He said yes, and then a minute later, his son turned up with a giant pot of tea and a loaf of bread for me. I was offered a place to sleep in a nearby house but turned it down and slept in the tent. I was sorry to disappoint the shepherd and didn't want to seem rude, but I really needed a night to sleep well and recover.

The next day, first day of June, started much better both physically and mentally. I followed a good road through the steppe and everything was much drier. I saw lizards and snakes, many of which are poisonous, giving a particularly large one, which was sleeping on the road, a wide berth. I reached a village and went to the local shop to stock up on supplies. One shop owner seemed delighted to see me and followed me around for about half an hour as I did my shopping. He walked right next to me and kept grabbing stuff off the shelves and handing it to me, which was really annoying. I knew he was trying to be friendly, but he was driving me mad and making everything take twice as long. It was difficult not to lose my temper. After shopping, I went to his restaurant in the village for a cup of tea and he seemed satisfied with that.

After lunch came a very long, straight climb in the Caucasus Mountain foothills. I was now in a hot desert and was getting bored with the scenery so invented a game to pass the time: *count the number of Ladas that drive past in a row.* I counted the Ladas that passed and restarted at zero if a non-Lada came past. Almost all the cars were Ladas. The highest my consecutive-Lada count got was twenty-three. It was only broken up by one car before another count of sixteen. *Boring miles in the desert.*

In the evening I reached a beautiful thick forest and was chased by two gigantic sheep dogs. This was pretty standard and I was used to getting chased by this stage. I jumped off the bike and stood up to one, which backed off nervously. The other circled me and walked straight in front of a car travelling on the other side of the road at about forty miles per hour. It flew about five metres through the air and hit the ground hard, whimpering. Incredibly the dog survived, and looked unhurt as it rushed off back to its master. I didn't feel too sorry for it as it would have bitten me if it had got the chance. The car was a mess though; the front of had caved in and the headlight was smashed. Thankfully they didn't blame me at all and I had a chat with one of the passengers who spoke good English. The driver just pulled out the large dent with his hand and drove off in good spirits. What a refreshing attitude.

That night I asked another shepherd, called Eziz, where I could camp. He took me to a bit of land surrounded by a river on one side and a fence on the other, which was accessible by a tiny thin bridge. I was safe from wolves here apparently! Eziz told me about the Caucasus Mountains that he loved and the wildlife on his land. He showed me a new born lamb and brought a group of small kids over to see me. I let them have a go in my tent then had tea boiled in Eziz's metal flask on a fire before going to bed.

Azerbaijan really started to grow on me. The scenery was spectacular and the people were incredibly friendly. Leaving my 'wolf-proof' camp spot, I passed through forests, mountains, plains and desert. It was one of the most varied days of cycling I have ever experienced. That evening, in a small village in the desert, I was told there were dangerous wolves about. This was my first big desert and I was worried about sleeping out on my own. In hindsight, and with desert camping experience, it would have been fine to sleep wild, but the stories of wolves had made me nervous so I decided to sleep in a town that night. After a few miles of isolated desert cycling, I found a metal shed on the side of the road with an open door. It would probably have been a safe place to stay but a town would be better if there was one close by. I flagged down a car to ask where the next town was:

"Salaam Alaykum," I greeted the driver.

"Assalam alaykum," he replied

Using my *'Point it'* book and map, I managed to communicate *'How far to the next village'.* He responded in Russian:

"Dva kilometre." (two kilometres).

I should have known by that stage, that Azerbaijanis are terrible at estimating distances. I believed him and continued. Ten miles later, I was shattered and it was dusk. Ahead was the tiny settlement of Cegrankegmaz, which was little more than a small farm and a couple of houses. As I had been hoping, one of the inhabitants invited me into his home. I gratefully accepted the invitation and was offered a shower and given a feast; *unbelievable hospitality again.* As we were eating, I spoke to one of the men, another guy called Islam. He could speak basic English and communicated to me that they didn't have any mains water there. They had to buy it at an extortionate price from a government run lorry that supplied their large water tank. It cost around fifty pounds a month and they were understandably very annoyed about it as the government had plenty of money. Azerbaijan has a fast-growing economy because of their Caspian Sea oil reserves. A lot of the money is spent on skyscrapers in Baku and much of the rest of the country is forgotten. Islam was hoping that in the next few years, they may be supplied with water from a pipeline. I went to bed quite early and offered to pay for the shower that I'd had; they of course refused. I was only forty miles from Baku so was expecting an easy ride the next day.

It wasn't. I fought a gale force head wind for nine hours and eventually arrived in Baku in the early evening. The ride through the desert was beautiful though; it was so remote along a hilly, winding road that passed sand dunes, in the heat of the day. My route took me from the middle of nowhere to the metropolis that is Baku, sticking out on a peninsula into the Caspian Sea. When I finally arrived in the centre of the city I asked at a tourist information office for the cheapest hotel around. They told me that the only one they knew of was the 200 dollar per night luxury tourist hotel next door, and that it wasn't their job to tell tourists about hotels anyway; they were there to give information about the historic old town. I wasn't in the mood to inform them that it is usual for tourist information centres to give travellers information about accommodation. I left feeling angry at their rude behaviour; they must have known of a cheaper hotel. I asked a taxi driver, using the worlds, *"Hotel"* and *"little money"*. He pointed me in the direction of the cheapest hotel he knew of (which wasn't that cheap). Baku is a very expensive city.

I was too tired to search for any more hotels, so I checked into the Soviet dinosaur that the taxi driver had suggested and hid away in my room. I scoffed some food, which I cooked with my petrol stove on the window sill, and headed out to try to get a ticket for the Caspian Sea ferry. I was absolutely shattered, leaving the hotel and walked to the 'Old Port' to try to buy my ferry ticket. I arrived at the ticket office only to be told that the tickets for the Aktau ferry were sold at the 'New Port' five miles away, even though the boat left from the Old Port. Only tickets to Turkmenistan were sold there. The ticket office at the New Port was closed until the next day so I would have to go back in the morning. I returned to my hotel after buying enough food to feed an entire family, and a couple of beers and had a feast in front of some Azerbaijani television that evening, taking a moment to think. I had reached the Caspian Sea and all I needed to do was get a ferry ticket, something that I would get eventually. With eight days still on my visa, I had enough time to get on one of the boats. I thought back to London and picking up my visa on that morning with Nan. *It seemed a world away.*

The Caucasus had been fantastic. I had absolutely loved Georgia, and Azerbaijan wasn't far behind. Georgia seemed to be a fairly stable country, at least in the areas

59

that I visited. I heard that the region of South Ossetia, which is under Russian control, is dangerous, but I don't think they let tourists in. Other areas in the north of the country are unsafe too, due to Chechen rebels operating in the mountains. My experience was that Georgia is a wonderful and safe place to visit. What I had learnt made me feel a bit sorry for Georgia though. Russia to the north doesn't get on with it. Azerbaijan to the east is much richer due to their oil reserves, and Turkey to the west is now a successful nation with a growing economy. Armenia to the south may have a lot in common with Georgia and is a country that I'd love to visit.

10. Baku and the Caspian Sea ferry

Difficulties are just things to overcome
- Ernest Shackleton

I wasn't expecting my ticket purchase to be easy, having heard nightmare stories of travellers being stranded in Baku for a week or more waiting for a ferry to Aktau. I was expecting pointless waiting and sucking up to 'important' officials to get a ticket. It didn't disappoint!

I left early in the morning, to resume my mission to get on board the Caspian Sea ferry, not having enjoyed my night in the grimy, overpriced, mosquito and cockroach infested hotel room. I was going to do all that I could to not have to stay there again. On the positive side, Laura and I had chatted for two hours over the hotel's internet until about four in the morning (Baku time). I got a taxi to the 'New Port' at eight o'clock, it was easier than trying to navigate my way through Baku on my bike to an unknown destination. I went to the ticket office to be told come back at midday. I said *"Okay, thank you"*. I waited in the hot sun and returned at midday and was told to come back at three o'clock. I said *"Okay, thank you"*. In the meantime I managed to befriend the guy who decided who was first in line for the next tickets. The befriending process involved drinking a bottle of vodka with a large group of Kazakhs who were delighted to have an English cyclist for company. 'Don Ferry Ticket' assured me I'd get the next ticket available. I was also offered a bed for the night from a lovely guy called Arif. The taxi back to my hotel was a Lada and I was pleased that I'd had a chance to ride in the Soviet Union's finest automobile!

I managed to leave just before one o'clock, which was checking out time, so didn't have to pay for another day and took the underground train to a bike shop, which turned out to be miles away and basic. I was hoping to buy some brake pads for my disc brakes, the ones I had brought with me were wearing out much more quickly than I had anticipated and only had one spare set left. These would last until the other side of Uzbekistan as it's pretty much flat and I wouldn't need to use the brakes much. Tajikistan on the other hand is over ninety percent mountains and I would need some new sets by then. I planned to email home and get some posted out to a city on my route when I got onto the internet next. It was strange because I had seen a couple of very nice looking mountain bikes being ridden around Baku. Perhaps their owners ordered spare parts from abroad.

At three o'clock I went back to the port, this time on my bike. On the way I tried unsuccessfully at almost every ATM in Baku to get some US dollars. I would need dollars in Central Asia to exchange for local currencies, as bank machines aren't very common in the Kazakhstan desert! After about twenty attempts, I finally found one containing 400 dollars, which I promptly extracted. Back at the port, the office opened at four and I finally got my ticket for 110 dollars, pretty pricey considering it was just a cargo ferry with a few rooms for passengers. The ferry company have a monopoly on the crossing and it was the only path between Kazakhstan, the Caucasus and Turkey, without having to pass through Iran and communist-run Turkmenistan, where foreigners aren't allowed to enter the country without an expensive guide. On being told that the ferry was about to leave, I packed up my stuff and cycled as fast as I could back to the Old Port. At the boarding check-in 'hut' they then told me the ferry wasn't leaving until the morning and I should come back at nine the next day. I hung around for a while and befriended the captain's assistant to see if I could board a boat that evening which may have been possible but tiring of waiting and complimenting officials, I cycled back to the New Port and Arif's house to take him up on his offer for a bed for the night.

Arif was the best host I've ever had. He welcomed me into his house and introduced his wife and baby. We, along with some other stranded passengers, had a delicious meal of spaghetti bolognaise and a few beers. Arif's wife washed all of my clothes and Arif gave me some of his to wear; a T-shirt, a vest and some brand new Y-fronts! Arif, a mechanic, let me use his vast array of tools to service my bike. He gave me a pot of grease to add to my toolkit. I turned the chain ring on my Rohloff hub around to give it a new lease of life and changed the chain, hoping that this maintenance would resurrect my drivetrain for the next 3,000 miles or so. Arif and I watched a hilarious Russian sketch show on TV, then I got an early night.

In the morning I tried to return my new outfit of clothes, but Arif insisted I should keep them, blown away by his generosity, I waved a very fond farewell to him and his wife, they were extraordinary people. They didn't want anything from me in return for food, beer, clothes and a bed for the night but were happy to hear my story and help me. Without their help my bike would have been in a much worse state, I would have had to spend significantly more money in Baku, and my clothes would still have been dirty for my ferry journey.

Back on the bike, I returned to the Old Port and finally boarded the ferry at about midday. I put my bike in the storage level and locked it around a pipe next to the train tracks in the hold. Freight trains are loaded into the lower level of the massive ship and transported across the sea to continue their journey through Asia. After performing a series of acrobatics, including jumping between gangways with a thirty foot drop to the Caspian Sea below, I finally arrived on the deck of the *'Professor Gül'*, walked up to the passenger area and found it was deserted. I was there on my own for a few hours until the other passengers with cars were let on. The trains were loaded on and the ferry eventually left at about seven in the evening. When I felt the engines shudder into life and saw the plume of smoke rising from the two funnels at the rear of the boat, I ran up to the deck and watched Baku get smaller as I began my crossing to Aktau. *The desert was waiting.*

I had to surrender my passport to an official for some reason. I was reluctant at first, because not only was it my passport, but it had 240 dollars worth of visas inside it. The other passengers handed theirs in though and I was told it would be returned when we left the ship, so I supposed I had no choice. On board the *'Professor Gül'* I had a great time. The ferry was full of Kazakhs importing German cars from the Caucasus. The import laws were changing; so many Kazakhs were buying old BMWs and Mercedes while it was still cheap to bring them into Kazakhstan. Needless to say there was a lot of alcohol on board the boat. I managed to avoid much of the drinking but not all of it. Luckily, my cabin mates were a guy who slept for almost the entire crossing and an Azerbaijani called Rashad who didn't drink much. I asked Rashad to write a note in the back of my diary in Russian, which explained who I was, what I was doing, that I was raising money for charity and what 'SOS Children's Villages' do, and finally saying that I would be very grateful for any help. It would come in useful for the rest of my time in the former Soviet Union. After this was done, I chilled out in my room for a while and read a book.

Feeling refreshed, I went to the restaurant on the boat and saw the group of people that I had befriended at the New Port. They waved me over and tried to teach me how to play a game of cards. Bizarrely, I won both games I took part in, despite having absolutely no idea how to play. We were an odd bunch; a Georgian, an Azerbaijani, a few Kazakhs and, most weirdly of all, a crazy English guy who'd come here on a bike. The Georgian provided some home-made wine and I was bought a beer, followed by a few rounds of tea. Despite a lot of pressure, I escaped drinking too much when the vodka arrived (having only one shot). After the frivolities, I went up to the deck and saw a blanket of bright stars in the clear sky above the sea. Massive oil rigs, lit up by bright lights, constantly surrounded the boat. It showed pretty clearly how the money is made in this part of the world. I lay on the deck alone, thinking about my journey so far and finding it hard to believe that I had made it this far. Europe, Turkey and the Caucasus were behind me and Central Asia lay ahead. I couldn't put off thinking about the desert much longer but needed to make some serious plans soon and resolved to look at my maps the next day. I wanted to know, in detail, how far I would have to travel between water points.

The next day the boat arrived at Aktau on time. We stopped about a mile out at sea at around ten o'clock in the morning, but stayed outside the port all day. Apparently there was no space for us to moor up. I used the time to look at my maps and to read. Nobody on board thought I had a chance of making it across the desert on a bike. This didn't make me feel any better about what lay ahead. I was told again that the road was utterly awful, most of the Kazakhs not knowing about the existence of a road linking Aktau to Uzbekistan. There was something there for sure though; I could see it on my map, and I had seen a line in the desert on Google Earth aerial photos. At the very least, there was definitely a track I could follow.

At about five o'clock in the afternoon, the captain announced that we would be spending another night on the boat because there wasn't room in the port. More drinking began, which I completely avoided this time, and inevitably tension was running high. Rashad was insulted by a drunk Kazakh guy, who had said something bad about Azerbaijan. The Kazakh wanted to start a fight in the restaurant. He was very drunk and had to be restrained by the other passengers. I escaped to the deck until it calmed down. The sunset over Aktau was spectacular. The enormous orange sun sank beneath the horizon and the sky turned a bright orange, with another cargo ferry sailing off in the distance. I looked over to the city, so near but so far away, unsure about what lay ahead. I almost didn't want the boat to reach the port.

The next day, we were finally let off the ferry in the early afternoon. I had been on board for over two days instead of the eighteen hours it was supposed to take. Clearing customs, and persuading officials to let me back on the boat to get my bike, took more time and I finally got to a hotel that evening. It was a good, clean hotel called *'Hotel Aktau'*, and was run by an Egyptian. He was very impressed by what I was planning to do. He thought that I wouldn't make it but gave me a free night in the hotel after I paid for the first. I promised that I would put the name of his hotel in this book, so if you ever end up in Aktau, stay in *'Hotel Aktau'!* My time in Aktau was spent preparing for the desert. I had to register with the OVIR office, an antiquated Soviet legacy which records where foreigners are in the country. I would love to know what they do with the files of traveller's passport details. They must have a huge storage warehouse full of them. In a modern shopping centre I found a cheap holdall to store water in, and a hat with a rim all the way round for protection from the sun.

After two nights in Aktau, I was ready for the desert and looking forward to getting moving again. This was the first time that I was worried about a part of the trip. The desert really would be entering the unknown. I called Laura and my family before I set off. While not expecting anything bad to happen I was concerned about my safety in the desert. It was very hot, barren and remote and road quality was poor. This was probably going to be the make or break part of the trip. If I could get through, I was confident of making it all the way across Asia on my bike. I was worried enough to make sure that I had a good long conversation with the people I loved though; *just in case*. Thinking sensibly, I promised myself that if I got into difficulties I would ask for help. It seemed, at least, that the odd lorry would pass, so if I was really stuck I thought that I should be able to hitch a lift.

11. Into the desert

Do, or do not. There is no 'try'.
- Yoda ('The Empire Strikes Back')

I was nervous leaving Aktau. People from whom I asked directions looked at me in an odd sort of way. Who rides a bike through a massive desert? Why would you risk it? I could see their point. I had no idea if anyone had made it across this desert on a bike before. Being determined to continue, I got back on the bike and pedalled out into the unknown. Riding felt strange at first because my already substantial load had been increased by twenty-three kilograms of water. I had decided, after much deliberation, that twenty-three litres was the right amount to take; wanting ten litres per day for two days plus three to cook with and to make tea in the evening. This was probably being overcautious, but definitely better than running out. The bike wobbled around the corners but was able to take the weight. I had been told that the road was good for the first sixty miles or so and by the time it deteriorated, my load would be substantially lighter.

The road followed the Caspian Sea coast for a while. I passed a spectacular Muslim burial ground, which was like something from Aladdin, with domes and minarets on some of the larger graves and temples over important people's tombs. Herds of camels were scattered across the barren desert landscape, which went on forever. There was nothing out there. The landscape was beautiful in its own way, isolated, desolate, but peaceful and infinite, and thankfully still fairly cool. This was because of the Caspian Sea. As I cycled away from its cooling effect, the temperature skyrocketed.

After twenty-seven miles spent following the road north along the Caspian Sea, towards Fort Shevchenko, I turned east towards Shetpe, the next significant town. Cycling until late, I found a little metal hut, to sleep in and was becoming ill with stomach problems again. This is not good for cycling, as it is difficult to absorb enough energy to ride all day when food passes straight through you. More worrying was making sure that I was taking in enough fluid, as I desperately needed to stay hydrated. Glad that I had brought so much water with me, I drank over two litres that evening. I hoped to reach Uzbekistan quickly in order to have my allocated full month to cross the country, get onward visas, and hopefully have time to do some sightseeing at the amazing-sounding Silk Road cities. If my illness became more serious, I didn't fancy my chances with any doctor that I might come across in the tiny and forgotten Kazakh desert towns and was worried about a long delay.

Having left my little hut at sunrise, I cycled away from the Caspian Sea and the temperatures increased, quickly reaching over forty-three degrees Celsius from about eleven to four o'clock. I reached the small village of Tauskgh, where the road to Shetpe turned off (fifty-six miles from Aktau). There was a shop there with cool water, hot food and fizzy drinks. A cool bottle of coke was so tempting but I resisted and didn't buy any water either, I still had plenty left, and everything was ridiculously overpriced. Turning right at the crossroads, I waved at some astounded looking police manning a checkpoint. The only people they ever saw here were lorry drivers heading to Aktau.

I stopped for lunch and ate my increasingly stale food. The heat was not doing wonders for the freshness of the large amount of bread I had bought, but the tinned meat was fine. I was still feeling ill and after another toilet stop, was worried. I had brought a bottle of coke with me from Aktau so I drank that to rehydrate, concerned about salt and sugar levels. I was starting to feel very tired in the heat. It was so hot that during my lunch break, my rear tyre exploded. The rim had heated up, without the cooling effect from the moving air that was generated by the movement of the wheel, and melted a hole in the inner tube. I fixed it with a large puncture patch from Baku and pushed on to Shetpe. Despite all this, I began to enjoy myself in the desert. The road was still pretty good and I had expected it to have deteriorated by now. I was in the most remote place I had ever been to, probably one of the most remote places there is and was completely reliant on myself to survive in the harsh environment. So far I was doing alright.

Thirty-nine miles after the last shop in Tauskgh, I reached Shetpe. The small town wasn't anything to write home about, but there was a decent bazaar, so I restocked with bread, jam, cheese and a new inner tube. The cheese was really salty so I ate a big piece of it at the market stall to try to restore my salt levels. I bought dinner and headed back out into the desert. Wanting to experience the desert fully and to camp out in the wild, I didn't stay in Shetpe that night but got another six miles done before looking for a place to sleep. There were a couple of mounds on the side of the road with a water pipeline running past. I lifted my bike across to the pipe and locked it around it; *you can't be too careful!* Completely out of sight, I unrolled my foam mat and put it onto the sand without bothering to pitch the tent; there was no chance of rain.

I lit up my petrol stove and started cooking dinner, watching a hillside that had some moving dots on it; wolves? Wolves where a worry as I had heard that were some out there in the desert that had recently attacked humans. I got out my camera and zoomed in on the animals. I couldn't be sure what they were, maybe goats but was confident that they weren't wolves. Lying down on my mat, I stuffed myself with pasta and cheese. I still felt ill but my appetite seemed to be back to normal. After eating, I lay on my back, watching the sky turn orange and then fade to black. The stars were a sight to behold, so much brighter than at home. Again, reminded how far from home I was, I felt very small. I was in the middle of a vast and barren landscape and very alone. Looking back on this part of the ride, I realise how important it was. It was a very valuable experience to push myself so hard and to attempt a challenge that I genuinely didn't know was possible.

The next day I felt much better, had a huge breakfast, went to the loo and was delighted to find that everything was back to normal. I felt as though I had loads of energy and I left my campsite in good spirits. Surprisingly, the road was still tarmac, but then, a guy in a big pick-up truck pulled up to talk. He couldn't believe I was there on a bike:

"Where are you going?" he asked.

"Beyneu," I replied.

"Beyneu? That's three hundred kilometres away, do you want to die out here! This road is like hell!" Then he drove off.

'Great, thanks for that,' I thought!

He was right and after the small town of Zharmysh (sixteen miles after Shetpe), the road deteriorated. It was just under two hundred miles to Beyneu, and the road would be like this all the way. It is difficult to describe it. I think if you tried you're very best to make the worst road you could possibly think of, this one would be worse. The Kazakhs have succeeded in creating an impossibly bad surface to ride on. It was corrugated, with gravel on top, huge ruts, sharp stones, sand traps on the sides and no shade from the beating sun. Riding the bike was slow going. I got up to maximum speeds of ten miles per hour on very good sections, but usually didn't move any faster than seven. Bizarrely, a few miles past the last bit of tarmac, I saw the second weirdest thing (after myself) in the Kazakh desert. A stretch Hummer was limping its way up the hill that I was limping down. What on earth was it doing there? Anyone rich enough to have a stretch Hummer would surely fly to Aktau. Maybe it was a successful former inhabitant of Shetpe, returning home to visit family. Maybe it was a rich oil baron who wanted an adventure in the desert. I speculated on the stretch Hummer for the next few hours and imagined the person inside drinking chilled champagne while I inched along the desert road. I thought he or she could have shared a bit with me...

My daily target was sixty-three miles, which meant riding from before sunrise until after sunset with only a short break. I had calculated that this distance would get me to Uzbekistan on the date that my visa was due to start. The physical side of riding this distance each day on the awful road was tough, but the mental torture was harder. I didn't have a conversation with anyone for days and only had my own thoughts to push myself on. Lorry drivers stopped sometimes to offer me a lift, but I turned every one of them down in favour of my stupid ambition to ride around the world on an unbroken chain. *'Why am I doing this?'* I had to keep telling myself: *'You can't give up now'*, *'You've come so far already'* etcetera. I wobbled along, constantly looking for the smoothest path. Sometimes there were dirt tracks along the side of the road that were often better than the main road, and so I swapped between the two. I ended up on the floor a few times after hitting a pile of sand, but it was a soft landing and I made steady progress.

On a couple of occasions it was really too hot to continue and I had to take a break and get out of the sun, sleeping in culverts (pipes) under the road during the hottest part of the day. I was worried about getting heat stroke and constantly drank lots of water, at least ten litres per day but stuck rigidly to my daily target. Once my speedo had ticked over sixty miles, I continued until the next pipe and slept there for the night. They really were a lifesaver, an instant comfortable and safe shelter; big enough to wheel my bike into and completely invisible from the road. I always checked for sleeping snakes and scorpions though! The comparative luxury of lying, dozing in the cool air away from the beating sun with not a worry in the world, made it very difficult to get going again.

Other rare comforts were the trucker's chaihanas (tea shops). I had no idea where they were so there was no mental comfort in easing myself on to the next one. However, when one did appear on the horizon I rushed to it and ordered a cold drink. Perhaps it was unwise in the desert, but beer had never tasted so good. The Russian lager, Baltika, was so refreshing when chilled, and I sat in the shaded chaihanas savouring it. I never allowed myself more than half an hour, fearing I would get too comfortable and never want to leave. Thinking about it, it was worrying that the chaihanas were selling beer. The only people who ever went there were lorry drivers. I imagine that the drink driving laws are fairly relaxed out there though.

The first chaihana that I visited was at the top of a long hill climb. This was pretty much the only hill between the Caspian Sea and the east of Uzbekistan. At the bottom of the hill was a sign that read *'The dangerous section'*. It was a steep hill, and as I climbed I got seriously hot. Not only was I having to work harder, I was also moving slower. Without the cooling effect from the moving air that is created when cycling faster on flat sections, I quickly turned into a sweaty mess. It was forty-three degree Celsius and the road was tough. I climbed past a couple of camels who thoughtfully watched me without any fear; they have no predators out here. They are so ugly, I thought to myself, and the camels probably though the same thing about me. All in all, I was a bit disappointed with *'The dangerous section'*. I was at least expecting a couple of wolves or a landslide or some big cliffs. It was just a long hill, but maybe it was dangerous if you were driving a Lada, which would have a serious chance of overheating or suffering a brake failure. Thankfully, at the top the chaihana was waiting. It was situated just past the top of some tall white cliffs; the relic of an ancient sea. The landscape was beautiful; the spectacular cliffs looked down on the endless desert, which stretched to the horizon in every direction. While I had been sat down cooling myself, two more holes had appeared in my rear inner tube so I replaced the inner tube with one I had bought in the Shetpe market. It looked like it was awful quality and I didn't fancy its chances against this ruthless sun.

Water was available here, forty miles from Zharmysh. The longest distance between water points was about sixty miles. The lowest my water supply got to was seven litres, so I could have got away with taking sixteen in total. However, it was obviously better to have too much and be safe than to run out. There was a small amount of traffic on the road, so I never felt too unsafe. The only worry I had was that one of the vehicles would contain an opportunistic thief who would mug me; I was carrying a lot of cash. If I got into any physical problems or had a mechanical failure, I would have been able to get help from a vehicle. A few passed every day.

Twenty-three miles down the road, I reached the settlement of Say-Otes; a small town with a railway station, a bar and a shop that seemed only to sell stale biscuits and vodka. I had camped just before the village the previous night so that I could use the water I had to cook dinner, planning to restock in the morning. I was happy to find that a tarmac road surface returned a few miles before Say-Otes and glided into the town along the mercifully flat road early in the morning. Having had to make a three-mile diversion to go there, I can safely say that it wasn't worth it. I needed food and water though and filled my panniers at the little shop. It was a forgotten place, with a horrible atmosphere, and I was pleased to leave. Here is what I wrote in my diary about it:

"Say-Otes is the most depressing place I have ever seen. There are a few houses, one shop and a railway station, which is probably too expensive for any of the locals to use. It's completely isolated and in the middle of the desert. The men that I saw there were drunk and were very aggressive to the women. I saw three men in the shop buying beer and vodka at nine in the morning, stinking of last night's drinking. They were aggressive to me and I didn't feel welcome there. I saw a little boy as I rode out and wondered about the life ahead of him. Barring a miracle, he will never escape this village."

Depressing thoughts, but that was the atmosphere of the place; *hopelessness*. I was happy to leave the village and was reminded of how lucky I was to have been brought up in England and not a desert village in Kazakhstan. Cycling away from Say-Otes I was treated to another few miles of tarmac until it deteriorated again into the awful road. There was a better dirt track off to the side of the main road, carved out by lorries trying to find smoother paths through the desert. I progressed through the steppe, but it was now becoming pretty tedious. There was nothing distinguishing about the landscape at all, just mile after mile of the same flat barren wilderness. The only highlight that day was a herd of wild horses that galloped alongside me for a few miles. Dust flew into the air as their hooves carried them forwards. They were a beautiful sight, and it is amazing that they are able to survive out there. In the summer it's difficult enough with the lack of water and sweltering temperatures. In the winter it would be even more difficult. The temperatures fall well below zero so their water supply would freeze..

By the afternoon of that day, the road was worse than ever and the wind direction had changed so I was now fighting a warm headwind. I was running low on water and gratefully accepted some from two separate passing cars whose drivers passed it to me out of the window. The ten litres remaining were hopefully enough to get me to Beyneu. Worryingly, I was running low on Kazakh money. I had dollars, but I wasn't sure that they would be accepted. There would be no problem exchanging them in Beyneu, so I would have to live on almost nothing until then.

After another sixty mile day, I found another culvert and settled down for the night, reckoning that it was one more day's ride until Beyneu and hoping tarmac would start again before the town. In the distance I could see a thunderstorm; the forked lightning was spectacular but menacing. I didn't want to get caught in a storm.

I woke up in great spirits, desperate to reach Beyneu and sleep in a bed that night. It turned out to be a very full day. After a large breakfast of stale bread and jam I left my pipe. Six miles later I reached Kemense, which was little more than a few houses and a truckers chaihana. I managed to exchange some dollars for an okay exchange rate of

140:1, instead of the official 145:1 and treated myself to a second breakfast and a bottle of Fanta. I had to buy some more water, and so got three bottles. Thankfully it was a cheap chaihana and everything had cost me six dollars, so not bad. I made steady progress on the appalling road and it looked like I would make Beyneu that day.

Unfortunately, the thunderstorm returned in the afternoon and some seriously heavy rain reduced the dirt road to a quagmire. It was so muddy that I was walking through a three inch deep sticky layer of gloop. It got everywhere, and jammed up my bike wheels every hundred metres or so. I had to push, straining my shoulders and arms for the short distance, stop to clear out the mud from around the wheels and bike frame, then carry on. This progress continued for about two hours, during which I covered only one and half miles. With over twenty-five miles until Beyneu I felt shattered and was beginning to despair. If it carried on like this I would have no choice but to hitch a lift. Even this was looking unlikely though as the lorries had stopped, unable to continue in the mud. This meant I didn't have enough supplies to camp out for the night to wait for the road to dry out. I continued pushing and dragging my bike until suddenly and miraculously, the tarmac returned! No-one I had spoken to mentioned it and it was a good road surface. I whooped with delight and stopped at a chaihana, where I celebrated with a pot of tea. A little boy ran after me and gave me a note that had been left for me. It read:

"We are two French cyclists heading to Uzbekistan. We heard that you are behind us and catching up. We will be in Beyneu tonight and will leave for Uzbekistan in the morning. If you would like to join us we can meet in Beyneu. Mark and Camille."

Company would be great, especially in the next bit of desert in Uzbekistan, which I expected to be even tougher. I had read that the road continued this way but became even more remote. It seemed I wasn't the only lunatic out there…

Preparing to leave the chaihana, I noticed that my little Nokia phone with my Kazakh sim card in was missing. I confronted the owner about it and he said it must have fallen out as I was riding. I said that I had definitely had it at my table. He looked genuinely insulted, so I went back to the bike to have another look in my bags. Nope, it wasn't there so I went back in and sat down, determined not to leave until I got it back. He took me outside to 'help' look for it then spoke to his son who incredibly appeared with the phone a few minutes later. I asked the owner where it had been found. He said on a ledge under the table that didn't exist. They had obviously taken it and hoped that I wouldn't notice. Not a great end to West Kazakhstan. I say West Kazakhstan because I planned to be back in the east of the huge country in a few months' time after crossing Uzbekistan, Tajikistan and Kyrgyzstan.

I sped off to Beyneu along the beautiful tarmac road (a relative description) and found the cheapest hotel in town, where I paid for twelve hours of accommodation. I could have done with a rest and a lie in but in Kazakhstan you can either pay for twelve or twenty-four hours, so I obviously took the cheaper option. This meant a six o'clock start in the morning, the day my Uzbek visa started. If I could cross the border some time the next day it would be perfect timing. Marc and Camille, the French couple were easy to find. I asked a group of kids if they'd seen any other bikers and one made a sign of man with a beard and long hair and another pretended to have boobs by pulling his t-shirt out with his hands. That would be them, I thought. I was expecting Sebastian Chabal, the French rugby player. I was disappointed to find a short bearded and not very long haired Marc sitting with the lovely Camille in a café. I shared a beer with them and we arranged to meet the next morning, so I disappeared for some much needed sleep. We were going to ride on together for a few days.

I managed to wash both myself and my clothes in the hotel, but didn't get much sleep because I had to check out so early in the morning. I stocked up on food, and more inferior inner tubes, in the bazaar. Beyneu is now a decent sized and well stocked town. It used to be a tiny village, but in the 1970s oil was discovered in the area and so the population grew. After leaving the bazaar I cycled over to meet up with Marc and Camille at their hotel. Marc was pumping up some new tyres that he had bought at the bazaar the previous day. They were absolutely awful quality though and ripped apart when the pressure got too high. He was understandably very annoyed and had to put his worn out old ones back on.

We rode out of Beyneu on another appalling road. If possible, it was even worse than before; corrugated with no dirt side tracks to ride on and nowhere to escape the bumps. It was great to have some company though and we talked about our rides. Marc and Camille had planned the same route as me except for the Pamir Highway in Tajikistan. They planned to go straight from Uzbekistan to Eastern Kazakhstan. Coincidentally, Marc is called Marc Beaumont, like the British round the world record breaking cyclist (Mark Beaumont). He had some funny email exchanges with possible sponsors who originally seemed very interested, until they realised that it was a different Marc Beaumont.

We cycled the fifty-three miles to the Uzbek border that day and planned to cross it the next morning. Their pace was a bit slower than mine and we stopped at all the chaihanas on the way, but I loved the company. It was so nice to chill out a bit but I needed to be pushed into doing so. The mindset that I had got myself into was that I needed to rush, rush, rush across the desert to get to Uzbekistan. I was right to push myself and would have continued to do so if I hadn't been cycling as a team. I was pleased to slow down and enjoyed the cycling again for the first time in a while. Crossing the border in the morning would mean that I would only have twenty-nine days in Uzbekistan. Mark and Camille had a more flexible visa than me, which didn't have a fixed start date, and they could cross the border with a full quota of thirty days. Considering the uncertainties between Istanbul and here, I was pretty pleased with my timing and predicted pace. It was a massive achievement to arrive on the border on the day my Uzbek visa started. Twenty-nine days wasn't long though considering what lay ahead in Uzbekistan. We had over three hundred miles of desert left until the next city, and if it was as slow going as the last stretch I really would be cutting it fine to get all the visas that I needed in Tashkent.

Unbelievably good news came our way when we met some Russian motorcyclists who were also waiting at the border. The road was all tarmac from that point on. At some point in the last few years they must have built a tarmac road across the desert. Nobody had mentioned this on any of the blogs that I had read on the internet. I was still expecting a very difficult week, but now my spirits soared and I started to think that I might actually make it to Tashkent in good time. We found somewhere to wild-camp in the desert and got ready for an early start the next day. Unfortunately, next morning, the 'twenty-four hour' border was shut until ten o'clock, followed by a load of pointless waiting and filling in more forms that took two hours. Every official wanted to prove their power by meticulously checking our passports. One, who couldn't speak any English, spent about ten minutes looking at the page where I had written my Nan's address for emergency contact details. Eventually he nodded and gave it back. I have no idea what he thought he was looking at!

Finally through the border, we got going in Uzbekistan. I changed one hundred dollars into about 200,000 Uzbek som. Ridiculously, the largest note they have is 2,000 som, which is worth about a dollar. I received a large and very heavy pile of notes, which I stuffed into my front pannier. Marc and Camille exchanged more money than I did and were literally millionaires! As we crossed the border, I was very pleased that there was a strong wind blowing towards the southeast; our direction for the next three hundred miles on a dead straight road. *Three hundred miles without a curve.* We rode at a good pace, sometimes in formation to minimise wind resistance, sometimes next to one another and chatting about our adventures and life back home.

Over the next few days, not much happened in the desert. We woke fairly early in the morning and rode until lunchtime, which we had in a chaihana if possible. I always got the cheapest food available and drank large amounts of chai (tea), which cost almost nothing. Thankfully, Uzbekistan was cheaper than Kazakhstan because the chaihanas were the only places that we could get food. After lunch, we took long afternoon breaks where Marc and Camille generally had a siesta. During these breaks, I escaped from the desert into other people's adventures. I read Fiona Campbell's book about her walk around the world, Aron Ralston's *'127 hours between a rock and a hard place',* and Alistair Humphrey's account of Uzbekistan when he had cycled here a few years earlier. He had not crossed this part of the desert, but his descriptions of the Silk Road cities of Samarkand and Bukhara excited me.

After lunch and a long afternoon rest, we cycled for a few more hours and finished early in the evening. Marc and Camille were cycling further now that they were with me; they told me I was pushing them on. I didn't know if I should feel guilty about this, but I needed to keep moving. On the first evening in Uzbekistan, we cycled around twenty miles and camped just off the roadside. I was more confident camping in sight of the road now that I was part of the group. Marc and Camille shared a large tent, with a bedroom compartment and a large porch area. My tiny tent was dwarfed by it, but I didn't mind. My tent was a constant source of comfort whenever I pitched it. *A safe haven from the dangers of the world...* That night, we were treated to an incredible moonrise. A huge, bright, orange disc appeared on the horizon and rose up into the sky, gradually shrinking and becoming whiter.

About midway through our desert crossing, the small isolated settlement of Jasliq provided a place to rest and to buy water. The chaihana there was very busy. We arrived at lunchtime and the whole place was covered in sleeping bodies. We found a place to sit and got some food. Finally the owner got very annoyed that everyone was using her chaihana floor as a bed and woke everyone up. One guy wouldn't wake up and was blocking the fan from moving round, so she grabbed his legs and dragged him out of the way. He groaned and went back to sleep. Everyone else started buying things as soon as they awoke and exchanged huge wads of cash. They don't use bank cards here so everything is traded in cash, which they carry round in large sacks. Dollars fetch more on the black market than they are officially worth, because they keep their value much better than Uzbek som. Inflation is a massive problem here and it reached a level of twenty-two percent in 2011. Imagining that is quite depressing; any savings you might have would lose their value by twenty-two percent per year. I imagined the locals buying a house or car; it must take ages to count the notes and they would need a wheelbarrow to carry enough.

We eventually left the chaos of the chaihana, and when we got back outside to the bikes all three of us had rear punctures. It must have been the heat again. After spending a long time fixing them in front of a crowd of about twenty-five very annoying and very eager-to-help locals, we escaped! The people there had no concept of privacy.

Jasliq is a settlement that has been built around the notorious Jasliq prison. Reports have come out saying that prisoners have been tortured to death there. Some of the crimes that the prisoners were convicted for are somewhat dubious, for example *'Infringement upon the constitution'*. According to human rights groups, Muslims and opposition activists end up in Jasliq for speaking out and demonstrating against the oppressive dictatorship government of Islam Karimov. In 2010, the Independent Human Rights Defenders of Uzbekistan reported the deaths of thirty-three prisoners, who had reportedly been physically abused. There are photos circulating on the internet, of a corpse of a man whose post-mortem undoubtedly proved that he had been boiled alive. We saw the prison set back from the road and it was a scary looking place, with a railway line leading to the gates. I cycled past it with thoughts of what it must be like to be imprisoned in a place like that. Apart from anything else, the local climate would make being a prisoner awful.

The ride across the desert was very hard and very hot, but one of the best experiences of my life. I loved looking across the barren landscapes, untouched by man, not seeing any human influence on the landscape in any direction. I saw marmots, scorpions, snakes, hawks and kangaroo rats; which are little jumping rodents. Although there is a tarmac road, this stretch of desert was more isolated than in Kazakhstan. It took careful planning and we needed a lot of water. The furthest distance without a water point was about one hundred miles, which took a day and a half. Using water sparingly, I reckon that ten litres or so would have been enough to safely pass this distance. I took thirteen litres, but Mark and Camille shared eighteen. They seemed to drink less than me.

The mystery of the new road was solved in a chaihana one day. We were talking about the huge number of *'Willi Betz'* lorries that had passed. An English speaker told us they were a Dutch haulage company who had been commissioned to provide NATO troops in Afghanistan with supplies. The road was about the same age as the length of the Afghan war. Putting two and two together, I would imagine that there was a significant economic incentive for the Uzbekistan government to build a road there. It is a shame that it took a foreign war to influence this. The number of lorries was quite staggering and really highlighted the scale of the operation in Afghanistan; I reflected on whether or not it was a useful way of spending taxpayer's money...

The desert continued in the same way for five days. When we finally got to Qongirat and saw green trees on the horizon, it was a wonderful moment. The three of us stopped and cheered, then took some photos. We were out of the desert! While celebrating in the last chaihana before civilisation, I made the difficult decision to carry on alone. Although it had been great to cycle with Marc and Camille, I needed to press on to get my onward visas, which would involve a long diversion to Tashkent. I hoped to meet up with them again in Samarkand but it was vitally important for me to get across the next desert stage quickly and to reach the cities in the east. That evening, I planned to reach Nukus, the capital of the Karakalpakstan region, and to stay in a hotel.

There is something special about riding a bike through a desert. Yes, it's a massive physical and mental challenge; the heat is torture and the lack of changing horizons makes it difficult to persuade yourself to keep going, but there is something so simple and pure about surviving in this vast landscape. It was just me against the world and nature. I had challenged myself and found myself equal to the challenge. To push myself this hard and fling myself into the unknown was probably my greatest achievement of the entire trip.

12. The Silk Road

We travel not for trafficking alone,
By hotter winds our fiery hearts are fanned,
For lust of knowing what should not be known,
We take the golden road to Samarkand.
- James E. Flecker

On arriving in Nukus I checked into a very basic Soviet hotel that smelt like a toilet. Despite this, I spent some time relaxing before finding an internet café where I could Skype Laura. The next morning, I had a look around the Karakalpakstan art gallery and museum. It is a bizarre location to have such a large and interesting art collection. A Soviet artist called Igor Savitsky collected it all and risked his life to protect it from destruction at the hands of Stalin's regime. Many of the artists who produced the art were executed by the Soviets or sent to the gulag. Savitsky survived and escaped imprisonment. He later set up the museum to display the lost art to the world. Out of the collection, I particularly liked the crazy wood carvings of people's heads using the tree roots as the hair. I also liked the famous painting *'The Bull'*, of a bucking bull with one of its horns decorated with cubic patterns. The artist, Yevgeny Lysenko, was thrown into a psychiatric prison for painting it and was killed whilst on remand.

The connected museum had an interesting article about the drying up of the Aral Sea. The once enormous expanse of fresh water was a vital part of the region's economy, supporting fishing and trading. In the 1960s the Soviets diverted the two rivers that fed the Aral Sea in order to irrigate the desert to grow rice and cotton. This caused one of the planet's worst ever environmental disasters and the Aral Sea, one of the four largest lakes in the world, shrunk to ten percent of its original size. There are now graveyards of ships that once sailed there. Ghost towns sited around the sea that once existed due to the fishing industry are all but abandoned. The Kazakhs in the north have built a dam to resurrect the North Aral Sea and a fishing industry is returning. The Uzbeks are more interested in exploring the dry bed of the South Aral Sea in a search for oil; *the black gold*.

I left Nukus about midday, bumping into Marc and Camille on the way out. They had just arrived. I directed them to my hotel, which was cheap and not too bad, the smell wasn't pleasant but I didn't see a single cockroach! The area around Nukus is irrigated and it was refreshing to be surrounded by fields and trees again. Lots of people were out and about and children were swimming in the irrigation channels. I headed south towards the border with Turkmenistan, which I would cycle alongside for a few miles until reaching the city of Khiva, an ancient Silk Road trading post. It was hard going, against a headwind, and still very hot. I was pleased to discover that the pipes under the road were still around though and had a nap in one for an hour at about four o'clock. Feeling better after my late siesta, I continued through a beautiful area around the Amu Darya River. The road was in perfect condition and the fields were full of people picking cotton; the area's main produce. The Uzbek women wore bright and colourful dresses and chatted loudly in the fields as they worked. I crossed the river on a floating bridge, which felt pretty unsteady. On the other side, I stopped at a market to buy supplies for dinner and to be entertained by a group of local people. They had a strange fashion sense: for some reason the women drew monobrows onto their foreheads with makeup! It looked very odd. Anyway, they were lovely people and they gave me a bag full of free fruit.

I carried on to a shop to buy the stuff that I couldn't get from the market and the owners invited me to sleep there that night. I gratefully accepted and followed them to a raised platform around the back where I could unroll my sleeping mat. They cooked eggs and sausages for my dinner (it seems to be a staple here) and then the neighbours asked if I was still hungry. When I said that I could eat a bit more, they came back with a very large second meal of plov, a greasy rice dish (the other staple). I hadn't been blown away by the quality of Uzbek food, but the people there were so friendly and hospitable.

The next day I passed through an agricultural area, including many more cotton fields. The most popular agricultural vehicle was a very odd-looking three-wheeled tractor. The two back wheels were normal, but the front was a small castor-like wheel under the engine. I supposed that for the flat fields around here, there was little chance of the tractor tipping over. In the early afternoon I arrived in Khiva, a beautiful ancient city, and in perfect condition due to a Soviet restoration programme. The buildings are stunning: colourful tiled mosaics, minarets, domes, huge city walls and archways. The atmosphere of the place has been sapped away though; it's like a big museum. I wandered around the amazing old streets, enthralled by the splendour of the place. It must have been a very rich city when trading on the Silk Road was at its height.

In a hotel garden, I met a Swiss couple who had been roaming around the world on bikes for three years. They had taken the train here from Tashkent and were having a break from the bikes. Coincidently, they had also met and cycled with Marc and Camille. We had a chat about our upcoming plans. They wanted to cycle through the Pamirs at around the same time as me. We would probably bump into each other again. I went to a shop, bought a beer and took it up to the city walls, where I sat and watched the world go by. I saw a group of women with gold teeth and colourful dresses baking bread in a giant round clay oven. A bright orange glow was coming out of the circular gap in the top. That was how they made the delicious round bread that I often ate for breakfast then. I drank the beer and watched the sunset; it was a wonderful moment as I sat, looking over the ancient city.

I had planned to spend another day in Khiva and wandering around the museums was an attractive thought, but getting back on the road was more pressing. I left the next day, having absorbed the atmosphere of the place. Although I did need a break, I really needed to get across the country as soon as possible and had decided that I would rather spend my time off in Samarkand if I had any spare. After a morning's ride I was back into the desert but still following the river. The irrigation had come to an end, so there were no fields in this part of the country, but there were plenty of towns, and the cycling was pleasant and easy. I reached a large town in the early evening and asked around for a place to stay. Some people who lived in a yurt next to a drinking water bottling plant waved over to me and I joined them. They had a manmade pool full of large fish and offered me one. A little boy caught it in a large net and gave it to his father. The man killed it and barbecued it for me, then covered it in breadcrumbs and spices. It was the best meal that I'd had for a very long time. I was allowed to sleep on a raised platform outside the house so I put up my mosquito net and got ready for some rest. I couldn't get the kids to leave me alone and had to answer the usual questions: *Where are you from? Where are you going?...*

Eventually they left and I put my head down, only to be woken up by the police. I was very worried about a large fine at first because all tourists are required to register in hotels every night in Uzbekistan. They had only come to look at me though. Someone had obviously told them about the weird white guy on a bike. I had to show them the bike, answer the same questions to faces with beaming smiles and golden teeth. It seemed that dental hygiene was not particularly good in Uzbekistan; everybody had gold teeth. Being cheery and friendly was hard work but I didn't want to annoy the police as they could have made me leave to a hotel in the next town. Eventually they left and I got some much needed sleep.

Unfortunately, barking dogs meant that I didn't sleep at all well and woke up tired in the morning. I had a large breakfast and was on the road by half past six. The morning went well, making fifty miles against a headwind and reaching a small town with a tiny shop by lunchtime, where I stocked up on supplies for the next desert stretch and talked with some very friendly people who kept giving me loaves of bread. I ended up with five! At least I could be confident that I wouldn't run out. After following the river up a valley in the desert I reached the same main road that I had left just after Nukus, to divert to Khiva. The road was appalling, sometimes consisting of tarmac that had been ripped up, sometimes melted tarmac, and sometimes no tarmac at all. Sand had been blown across in drifts and it was really hard work. It was even hotter than the last desert, up to forty-five degrees Celsius, there was absolutely no shade and no culverts under the road to sleep in. It was also sandier and drier; my mouth was constantly parched no matter how much water I drank. I got into a routine of cycling two and a half miles, taking a swig and then getting going again because the only way to keep cool was by moving so that I was creating a breeze. There were also loads of flies to make things worse, oh, and a headwind for three days!

I slept under an abandoned truck for an hour that afternoon; it was the only shade available. I woke up feeling awful; nauseous and exhausted but had no choice other than to push on. I met an Uzbek cyclist going from Tashkent to Nukus and back. He was in a bit of a rush and stopped me for a photo, didn't speak, and then sped off mentioning something about an interview. I bought a couple of large bottles of coke from a chaihana and pushed on into the desert. I was definitely ill again and my bowel problems were back. It might have been something I ate or drank, or just exhaustion. There was plenty of water available in the chaihanas, which were more regular than in Kazakhstan, so I drank as much as possible but was still dehydrated and there was nothing I could do about it. I vomited in the afternoon and was running on coke because I couldn't eat anything solid. I didn't eat that night and finished riding just before dark before collapsing into my tent.

Thankfully, I felt better the next day and my appetite was back. It was a shame that I only had stale bread and chocolate spread to eat. At the first chaihana, I had eggs, sausage, soup and bread. I ate and drank so much that day and felt much better, although was absolutely shattered by the afternoon. More miles passed in much the same way over the next couple of days the desert was coming to an end. After one very hard day's ride, I was looking forward to a meal of pasta that I had managed to buy from a rare shop. As I opened the bag, it split and went everywhere. I was gutted; but picked up all the pasta pieces. Not having enough water to rinse them, I had a very sandy and gritty dinner.

This desert crossing was mental torture for three and a half days. I didn't enjoy it at all, but it was great to overcome the challenge. I could have gone slower or stopped when illness was upon me, but my determination to make it round the world using only a bike was growing. *I had to get to Tashkent in time to get the Tajik visa.* I was delighted with my performance across the second desert stage, averaging over eighty-five miles per day, a brilliant achievement given my illness, the headwind, the road conditions and the heat.

Finally across the desert, I reached another oasis: Bukhara. Arriving at around five o'clock, I checked into the cheapest place in town; only five dollars a night and not bad at all. I had a day off in Bukhara, which was wonderful. The buildings are incredible: huge ornate madrassas (the Arabic word for an educational institution), giant mosques and towering minarets, often coated with coloured tiles and topped with bright turquoise domes. There is a giant old fortress called the Arc, where the old Khans used to live. Unlike Khiva, Bukhara is a bustling city, full of life, with a large central square and pool with restaurants all around it. This pool was one of many in the nineteenth century. Bukhara was famous for plagues during this time, because the water was only rarely changed and was left to stagnate. The life expectancy for an inhabitant of Bukhara at that time was just thirty-two. The Kaylan minaret was impressive; fifty metres tall and nine metres thick at the base. It is nicknamed *'The Minaret of Death'* because for centuries, criminals were executed by being thrown from the top. Continuing that slightly morbid theme, I visited the city prison, complete with its *'Bug Pit'*. This became an infamous place in the 1840s when two British officers ended up on the wrong side of Khan Nasrullah. Colonel Stoddard was on his way to India when he made the mistake of riding, rather than walking into the Arc. He had no gifts from Queen Victoria for the Khan, and as a result was thrown into the *'Bug Pit'*; so called because it was full of rodents and insects, including rats, spiders and scorpions. He was there for two years before another British officer, Captain Connolly, came looking for him. He also rode into the Arc so was chucked in too! They were both kept there for another year before being executed on the square in front of the fortress.

I spent the day wandering around the ancient buildings and eating good food, even having a couple of beers in a restaurant overlooking the minaret and domed madrassas either side. It really was a spectacular place. I met a few other travellers in the cheap 'B&B' I was staying in. I use quotation marks because there was neither a bed nor breakfast, despite being called *'B&B Bahodir'*. Guests sleep on a mat on the floor and the owner seemed surprised when I asked if breakfast was included. He was an interesting guy; an ex-Soviet Olympian. He had enjoyed a good career as a sprinter until he injured his leg, so became an Olympic coach. I needed a day off and forced myself to take one even though my instincts told me to push on to Samarkand. I spoke to my Dad on Skype and he arranged to get a letter of invitation to Russia from a travel agency, so that I could get a visa from Tashkent. I hoped that it would work out.

The next morning, I woke up feeling well rested and great again. As I left Bukhara, I met a team of Chinese runners. They were running the Silk Road from Istanbul to Xian, China. It would take them five months, averaging about forty miles per day. I chatted to their Australian medical support team for a while as I rode along, through the open window of their support vehicle. I can't imagine how difficult it must be to run that distance in the desert heat every day. Those guys were seriously fit.

I also felt very fit and managed over sixty miles before being stopped at a police checkpoint and asked to show my registration papers. This was a worry because I only had a couple of nights in registered hotels, but they didn't check them properly and were more interested in Nino the giraffe which was still attached to my front pannier rack. In the afternoon, I passed one hundred miles for the day with a cheer and cycled on to the next town, where I was offered a bed in a chaihana. I had managed 105 miles, the biggest day in a long time. That night, I provided entertainment for the six kids who lived there. They were amazed to see a crazy, dirty, smelly, British cyclist turn up at their quiet village tea house. I ate tasty Jasliq (mutton kebabs) and slept in a back room. The toilet was the worst one yet and I had to hold my breath when I used it. The four surrounding houses shared the single long-drop toilet, probably between about twenty people.

The following day I rode about fifty miles to get to Samarkand, which took me until two o'clock, despite setting off at dawn. Fighting a headwind all day, I climbed through hills along a beautiful country road surrounded by cotton fields. I was getting frustrated because I wanted to get to the station in Samarkand in time to get a train to Tashkent that evening. It was Sunday, and I needed to go to the Tajikistan embassy on Monday to give myself a full week to get visas. It was annoying to arrive at Samarkand and have to leave straight away; I'd been looking forward to seeing the city for so long. I planned to go to make the return journey to Tashkent by train, get all the visas I needed then return, hopefully with some time for sightseeing. From Tashkent I would then continue by bike from Samarkand.

I arrived in Samarkand unhappy and shaken thanks to some extraordinary driving: blind overtaking around corners, swerving randomly across the road, pulling alongside me for a chat and holding up a line of very impatient angry drivers who then chose to make an outrageous overtaking manoeuvre rather than waiting ten seconds for a safe overtake. Added to this was the constant refrain of horns doing their best to deafen me! The Uzbeks have definitely won the *'Worst driving in the world award'* so far, but I had heard that the Chinese would give them a run for their money.

Eventually, I arrived alive at Samarkand station at about half past two and bought a ticket for a train at five o'clock. It was supposed to take three and a half hours, scheduled to arrive in Tashkent at half past eight. After a five hour breakdown, I got into Tashkent at half past one in the morning, without a hotel booked. The train journey was very interesting however, as I shared a carriage with very friendly Pakistanis, one of whom spoke excellent English, and talked with me for about three hours. I was welcomed as their guest so wasn't allowed to pay for any drinks or food on the train. Amjedali (the English speaker) and I discussed Pakistan/UK relations. He told me that in general the UK was viewed well in Pakistan, although there is a minority of extremists who are very anti-UK. The Pakistanis are grateful for the infrastructure that the British built during colonial times, and many of the older generation remember a better life back then. Unfortunately, due to corruption in government, the country has gone backwards since that time. They are looking over their shoulders at a much more successful India and frustration is growing with the current regime. When the British left Pakistan and India, the Indian and Pakistani rupees were worth the same; now the Indian rupee is almost twice as valuable. He also told me of the problems that relations with the West (particularly America) have caused. Terrorist attacks are common from Afghan and Pakistani extremists due to the country's collaboration with NATO forces, and the country has become much more unsafe due to its partnership with NATO during the Afghan war. He found it incredibly unfair that Pakistan had received such bad press over the possible sheltering of Osama-Bin-Laden, but admitted it was very unlikely that someone in Government didn't know he was there.

We talked about America, and the opinions towards that country in Pakistan. Some of the things that he was saying about America were as a result of anti-American propaganda, which he acknowledged, but in general the view of America in Pakistan (according to him) is basically hatred. He mentioned the deaths of civilians in the bombing of Kabul and I could see his point. The Pakistanis sympathise with the Afghan civilians who were needlessly killed by American bombing missions. From their perspective, George Bush is a terrorist. I found myself defending America and although I'm against the Afghan war, I talked him round to agreeing that we do need a way of policing countries if things turn bad and that George Bush had to do something in the wake of September 11th, even though if what he did do was possibly not the best course of action. It was a very interesting conversation and I enjoyed learning more about Pakistan, which is a country that I would love to go to if things settle down in the future.

The breakdown of the train was awful. There was no information about how long the wait would be. I was getting worried about turning up in Tashkent after midnight, finding a place and securing my bike. The worst bit was that the air conditioning was turned off.

The power saving didn't stretch to turning the Uzbek pop music off though so I was sitting in a sweat box with an assault on my ear drums for five hours. Eventually the train started moving with a round of applause from the much-more-patient-than-me other passengers and we finally pulled into Tashkent. Luckily there was a very cheap hotel at the station (seven dollars per night) where I stayed for the next five days. I got to sleep at about two o'clock that evening, planning to get up at seven to go to an internet café to print off the visa application forms, then cycle to the Tajik embassy for nine o'clock.

Everything went to plan on my first day in Tashkent. I arrived on time at the Tajik embassy, with my application form filled in, and was called to the front of the long queue because I was a tourist. There were lots of Tajiks there because when the Soviet Union broke up, many Tajiks still lived in Uzbekistan and vice versa. This has caused many problems and violence ever since. An official showed me to an office around the back of the embassy where I had my passport photocopied and was helped to write a letter on a Russian form saying how wonderful Tajikistan is and why I wanted to go there. I handed in my passport and was told that I would get it back at five o'clock, with a visa and GBAO permit for the Pamir Highway. Unbelievably easy!

The rest of the day went well too. I found a DHL office in a good hotel, and was told that my parcel containing bike spares, including disc brake pads, was on its way and if it wasn't here by Friday then I could redirect it to Samarkand (thanks to my brother Oli, for posting that to me). I found a large and very well stocked bazaar for lunch and managed to withdraw a wad of dollars from a bank at a very reasonable commission rate. I picked up the visa at five then went to meet Paul, the Dutch cyclist whom I met at the Uzbek embassy in Istanbul. We had kept in touch and had arrived in Tashkent at the same time. Now we were planning to ride the Pamir Highway together and I was looking forward to company again. I hadn't committed to anything at this stage because I needed to make sure we were riding at a similar pace before planning too far ahead.

Paul had cycled a completely different route to me. He had gone through Southern Turkey and seen the famous cave towns of Cappadocia. He had been very ill, so had taken a bus for six hundred miles to get to Iran in time for his visa. I could see he had lost a lot of weight since Istanbul and was now very lean and skinny. He had cycled across Iran and Turkmenistan, then entered Uzbekistan, had cycled to Samarkand and, like me, had come to Tashkent on the train. Iran had been his favourite country; I wished that I had the chance to see it but I didn't regret taking the route through the Caucasus.

We enjoyed a meal and a beer then I left for bed. The next day I headed to the Russian embassy with the 'Letter of Invitation' that I had bought from Stantours, a Central Asian travel agency. Stantours were incredibly helpful and had given me loads of free advice that had worked out well. Unfortunately, on this occasion they got it wrong though. At the Russian embassy I was told that British people couldn't get a Russian visa here or anywhere abroad. I explained that I couldn't get one in the UK either because you have to apply less than three months before entering the country. I showed them the note that Rashad had written in Russian, on the Caspian Sea Ferry. The lady read it and looked very sorry that she couldn't help me but was unable to overturn the rules, so I left feeling very down and not knowing what to do next. The options were:

1. Try again for the Russian Visa in Dushanbe, Osh, Bishkek or Almaty (unlikely I'd get one though).
2. Send my passport home for a Russian visa and stay in Tashkent for two weeks. This wasn't really an option because I didn't have time on my visa and it would be too expensive to stay in a city for that long. I couldn't leave Tashkent without a passport because I needed it for police checks, which were pretty frequent on the Uzbek roads.
3. Scrap the idea of going through Russia and fly over the small region separating Kazakhstan from Mongolia, not ideal because I had got this far only using my bike and it had been very difficult. I didn't want to have to use a plane.
4. Scrap going to Russia and Mongolia and cycle through China, crossing either from Kyrgyzstan or Kazakhstan. Not ideal because I really wanted to go to Mongolia.

I decided to go to the Mongolian consulate to see if it was possible to get a visa there before making a decision and found the consulate after cycling halfway across the city to the wrong address provided on the internet, then taking a taxi to where the consulate actually was. It turned out that they don't issue any visas in Tashkent, and the guy helpfully told me to go to the consulate over six hundred miles away in Almaty in Kazakhstan. He did give me a cup of tea though! This made my mind up. Mongolia would have to wait. I was gutted, but promised myself that I would go back to cycle across Mongolia another time. It had been the country that I had been looking forward to visiting the most, *the great wilderness*. China, however, would be fascinating, and it would mean that I would succeed in my round the world ambition. As it turned out, this was more important to me than visiting Mongolia (although at the beginning of the trip I may well have made a different decision).

My plan was to go to the Kazakh embassy the following morning. If I could get a visa in one day, I would go through Kazakhstan to China, but if it took more than one day I would scrap going back into Kazakhstan and cross from Kyrgyzstan. My preference was to cross the border from Kazakhstan because that would mean that I would be able to cycle through the whole of Kyrgyzstan, a country that I really wanted to see. It sounded like a mountainous version of Mongolia, full of yaks and nomads in yurts. If I took the Kyrgyzstan border crossing, I would only be in Kyrgyzstan for a couple of days however I was tired of tip-toeing around bureaucrats, whose arrogance had driven me mad one too many times and learnt that any route I took would throw up amazing experiences, no matter which country I was in.

The next day I got my Kazakh visa, and the following day I got a three-month Chinese visa. It was almost too easy. Maybe it was fate, if you believe in that kind of thing, but my route had been decided for me. My path around the world was now set and I didn't have to deal with any more frustrating embassies. I had every visa that I would need.

Despite having a lot to do in Tashkent, I really enjoyed my time there. It is a lovely city, with great bars and restaurants. It is modern, very clean, well looked after, the people are very friendly and it is a 'purpose built' Soviet-style city with large roads and no congestion. The last night in Tashkent was fun. Paul and I went to a few bars, including an appalling imitation German beer hall and a great little 'ex-pat' bar with the Wimbledon semi-final on. Predictably, Andy Murray lost to Rafael Nadal; *better luck next year!* We ended up in a rock bar with a Swiss guy called Rene, who worked in Tashkent. I lost Paul at about one o'clock and walked back to the hotel assuming that he had gone back there. At five o'clock I woke up and Paul still wasn't back. I was a bit worried. We had a train booked at seven o'clock to Samarkand. At half past five, a very merry Paul turned up, having slept in a field in front of the President's house for a couple of hours! It was hilarious going to the train with him; I was tired and he was drunk, trying to talk to the Uzbeks in the station. At least we slept for most of the journey...

13. Samarkand and the end of the desert

You can travel through the whole world, have a look at the pyramids and admire the smile of the Sphinx;
You can listen to the soft singing of the wind at the Adriatic Sea and kneel down reverently at the ruins of the Acropolis;
Be dazzled by Rome with its Forum and Coliseum;
Be charmed by Notre Dame in Paris or by old domes of Milan;
But if you have seen the buildings of Samarkand, you will be enchanted by its magic forever.
- An ancient poet

I was hugely excited to be in Samarkand, the city that I had been looking forward to visiting more than any other on the trip having read about it, I had visualised it in my head to be the most magical, beautiful city in the world.

Samarkand is an ancient city, with a fascinating history as a major trading post on the Silk Road. One of the oldest inhabited cities in the world, having been founded in 700 BC, it has passed between different empires ever since, including; Alexander the Great's Greeks, Genghis Khan's Mongols, Arabs, Turks and Persians, until relative stability came when Timur made it capital of his empire in 1370. Artists and craftsman moved to Samarkand under Timur and the population exploded. Bukhara then became the Uzbek capital and Samarkand went into decline before being abandoned. In the nineteenth century, the Russians took control and it became the capital of Turkestan and then the Uzbek Soviet Socialist Republic, before being replaced by Tashkent in 1930. The Soviets restored the majority of the buildings in the city; it became a tourist destination and is now a wonderful place to visit.

I arrived at the most popular hostel in town, which was full of other travellers, including Damian and John, whom I had met in the 'B&B' in Bukhara, and Marc and Camille, who arrived during my first afternoon there. It was great to see them again and we had a few days to wait over the weekend until my parcel arrived. There were about twelve other cyclists there; Samarkand is on everybody's route through Central Asia. It was good to relax with like-minded people, but the large number of other tourists did make the whole experience feel a bit less of an adventure. Over the weekend we visited most of the sights of the regal Registan, with its giant, ornate madrassas and tilting minarets; the gigantic unrestored Bibi-Khanym Mosque, with its crumbling dome; the magnificent tomb of Timur, and the eerie avenue of tombs at the Shah-i-Zinda necropolis with its mosaic tiles, domed crypts and endless gravestones. One night we bribed the guard to let us up one of the minarets in the Registan at sunset. It was a dark climb up a narrow spiral staircase, and at the top there was only room for one of us to poke our head out at a time, for a beautiful view over the magical city. After coming down from the minaret I wandered in awe around the Registan. The low light was being reflected by the mosaic tiles and the shadows of the minarets and domes were cast on the towering, crooked ancient walls. They were magnificent, the most beautiful buildings I have ever seen. The city at the end of the golden road had fulfilled and exceeded all my expectations. I remember reading James Flecker's poem *"The Golden Journey to Samarkand"* (quoted at the beginning of chapter 12), while I sat in the square surrounded by the Registan's three madrassas. I haven't experienced manmade beauty to rival Samarkand's anywhere else in the world.

My parcel finally arrived at the DHL office on Tuesday and Paul and I planned to leave the following morning. I fitted new disc brake pads, serviced my bike and photocopied maps of China from other travellers so I could plan my future route as I cycled through the rest of Central Asia. Paul and I had a goodbye meal with Marc and Camille, who were heading north to Tashkent. We left early the next day with a Portuguese couple who were also on the way to the Pamir Highway. I had enjoyed my two-week break from the bike, but was really looking forward to getting on the road again. Crazy bureaucracy couldn't stop me now; my pathway around the world was mapped in front of me.

The ride out of Samarkand was beautiful. Quickly the road started climbing up into the first mountains that I had ridden through for months. I had been stung by a bee the previous afternoon and my arm had swollen up. It was really painful, forcing me to ride one-handed over the bumps to avoid the shooting pains. It was so refreshing to finally be out of the desert and to see lush scenery again. Small mountain villages were teeming with people on the streets going about their day-to-day business. We watched women washing clothes in a large tractor wheel full of water, and children playing in a fountain. We stopped at a shop and bought eggs to cook for lunch then had a siesta for an hour or so. Over the top of the pass, the road snaked its way down to a plain and the city of Shahrisabz; Timur's birthplace. We stopped for a chai before riding down to the city, arriving at dusk. An old man who was cycling in the city centre offered us a place to sleep so we followed him on our bikes to his beautiful house. He and his wife grew vegetables in their garden and had a cow for milk, so they didn't have to buy much food. Stacked up against their long-drop outdoor toilet were piles of cow dung moulded and shaped into thick plate-sized circles. The dung burns hot and for a long time and is used in the stove to heat the house during the winter, and also for cooking. The man's wife quickly made us some delicious laghman soup. We slept outside under grape vines.

For breakfast, we were given homemade yoghurt and a glass of fresh warm milk. We waved a fond farewell to our latest hosts and visited Timur's tomb, which was built for him before his death. Unfortunately for the builders, he wasn't buried in it. The mountain pass (that we had just crossed) was covered in snow when he died so he was buried in Samarkand instead. The gatekeeper gave us a free tour of the site. There was another ancient mosque and ruined palace in the same architectural style as Samarkand, but unrestored and crumbling. We were taken down to the tomb in a crypt under the mosque which was a grand burial chamber with a central coffin, where one of Timur's relatives was buried instead of the great man himself.

The next couple of days were fantastic. We didn't cover much distance, but ate lots of food and drank huge amounts of chai in many different tea houses. One night we stayed in the garden of a chaihana, and the next in a farmer's field. All the time people offered us food, and one even gave us money, despite our protests. It was more relaxing cycling with Paul. We rode at a good pace, but took longer breaks and finished earlier. I was in no particular rush at that stage, as I had until the first of August to get to Kyrgyzstan and it was early July. That would give me about four weeks to cross the Pamir Mountains and the country of Tajikistan.

We cycled through a mountainous and remote desert landscape, where I saw a vulture circling overhead. The road surface was good and it was great to be going up and down and around corners again for the first time in weeks. The flat straight roads of the Uzbek desert were over now and the cycling was much more interesting. At the end of the day, we reached a chaihana and were asked if we wanted to stay there on one of the outside benches. We accepted the offer straight away and ordered a large pot of green tea. Unfortunately, that night the man of the house returned very drunk and had a loud party with his friends until the early hours. When alone he played music very loudly through speakers that were right next to us, as was the noisy generator that powered them. He had no concern for us and the music kept us awake almost all night. His wife was probably mortified that we had not been able to sleep after her invitation to stay. There were young kids trying to sleep there too, and by the sounds of things were struggling to do so. Tired, we left the chaihana early in the morning and headed towards the Tajik border.

On the last full day in Uzbekistan we crossed another desert landscape near Boysun. At a viewpoint, we stopped to look out over an area with hundreds of pillar-like spectacular rock formations and canyons carved out by an ancient river. One large pass in the desert was very remote and we underestimated the distance between towns. I had to be very sparing with my water and only drank a small mouthful every half an hour or so. I was feeling great and sped up ahead of Paul. We passed a blown up tank with a turret missing, from a recent war. Paul met me at the top of the climb then shot off downhill. I could barely keep up with him on the descent; he has no fear! It was a tough day with lots of climbing, but sixty miles later we arrived at a farm where we were given permission to stay for the night. That day, we had (despite our protests) been given three large (and very heavy) melons, 6,000 Uzbek som (about three dollars) and two loaves of bread, by one wonderfully generous person after another. We camped underneath some trees in an orchard and were encouraged to eat as much of the fruit as we wanted. Paul was great company, we were getting on very well and decided to cycle together for the whole of Tajikistan.

On the final day in Uzbekistan we set off at about five o'clock and passed the city of Denov, a bustling and infuriating market town. I looked after the bikes while Paul went to get his passport copied for his Kyrgyzstan visa, which he needed to get in Dushanbe the next day. Within five minutes I was surrounded by a crowd of about two hundred; it was unbelievable. They were all over the road and the cars couldn't get past. They just stared at me until some policemen came and moved them away. They only did this so that they could have a look at the tourist too though! I made a mental note to get my own back on Paul for leaving me in this circus. I thought that maybe a couple of large rocks in his panniers would be suitable revenge (although I unfortunately forgot to do this). The behaviour of the locals was understandable though; many of them may have never seen a white person before. Not many cyclists pass this way because most cross the border between Samarkand and Penjikent. It was closed at that moment due to civil unrest, so we had to detour through Denov. I was clearly a novelty who definitely entertained the locals. After this unpleasant experience, we escaped from the city and got to a chaihana ten miles from the Tajik border. My love of Uzbekistan was restored when we were invited over by three old men who bought us a huge lunch, and then tried to give us vodka. We resisted.

Soon we reached the Tajik border and crossed it easily, with no fine for our lack of registration papers. Uzbekistan had been a brilliant experience, infuriating at times but on the whole great. I had no idea what to expect and experienced lovely people, absolutely incredible cities, desert crossings, mountains, great company, visa success and unbeatable hospitality (unless you go to Georgia). The downside was intrusive staring, being treated like an attraction rather than a person, unbelievably bad driving, bad food, terrible heat and illness. That is travel though, and the good definitely outweighed the bad.

14. The mountains at last

It is by riding a bicycle that you learn the contours of a country best, since you have to sweat up the hills and coast down them. Thus you remember them as they actually are, while in a motor car only a high hill impresses you, and you have no such accurate remembrance of country you have driven through as you gain by riding a bicycle.
- Ernest Hemingway

After crossing the border to Tajikistan, we cycled along a quiet country lane for a couple of hours, until reaching a large river. We asked for a place to camp but instead were invited to stay in a shelter by the river which belonged to a large family who lived in the nearby house. One of them spoke English and brought us a second dinner of plov. Plov was clearly a staple in Tajikistan as well as Uzbekistan. We had already cooked and eaten our first dinner, but cycle tourists never refuse food, so we tucked into a second with six Tajik teenagers. Not a bad start to a new country. We sat cross-legged on a carpeted platform with cushions all around us. The English-speaking guy told us about his country. He was fiercely proud to be Tajik and seemed to be doing well, studying English at university in Dushanbe. He told me that a lot of adults in Tajikistan work in Russia and send money home for their families. It is a big problem and means that there is a lack of skilled workers in Tajikistan. The economy suffers, and as a result, the country is the poorest of the former Soviet states.

An early start and a very fast ride for the first three hours of the day got us through the thirty miles to Dushanbe by nine o'clock. Paul went to the Kyrgyzstan embassy and came back half an hour later with his visa; unbelievable service! It had taken me four days in Istanbul. We bumped into the Swiss couple whom I had met in Khiva, so we had lunch with them and spent about four hours talking, before finally leaving for the Pamir Mountains. Finally I was starting the leg of the trip that I had been looking forward to most. I had spent hours looking at the Pamir Highway on Google Maps whilst planning the trip; it was difficult to believe I was almost there. Dushanbe is the capital city of Tajikistan and was very different from the purpose-built, Soviet-style city of Tashkent. It wasn't as well kept or as clean, and had a busy, bustling feel to it. The history behind its name was that it grew from a village with a popular Monday market; Dushanbe means Monday in Persian, the language that is spoken in Tajikistan.

After leaving Dushanbe, we passed a power plant belching out a disgusting amount of pollution, and arrived at a small village. We asked one of the inhabitants for somewhere to sleep, and after about forty-five minutes of deliberating (I have no idea what they were talking about), the elder of the village introduced us to our host, Rhadijon. We walked with him for about a mile, followed by a trail of children, including one who had been ordered to carry a watermelon as a gift for us. It was massive, and the poor boy was obviously struggling to carry it all the way to the house. We were shown to a room and served a delicious dinner of pasta, watermelon, nuts, yogurt, sweets and the inevitable chai. This all happened without any show of surprise from the locals, they were just happy to help us. The next morning we were given a tour of Rhadijon's land. They had a few cows and stockpiles of dry dung, which, like in Uzbekistan, was shaped into conveniently sized circles for burning. They had crops, and it looked like they were also almost completely self-sufficient, using their relatively small plot of land to its full. Rhadijon was an official in the village; he called himself the '*President*' and had a stamp which he proudly used on my diary. Looking around the neighbourhood gave me a great insight to these people's lives. In the West, we think of people like this as under-developed because they have fewer things than us. Are we really any better off? Everyone here seemed very happy, they have better social and family values, and they are far less reliant on other people than we are. People were far friendlier and more hospitable, and their life looked very comfortable. The material possessions we are so obsessed with back home are nothing compared to these assets.

We left the village and Rhadijon, climbing up a lush green river valley with towering mountains on both sides. It was a good quality road and I enjoyed the cycling. At every town we stopped for an ice cream; they were very cheap. In the early afternoon we came across an irrigation canal where a large group of kids and teenagers were swimming. I had a wash; an aqueduct with holes in the side formed a perfect shower. There was a fairly deep pool where the kids dived and flipped to show off to the weird foreigners. After a while, three older guys wearing aviator sunglasses showed up in a Lada, blaring out hip-hop. It was very funny; the kids were obviously in awe of them. They proceeded to do a workout in the canal, and then shared a watermelon with us. I had a swim in the pool and cooled down for the first time in days.

Feeling refreshed, we continued up the road, which climbed through the valley, passing many more small villages. The villages were built linearly along the road and didn't stretch back far but were sometimes quite long. They were very peaceful, and the inhabitants convened on the main street. The Tajiks were different to the Uzbeks; just as friendly, but much more reserved, which meant that they appeared very polite in comparison. That night, at a beautiful riverside campsite, a small boy galloped up to us on a horse and stared at us; he had evidently never seen anything as strange as two very white people speaking in a strange language and sleeping in two weirdly shaped cloth houses. We had almost no interaction, but the experience was memorable.

The next day, we continued up the beautiful valley and over a small pass, before whizzing down to the town of Obi. We stocked up on food and Paul put his phone on charge in a shop saying: "*I must remember not to forget it*". We left the town, and after ten miles of fantastic descending, Paul cried "*Arggghhhh*"; he had forgotten his phone. It would take a lot longer to climb back up the descent than the ride down had taken. He hitched back up to the town while I watched the bikes and returned in a lorry with the phone an hour and a half later. We climbed all afternoon up another, more wild and rocky valley, with a fast-flowing river snaking through a gorge at the bottom. The river's high flow-rate was fuelled by melting snow in the high mountains that lay ahead.

At the village of Kosmolobad, we paused for a break. One of the older men in the village insisted on giving us a tour. There wasn't much to it, but he took us to an orchard and presented us with as much fruit as we wanted. Then we were taken to a giant gnarled tree that he said was over three hundred years old. A rickety iron bridge took us across the river and the road continued up a new side valley, following a large tributary until we reached a picturesque farm, where we set up camp, then watched the sunset. A low light lit up cliffs on one side of the valley until the sun set behind the mountains. The golden cliffs became dark as sunlight moved up and up until the last rays disappeared, leaving a golden sky. We cooked dinner in the twilight whilst the mountains became a ghostly silhouette as the full moon rose over the valley.

The morning saw more climbing and descending on tarmac, dirt roads and rocky tracks. In Soviet times, the road would have been better than this and completely paved, but it wasn't too bad. There were sections of eroded tarmac and the dirt sections were pretty smooth. My bike had definitely survived worse than this in Kazakhstan. The river in the valley was flowing even faster now, and had raging rapids and white water. After passing two police checkpoints, where we had our passports checked, the bumping got the better of one of Paul's rear panniers. The clip that held it onto the rack broke and he had to tie it on with a piece of rope that we found on the road. It was a pretty good bodge though and no cause for alarm. We found a place to camp on a grassy bit of land that jutted out into the wide river. There was a powerful flow sweeping around the peninsula. A storm arrived with very heavy rain and lightning. This was bad news for Paul, who had only pitched the netted inner part of his tent. He had to get up in the pouring rain in the middle of the night to attach the flysheet. I was worried about the level of the river, because the road ahead looked likely to flood. Our campsite was safe enough, being a few metres above the water level, although it was difficult to sleep due to noisy storm.

The next day was one of the best of the whole trip. We started fairly late and had to cycle across the flooded road because the river level had risen slightly. It wasn't deep, but it was disconcerting that we had to cycle in the fast-flowing water. We crossed without incident though and the laid-back start continued after four miles when we stopped for a second breakfast in a chaihana. The road contoured around, and then climbed an alpine valley as a dirt track. Unfortunately, visibility was limited by a hazy mist, but what we could see of the view was beautiful: the fields on the side of the road were covered with wild flowers and the scent of herbs hung in the air; herders walked after donkeys, calves and herds of goats, ushering them along the road. We were surrounded by a panorama of mountain peaks and valleys. It was absolutely spectacular.

We met a Ukrainian journalist who was cycling the Pamir Highway and writing about his experiences. He was talking to a girl who had cycled from New Zealand on a four year trip. She was riding the Pamir Highway in the opposite direction. I had a lot of respect for a solo female cyclist, because the hospitality that I was being shown would be much more difficult for a woman to experience. Muslim men would not approach a female stranger and would certainly not be allowed to put one up for the night. I imagine she must have had more contact with Muslim women, but they were a rarer sight in public places than the men, and much less approachable. Not many women would feel safe enough in these countries to travel alone.

The road was all dirt at this point, with no tarmac. It didn't matter about the bumps on the uphill sections because fighting the gradient meant that we were moving slowly anyway. The road climbed the northern side of the valley, crossed a bridge, and then continued to climb the southern side, gaining altitude quickly. It was hard work, but the gradient was shallow enough to make it all possible to ride. We stopped for a chai as the road left the valley and were told that the top of the pass was close by a group of truck drivers. Every now and then we saw a lorry on the road; I couldn't imagine driving a large lorry along the badly surfaced, very steep and precarious track. It must be a dangerous job. After passing a couple of false summits, the real one finally appeared. I was ahead of Paul and felt great despite the increasing altitude, sprinting the final hundred metres to the top. Lying down at the bottom of the sign marking the height of the pass (3252.8 metres), I savoured the aching in my legs and the blood pumping around my body as I looked around at the mountains surrounding me and watched Paul cruise to the top with his smooth cycling style.

Paul and I cycled differently; I preferred to rotate my legs slower, cycling in a higher gear. Paul's pedals spun much faster and he looked smoother, with his long, lanky legs. On the whole I was slightly faster than Paul, but there wasn't much in it and I valued the rests that I got while waiting. Paul descended fearlessly and I struggled to keep up with him on the rocky descents. This was partly because I was worried about damaging my bike and panniers; not wanting a serious mechanical failure on the remote Pamir Highway.

Over the pass we rode a great descent down a rocky road. It clung to the cliff edge, above a bright blue river below, first passing rocky outcrops, and then skirting the edge of a gorge, where the river turned into a spectacular waterfall as it plunged over a high cliff. We carried along the track, with a drop of at least 1,000 metres on the right and a cliff face on the left. The road reached less precarious land and weaved backwards and forwards down a series of switchbacks to the valley floor, where it followed the river down to the town of Kalaikhum. We had dropped 2,000 metres of altitude in one and a half hours. It was the best descent I have ever done; an exhilarating high speed race to the valley floor on a bumpy track that followed the rushing white water . I managed to keep up with Paul by cycling uncomfortably fast and putting Sandy through her paces. She responded well, as ever, and tarmac finally returned as the road approached Kalaikhum. We found a cheap bed for the night in a homestay and started regaining some of our calorie deficit with a huge feast from the local shop.

In the morning, we joined the raging Panj River on the border with Afghanistan, following a good road along a gorgeous valley and passing through pretty villages growing fresh fruit, which kids sold to us. Their mothers let us barter with them and we taught them how to negotiate as they started far too low in our opinion! I got two flat tyres because I was still using the poor quality inner tubes from the Denov bazaar. I put my final tube in, hoping it would last until Khorog. It had a hole in it that I fixed, praying it would survive a couple of days, as I realised that I had run out of puncture repair glue.

We had a large lunch on the side of the river and watched the world go by. A Tajik girl was playing a game with two Afghan boys who were standing on the other bank. They were throwing stones into the water, and communicating with each other across the river despite the nearest crossing being over twenty miles away; a lovely sight. Despite this friendliness among the younger generation, we were told by some locals that there is great mistrust of the Afghans here. When the river freezes in winter, they sometimes come over to Tajikistan and steal food, probably out of desperation rather than any other reason. This predicament was actually partially caused by the UK. The area that we were cycling in, the Wakhan Corridor, is 140 miles long and between ten and forty miles wide. This small strip of land separates Tajikistan from Pakistan. It was a political creation of *'The Great Game'*; a conflict between the British and Russian empires in the Nineteenth Century. Its purpose was to separate the two empires by a buffer zone, which was part of Afghanistan. Now the 12,000 inhabitants of the Wakhan Corridor are very cut off from the rest of Afghanistan and, as a result, are very poor, have little to eat and have to fend for themselves; *a reminder of our glorious past.* I saw a very old man ploughing his field with a horse and a single-bladed plough that he operated by standing on a platform above the blade. Life looked very bleak on *the other side.*

That night we cooked our culinary highlight as 'Team Beer', a sensational fish curry. We had been christened *'Team Beer'* by Mark and Camille in Samarkand, after stories of our heavy night in Tashkent. A villager had given us permission to camp that night in an orchard that had a beautiful stream passing through the middle of a flat copse. We pitched the tents and started cooking the curry. A small waterfall at the back of the orchard formed a perfect shower. It was an exhilarating experience to stand under the very powerful and freezing flow of water, but difficult not to lose the soap down the stream. Clean and well fed, I lay in my tent very content. The adventure was progressing brilliantly, Tajikistan was even better than I had expected because not only had the scenery surpassed all expectations, the inhabitants of the area were some of the kindest and hospitable people I have ever met. *Life was good.*

One night in the valley, we camped just across the river from Afghanistan and were invited to a concert of traditional Tajik music in the village that we were staying next to. We arrived and weren't allowed to pay for the entrance ticket. I was quite pleased about this in the end because the music was truly terrible; with the exception of one performer, none of the guys could sing at all well. The only girl on stage introduced the acts, speaking into a microphone that was put through an echo synthesizer for some reason. The highlight of the show was two rappers who were trying to be as American as they could, with aviators and baseball caps. They seemed good until the backing track skipped and we found out they were miming! The evening progressed into a great experience for us and the locals loved it.

A short ride the next day brought us into the town of Khorog; the capital of the Pamir region. It is a well-developed town, considering the location and owes its existence to the Aga-Khan, head of the Ismailly Muslim religion. He is Swiss born, a man regarded by some Ismailly Pamiris as a living God. His charity donates a lot of money to the town and has prevented certain famine in Khorog and the surrounding area for a number of years. He has also opened schools throughout the region as well as a university. On the way into Khorog I got stung by a bee again, this time in-between the eyes. I managed to head-butt the bee when riding downhill at about thirty miles per hour. During my stay in Khorog I had to go to the hospital that the Aga-Khan had funded, because my face had swollen up so much that I couldn't see and had to stay an extra day in the hostel in Khorog too due to terrible stomach problems, vomiting and fever. I met a young British guy called Alex in the hostel, he had been blinded in a car accident a few years ago and was travelling from Beijing back to England by public transport, visiting some of the places he had been to when he was able to see. I thought this was inspirational and incredibly brave.

Paul had to leave without me because he had to get through the country before his visa expired; we hoped to meet up again on the road. I left Khorog thinking I was on the mend after spending a day and a half in bed, having been told that the town of Ishkashim was a couple of days away and that it had a hospital so I could rest there if needed. It was good to be cycling alone again. Paul had been great company, but there is something special about experiencing a place like this alone. You feel more of a part of it somehow. On the way out of Khorog I went to the market and stocked up on decent food for the last time in a couple of weeks; supplies would be hard to come by until I reached Murghab in the Eastern Pamirs. I bought a litre of petrol to cook with for about five pence, and then entered the famous and spectacular Wakhan Valley.

The river was much narrower here, only about ten metres wide. In some of the shallower parts I thought it would be very easy to enter Afghanistan. I was almost tempted to try to cross at night; it would be a great story to illegally cross the Afghan border but I decided not to risk it, imagining that Afghan prisons aren't great places to be. The road was half tarmac, half dirt and riding was tough, especially with low energy levels because of my illness. I was managing to make slow progress, but needed to get better in order to get through Tajikistan before my visa expired.

At the first police checkpoint I cheered up. The police handed me a pot of tea and some bread, which really helped my morale. This is typical of Muslim hospitality. No questions like *"Would you like some food?"* They just know that you do and give it to you. Unfortunately, six miles later I was really low again. I had no energy at all, so I gave up and lay down on a warm boulder on the side of the road and slept for half an hour. I woke up and managed another six miles to the next village and asked for a place to camp. They showed me to a lovely orchard, where I pitched my tent and unloaded the bike. I was feeling very ill, and to make things worse, I discovered that my rear pannier rack was broken. The hole through which it is screwed into the frame had snapped. I swore loudly and the two teenagers who had taken it upon themselves to look after me came to investigate the problem. I said:

"Problem," pointing to the damage.

"No problem," one of them replied.

He took the broken component away, and after an hour came back with a new part that he had made in a workshop. It fitted perfectly and the rack was as good as new. I gave him a big smile and thanked him before crashing into bed.

The next day I was woken at half past six by an overexcited teenager who had brought me a kettle full of chai for breakfast. I went to use the village long-drop toilet and was followed. He waited outside while I was on the loo, and then escorted me back to the campsite; very strange. Anyway, I left in better spirits, but still not well, and limped on to another village before throwing up my breakfast. I managed to eat a bit at lunchtime and then slept in a bus stop before I was awoken by some middle aged women shouting *"tourist"* at me! Very annoyed, I carried on and struggled into Ishkashim, where I bought some antibiotics. Thinking about it now, I don't know why there was a bus stop because I never saw a bus while I was there.

In Ishkashim, I met a Polish cyclist called Paul, who rode with me to the next village. He knew that a doctor lived there and took me to his house. We knocked on the door and were ushered in. Paul could communicate with him in Russian and explained that I wasn't well. I lay down on a mattress in his beautiful open plan Pamiri house which had five pillars, to symbolise the pillars of Islam, with the kitchen, a TV, chairs, a table, and roll out beds in one room. It was a lovely place to recover. I was absolutely shattered, with no energy at all and could see that I had lost weight by the fact that my ribs were visible. I really needed to get better quickly if I was going to get through the mountains before my visa expired.

The doctor made me some herbal medicine, which I drank, and then he fed me some rice and milk. I had a shower and then fell asleep. The next morning I felt a lot better so something had worked. I still wasn't one hundred percent, but was ready to get going again. The doctor was yet another example of amazing kindness from a complete stranger. In the morning, just before I left, a baby with a bad cough was brought to the doctor to be examined. The doctor checked him over and didn't ask for any payment.

I left the house and rode up the most beautiful valley that I have ever seen. The side valleys over the river in Afghanistan showed off views of the Hindu Pradesh Mountains in Pakistan, with snow-capped peaks of over 7,000 metres in height and bright white rivers falling from them into the valleys below. The road turned into an appalling dirt track, which I climbed for an age, and then had another energy crash. I struggled to a shop and found some coke, biscuits and CRISPS! I hadn't had any for a long time and craved them, so bought four packets, got my salt and sugar fix and was able to continue.

The next morning I was better. Tummy troubles finally over, I cycled along on increasingly worsening roads, but through even more beautiful scenery. I passed a museum with a traditional Pamiri house and a solar calendar from the nineteenth century. There was a stone with a hole in it that could somehow be used to tell the date. In the afternoon I found another waterfall and had a refreshing super-power-shower under it. I collected a couple of litres of water in my bottles from the stream and was planning to drink it. Luckily some locals, whom I met on the road, told me that the water from that stream wasn't safe. A white algae was growing which is poisonous and would have given me bladder problems. I made a mental note to check streams for the algae from now on. Further along the valley was a mineral water spring. It was delicious, with naturally sparkling water at about bath water temperature flowing out of a crack in a rock. It tasted sweet, and the fact that it was naturally carbonated amazed me. I filled all my bottles up.

The valley widened and the road was good until the village of Langar; the last settlement in the Wakhan Valley. There was only one shop, which seemed to be priced based on the fact that cycle tourists had no other place to buy food for the next three days. Local people had one price, I had another, and there was nothing I could do about it. I stocked up on three days of food, asking the price of each item and bartering the shop owner down until it was a reasonable rather than a complete rip-off. The next section would be very remote until I reached the main Pamir Highway so I needed a lot of food but reckoned that I would be okay for water as I would be following the river. I was sure to find streams flowing into it, and if not, I would purify water from the river with my chlorine pills.

The road climbed out of Langar to reveal yet more spectacular views of the mountains in Afghanistan and Pakistan. I cycled up a series of switchbacks. The local boys pushed me up from behind to give me a boost then demanded money for the privilege. I refused to give them any. Paying them would teach them that bike tourists were a source of money, and then the annoying kids from Uzbekistan who demanded money from white people on sight would be born here too. The road surface was bad again, gravelly and sandy with no tarmac. There was very little passing traffic, and that evening I didn't see any vehicles at all. I found a flat bit of land on the inside of one of the switchbacks and lay down on my foam mat; there was no need for a tent. I made a delicious soup for dinner out of fresh vegetables and chicken stock, and then fell asleep under the clear night sky. Three shooting stars passed by and the Milky Way was as bright as I have ever seen it. From my sleeping mat I could see three countries: the fertile fields and good road on the Tajikistan side of the river, the poorer farms and donkey tracks on the Afghan side, and the enormous snow-capped mountains in Pakistan looming above the side valleys off the main river.

The next morning, the road continued to climb up to an altitude of 3,000 metres. It turned into a terrible sandy track, which wasn't all rideable. With a mixture of pushing and slow riding I managed around thirty-five miles a day for the next three days. The road climbed up the river valley and was as beautiful as ever. I saw some rare Bactrian camel on the Afghan side of the river. They have two humps rather than one and are classified as critically endangered. The Bactrian camel was the camel of choice for traders on the Silk Road in ages past because itcan cope with cold, heat, drought and altitude. Apparently there are now only around 600 wild Bactrian camels left. I felt very privileged to have seen a group of them.

There was really nothing around me except for nature and beautiful scenery. The only sign of human influence on the landscape was the track that I was riding along and that day I saw no other traffic at all. This track continued for a very tough but fantastic three days, which gave me a real sense of adventure; what I had left home for. Along with the Kazakh desert, this is the most remote place I have ever been to. It was me against the mountains. All I had to do was eat, drink, sleep and make progress uphill on my bike. It was a simple life, but wonderful.

After the final police checkpoint of the Wakhan Valley, I started the difficult climb up to the 4,320 metre Khargush Pass, which would take me up and over the mountains on the north side of the valley, to the Pamir Highway. The altitude was really affecting me now. My breathing became short and I had to keep stopping to get my breath back. The climb was hard anyway but made very, very difficult due to the altitude and the appalling road surface. After a few hours of panting up the climb, I eventually reached the summit and bumped into Martin there, a German cyclist whom I had met in Khorog. I met him at a rather embarrassing time; he was clearly suffering from the same tummy problems that I had been a few days ago! I turned my back and took some photos of the scenery behind me, then approached him and we caught up. He had loved the Wakhan Valley as much as I had, but was struggling with illness that day.

We had lunch together and celebrated beating the pass. He was moving slowly because of his illness and I had to push on, so I went ahead to begin the descent to Alichur. It was just as difficult as the climb up the pass because I was cycling in sand, had to push a lot of the way and struggled to ride the rest. Eventually the sand ran out and the tarmac returned. I let out a cheer as I cruised along the perfectly smooth road surface. I almost kissed it! It was great to be moving fast again, having beaten illness and the Wakhan valley, and experienced the most beautiful scenery of the ride so far. Next up was the Pamir Highway proper. I decided to finish a bit early at the lake on the Pamir plateau because it was a perfect place to set up camp, with a view over a plain surrounded by giant rugged mountains in every direction. I set up my tent, got my cooking equipment out. I had a nasty surprise when I emptied the bag of pasta that I had brought with me from the last shop in the Wakhan Valley; it was full of rodent droppings. The shop had clearly had a problem with mice (or worse) and the pasta was ruined. I ate what I could from my low food supplies, knowing that the town of Alichur was coming up the next day. I had sweets, vegetables and the last of my bread, leaving a few things for breakfast, hoping that Alichur was nearby so that I could eat a proper meal in the morning.

15. The Pamir Highway

I believe in one thing only, the power of human will.
- Joseph Stalin

The Pamir Highway has been used for centuries and was once part of the ancient Silk Road; it was developed by the Soviets, and it is thanks to them that I was now cycling on tarmac again. Say what you want about the former Soviet Union, they made this part of the world vastly more accessible for cycle tourists!

I woke up to the stunning view of the 4,000 metre high lake on the Pamir Plateau. Looking back, one of my favourite memories is waking up in the morning and unzipping my tent door to a different view most days. Today's was arguably the most beautiful of all, with rugged mountains surrounding the lake on one side and the Pamir plateau stretching out into the distance on the other. Unfortunately, my breakfast wasn't as good as the view, consisting of last night's leftovers. Fortunately, after around half an hour, I reached Alichur which was bigger than expected. I stopped for a proper breakfast in a chaihana, where I met Martin again. Over a cup of tea, we decided to cycle together for a while. Our journey as a new team began with a 4,100 metre pass, although having ascended from 4,000 metres, it was a pretty minor climb. At the bottom of the short descent, we were beckoned over by a family living in an isolated house in the middle of nowhere. Martin decided to carry on because he had some lunch in his bags. I went into the house, not wanting to miss this opportunity to visit a family in such a remote place.

Inside the house, it was really warm because their stove was burning yak dung. There were fourteen people in one small room. The family living there were two brothers and their wives, their ten children and their mother and father. Sixteen people living in one tiny house. They were almost completely self-sufficient because they had no way of getting to the other towns; their only contact with the outside world was the road and the passing traffic. One of the men told me that they buy food from a passing lorry sometimes, but basically they ate food made from yak milk, bread and eggs. They can't grow fruit and vegetables in this climate. They gave me bread, yak cream and apricot jam. The apricots had come from the lorry and were probably grown in the Wakhan Valley, I thought. All the food was delicious, especially the cream. I thought about what the future holds for the kids in that house. There was nothing for them there. Would they just end up staying there for their whole lives and never get an education or know anything except for that barren plateau? Maybe they would be happy there; the family was very close. Or maybe they would marry someone from Alichur or Khorog and move there.

I left the house and gave the rest of my sweets to the kids, before meeting up with Martin again. He had stopped for his own lunch and, once he'd finished, we cycled on together. I noticed that the altitude was affecting me because my breathing was much heavier than normal and it was a fairly flat section of road. Other than this, I didn't seem to have any problems with the altitude. Acute mountain sickness (altitude sickness) affects people above 3,000 metres and can be fatal. It is rarely dangerous if you acclimatise properly and I had ascended to this altitude over a couple of weeks, so was pretty well used to it by that stage.

The mountains were now grey and rocky, not green and snow-capped like in the Wakhan Valley. The landscape was like nothing I had ever seen; beautiful but so barren and imposing. Unfortunately, we had a strong headwind to battle against, but we made good progress. The road was mainly flat, with a few small climbs until a large one up a windy valley late in the day. From the top, we began our descent to Murghab, the largest town in the Eastern Pamirs, following a river then rounding a corner, which hugged a cliff. It was early evening when we finally saw our target (Murghab) ahead, about ten miles away. The wind was brutal and it was getting dark as we arrived at the police checkpoint on the way into the town. It was very funny; the police checked the passports from their beds where they were napping. It didn't look like a particularly difficult job! After being cleared to pass, we struggled into Murghab absolutely shattered and stayed in the first homestay we could find.

The next day I headed up to the Murghab EcoTourism Association (META) building, which was a really interesting place built in a traditional style to resemble a Pamiri house. There was a shop with traditional craft products for sale and a very dodgy internet café, which ran very slowly from a petrol generator. I managed to buy Laura a good luck card for her new job from a website, but it took over an hour because of the slow connection. META promotes traditional living and provides community schemes in Murghab and the surrounding area, offering employment to a few people who make traditional souvenirs for tourists. I bought Laura a gift; a yak wool wall decoration. At lunchtime I headed to the bazaar with Martin and bumped into Paul there. I had finally caught up with him and was delighted to see him again. Now a team of three, we bought provisions and set off into the mountains once more. The headwind was roaring again, so after struggling along a valley, we stopped at another wonderful campsite on a lawn of grass by a river and cooked a delicious meal of homemade chips and plov.

After a late start the following day, we set off for the highest pass on the Pamir Highway and of my entire trip around the world. It took a while to get going as we'd had to fix a broken spoke in Martin's rear wheel. It reminded me that I hadn't had one for months. Before Georgia, three had snapped, and then in Tblisi I spent some time adjusting the spoke tensions in the wheel. It must have worked okay because it had been fine ever since. Once the wheel was mended, we set off to tackle one of the highest road passes in the world. The Ak-Baital (White Horse) Pass climbs to an altitude of 4,655 metres, so I was expecting a tough day. At least the wind had died down a bit though. We climbed all morning, had lunch, and then set off at our own paces for the final part of the climb. About 300 metres of altitude from the summit I met Polish Paul again and he looked freezing; it was snowing heavily. He had turned back halfway up the final climb to the top of the pass because his rear wheel was damaged. He planned to cycle to Murghab, and then get a jeep taxi back to Khorog, saying that the weather had caused him to turn back. Apparently it was awful at the top. I didn't have this option so had to carry on through the snow. Taking a taxi didn't occur to me as a possibility. I carried on up a gravel track that got really steep, cycling as far as I could in stints, before stopping to let my breathing and heart rate drop, then carrying on again. After a very steep final switchback I made it to the top; *4,655 metres*. There was a blizzard blowing, but I didn't feel the cold, exhilarated to have got to the highest point of my trip. *I felt like I was on the way home now.*

I waited for the others and the sun came out. When they arrived we celebrated, shook hands, took loads of photos and then descended into yet another beautiful valley on the other side. It was freezing cold and the wind was back. I put on all my clothes and made it to the valley floor with numb fingers despite my thick gloves. As we descended, I remember hearing what I thought were birds screeching but they turned out to be marmots. There were hundreds of them, standing by their holes and, I assumed, sending warning signals to each other when they saw, heard or smelt us coming. We found a yurt to stay in for about the equivalent of three pounds. It was so warm inside and the people who lived there brought us delicious food; noodles and mutton. We lay around snoozing and talking about what an amazing place we were in; the Pamirs really had surpassed all of my expectations. The yurt was covered in fur, the inside hung with decorative material and carpets. In the middle there was a chimney and a large cast-iron stove that burned animal dung. It was extreme luxury to me and the cosiest place I have ever been. I thought of Martin, who had flown directly to Dushanbe and was finishing in Osh at the end of the Pamir Highway. He had come straight from Germany into this remote but wonderful place. It must feel very different for him in comparison to my experiences. Having gradually eased myself into this world, it probably felt much more normal to me. I had to remind myself where I was, how lucky I was to be there and how far I had travelled to get there. My speedometer read 6,313 miles; *I was nearly halfway around the world...*

In the morning the sun was out and we could see back up to the pass. The view of the surrounding mountains, the yaks in the pastures around the yurts and the bright sun in the blue sky made for an excellent photo opportunity. I spent an hour happily taking photos, before remembering that time was limited and that I needed to get to Kyrgyzstan the next day. There was still a fair distance to the border. Despite the sun, it was very cold, and I dressed in a few layers before setting off. After a slow start, we headed off again into the ever present headwind. After lunch, we bumped into Brigitte and Clemance, another very friendly Swiss couple, whom we had met in Khorog and were cycling to China. As a group of five we carried on to Karakul, the highest lake in Central Asia. Karakul is also the name of the small town by the lake, which was not the most beautiful place. It looked like it had been hit by a bomb, with half collapsed buildings and rubble lying around on the ground. We found a homestay, where Brigitte and Clemance planned to stay for the night, and ordered some food. Clemance showed me his lower arms, which had swollen up with fluid. An unusual reaction to the prolonged exposure to high altitude had started. He and his wife were very worried, but had decided to push on because they would be descending soon. An ancient looking man with a beautiful weather-beaten face and a pointy white beard allowed me to take a photograph of him. What was his story, I wondered? He had probably lived in this isolated settlement for his whole life. People spoke Kyrgyz here rather than Persian and used Kyrgyz money. We were getting close to the border now.

Leaving the Swiss at Karakul, we continued around the lake. It was gorgeous; maybe the most beautiful part of the Pamir Highway. The lake is vast, and surrounded by snow-capped mountains as far as the eye can see; some more than 7,000 metres high. The wind was unbelievably strong, and we struggled for ten miles until we found a relatively sheltered campsite behind a sand bank. The terrain was high altitude desert now, loose sand and little vegetation, with no water sources. We had plenty in our bottles, but had to carry more than usual the following day, because we couldn't guarantee finding streams anymore.

The last day in Tajikistan started at five in the morning. I decided to get going early to make sure that I would reach the Kyrgyz border post before it shut that day. The others seemed to think this was a good plan, so they also got up early and we set off together. We had yet another giant pass to climb first thing and I was feeling great, so tried to make it in one go without getting off the bike. I was delighted to be feeling so fit again after my illness in the Wakhan Valley, and thought my acclimatisation must be complete. The altitude had affected me a bit, with headaches for a few days and a loss of appetite, but on the whole I had coped with it well. Paul arrived at the top shortly after me and we sat down to wait for Martin. We waited for an hour and he didn't arrive, so we left a message in the road with stones that we would meet him in the next town and then carried on. A passing car had told us that there was a group of four cyclists coming behind, so we knew that he would be okay and assumed that he had suffered another broken spoke.

Needless to say the wind was still in our faces, and after lunch in the shelter of the raised road, Paul and I carried on. Looking back we saw Martin behind us. He had suffered from an energy crash on the climb and got really dizzy and had to lie down for an hour before continuing. This was probably an effect of the altitude combined with his illness. Martin had a heavy load and Paul and I had thousands of miles of training behind us. He was doing incredibly well considering. The times that I had been ill had really sapped the strength out of me. During these times, the last thing that I wanted was to cycle up huge mountain passes.

I made a difficult decision to break from the others. We were cycling at different speeds and I needed to get into Kyrgyzstan that day. Cycling at a pace that isn't your own is difficult. It is important to find a rhythm and to keep plugging away under your own steam. This was particularly relevant as the next climb was the hardest of the entire trip for me. After leaving the others I battled up a gravel track to the Tajik border control. It was tough, mainly due to the wind and the poor road surface. I struggled up for what seemed like hours, making slow progress, until finally rounding a bend to see Tajik customs ahead. I got through pretty quickly and continued the final mile or so to the top of the pass, which was much more sheltered. At the summit was the border. It felt great to reach Kyrgyzstan; it was all downhill to Sary-Tash now, the first proper town since Murghab, and a chance to resupply.

The descent to Sary-Tash was spectacular, from 4,260 metres elevation down to 3,200. I was off the Pamir Plateau and it was green again. A glistening river ran down from one of the giant mountains, with a glacier hanging from its snow-capped peak. There were Kyrgyz yurts and herds of yaks dotting the green pastures in the base of the valley. The road was also great fun to cycle on, since the gravel and dirt surfaces with switchbacks and river crossings made for a challenging, technical descent. About fifteen miles later I was at the Kyrgyz border control, where I was given some dough dumplings to eat by a Chinese lady who was travelling in a truck with her husband. I cycled through the valley to Sary-Tash, into the wind again. There were many nomad families there and kids ran up to the road to demand photographs, which I happily took. Birds of prey perched on telegraph poles and swooped through the sky. The landscape was endless. I looked back up to the glacier, at the river widening into hundreds of snakelike channels as it reached the plain. The barren rocky landscape was over, it was lush and green here.

I arrived at Sary-Tash at around six o'clock and found a cheap homestay. Paul turned up shortly after, and later on Martin arrived, what an incredible recovery! I was starving, so I gorged on chocolate from the first decent shop in weeks. The Pamir Highway was definitely the highlight of the trip and it was fantastic to have completed it successfully. *I'd turned dreams and plans into memories and photographs.* I still had a lot to look forward to over the next few days though. Kyrgyzstan was another country that I really wanted to visit. I imagined a nation of nomads, pastures, mountains, horses and yaks.

16. Nomads, yaks and a snowstorm

Not all those who wander are lost
- J. R. R. Tolkien

I left the homestay in the early hours, saying goodbye to Martin and Paul for the last time. I was in more of a rush than they were because my plan was to meet my cousin Phil in Urumqi, China in three weeks' time. I also wanted to spend three weeks alone because they were to be the final three weeks of solo cycling of the trip. If all went to plan, my friend Harry would join me for the crossing of North America. Solo travel has its advantages, and I wanted to be able to make selfish decisions. With a long way to go in three weeks, I needed to be able to put big days in when necessary but wanted to balance hard effort with time to relax.

With the spirit of adventure returned to me, I left Sary-Tash and began realising the treat this country had in store for me. Like Tajikistan, it was even more beautiful than I had imagined, but it was a different sort of beauty, not as ruggedly spectacular, but prettier, with fertile landscapes rather than desert and more wildlife and people around. For 2,000 years, the people of Krygyzstan have been nomadic, only beginning to settle in cities during the last century. A large proportion of the population still live in the traditional way; in yurts, moving their animals with the season to follow food sources. Some yurts are sited alone and some are near groups of others. Some nomads must prefer solitude, while others prefer company. I wanted to speak to some of the local people, to be invited into the yurts and to find out what it is like to live the way that they do. I thought I had something in common with them, however, my nomadic existence was only temporary while theirs is permanent.

The road between Sary-Tash and Osh begins by climbing over a long double-headed pass (a pass with two summits in quick succession). Compared with what I'd just conquered in the Pamirs it was a piece of cake. I had a load of extra red blood cells from all my training at altitude and would probably never be this fit again. It felt great to make it to the top so quickly and I sat down, ate a snickers bar and admired the view, watchingbirds of prey swooping around looking for rodents to eat and shepherds going about their business around their yurts on either side of the road. The descent from the top of the second pass wove down the hillside into a valley with bustling towns, shops, cafés and people. It was great to be back in civilisation again.

The headwind was still blowing though. It seemed it didn't matter which direction I was cycling; there was always a bloody headwind! I met a couple of Americans cycling in the opposite direction, who were loving the tailwind as they headed towards the Pamirs. They were almost getting blown up the hill that I was cycling down. I had to pedal hard to make progress downhill, which was really frustrating. At the end of the day, I passed through the fair-sized town of Gulcha, cycling along its high street, named 'Lenin Street' (a reminder that I was still in the former Soviet Union) and reached a river, where I asked a farmer if I could camp in his field for the night. I had a wash in the river, washed my clothes, cooked a decent soup for dinner and enjoyed a good night's sleep.

The next day started with another long climb, up the final pass on the road to Osh. There was a tea shop near the top so I stopped to refuel and talked to the shopkeeper about the Pamir Highway. He had travelled to Khorog a long time ago but I don't think he was quite as amazed by the experience as I was. He talked about it as a chore and told me he wanted to get back home as soon as he could when he had been there. I drank an entire kettle full of green tea, and then climbed the final couple of miles to the top of the pass. That was followed by a very fast thirty mile descent to the city of Osh. Osh is an ancient Silk Road city, older than Rome according to the locals (although I'm not sure that this is true). It is a busy, bustling town with a good market, but there was a nasty feel to the place; residual tension following the 2010 Kyrgyz Revolution. In 2010, President Bakiyev was ousted from the capital city, Bishkek. This led to conflict between the Kyrgyzstanis, Uzbeks and Tajiks living in Osh and the surrounding area. Mass riots began and buildings were burned down. Estimates are that 2,000 people lost their lives and that 100,000 Uzbeks and Tajiks fled to Uzbekistan. Killing, gang-rape and torture took place. A little over a year down the line, Osh still has underlying unrest. Not feeling safe there, I decided that it wasn't worth staying in Osh long, so I left the next morning, into the Fergana Valley.

The Fergana Valley is the 'heartland' of Kyrgyzstan and stretches into Uzbekistan and Tajikistan too. It is called a valley but really it is a plain between two large mountain ranges. I was heading to the Tian-Shan in the north of the country, a mountain range that extends into Kazakhstan and China. The ride through the valley was very hot and temperatures were as high as they had been in the deserts of Uzbekistan. It was humid, so I sweated profusely and needed to drink even more water than during the desert crossings. I cycled all morning, then was invited over to a stall selling melons. The melon sellers gave me chai, some melon slices and shelter from the sun for a while. I left them at about two o'clock, but it was still too hot to be riding, so I went for another chai in a café and had a siesta for a couple of hours. I had worked out that around sixty-five miles per day would need to be completed to arrive at Urumqi in Western China in time to meet Phil at the airport. It was a fairly fast pace, taking into account all the mountains that needed to be crossed, but if I got up early every day, there would be enough time to chill out a bit and take siestas in the midday heat.

That evening I found a phone on the side of the road and did my good turn for the day by finding an English speaking woman (very rare in Kyrgyzstan), who I explained the problem to. She called the last number and arranged to leave it in a shop while the owner came to pick it up. Karma must have been favouring me after that because I found a great place to stay. An old man and his wife invited me into their home and gave me a delicious meal of potatoes mashed up with bread and meat, followed by laghman soup. After dinner, the old man played his home-made three-string guitar, or 'komuz', for me and sang. It was a lovely moment. All the children in the house had a great deal of respect for the old man and woman. They must have been at least in their seventies, an age which is an achievement to reach in this part of the world. They had their children and grandchildren around to look after them and it seemed like a very happy old age. We sat together for a few hours, then I slept on their patio with my mosquito net protecting me from the hundreds of mosquitoes that buzzed around outside. Their cat came over and curled up next to me.

The next day, I left my latest hosts after a quick breakfast, and rode until lunchtime, when I stopped for a siesta at a chaihana, ate another melon and read a book. It was too hot in the middle of the day to eat too much; I just tended to snack on stuff all day rather than have a big meal. The humidity and hill climbs made the temperatures more difficult to cope with than in the dry, flat desert. There were also many more places to pull over and to relax, so it was much more tempting to stop. I was in a lazier mind-set and didn't have the visa concern that I had experienced in Uzbekistan. My only deadline was meeting Phil in Urumqi, but if I was a day or so late, I thought that he could entertain himself or hitch a lift to where I was.

In the evening I started climbing again and at dusk, asked at a petrol station for a place to camp. The petrol pump operator said that I couldn't cook near the petrol station because of the fire risk (as he puffed away on his cigarette). The owner took me to a nearby house and asked if I could camp there. The family who lived there let me put my tent up in front of the entrance and I started cooking. They kept bringing me food, bread, cucumbers and tomatoes. I had just started eating my pasta when the lady of the house said I should come and eat with the family. By that stage I was ready for bed. In situations like this it was difficult because I felt like an 'ambassador' for my country. The chances were that they had never met an Englishman before. Their opinions on the English would be based on me for years to come. If I came across as a grumpy antisocial guy who slept in a tent, would they think that that is typical in England?

So I went to their house and left the pasta for breakfast. What was for dinner? More plov! I didn't want to be ungrateful so I ate it, but the greasy rice dish that everyone in Central Asia seems to eat was really getting to me now. It was okay, but eating it for every meal was a bit much. I thought of my pasta, which I would have much preferred. Anyway, the family were lovely and the kids tried out the English they'd learned at school. Much to her embarrassment, the thirteen year old girl told me she was thirty and everybody laughed! They brought a watermelon for dessert and I had a beer that I had bought earlier. *Luxury!*

In the morning I was woken by one of the children, who brought me chai. I started eating my pasta again, but then last night repeated itself. I was invited to breakfast with the family, who washed up my pans and threw my pasta away while I was in the loo. When I found out I was gutted, even more so when breakfast materialised. MORE PLOV! Anyway, it was very nice of them to wash my pans for me and the lady washed my shirt. It must have smelt pretty bad because she didn't ask me if I wanted it washing.

I left the house and signed autographs for the children. The morning was spent climbing up to a beautiful blue reservoir in a dry brown desert landscape. I had lunch at the water's edge on a carpeted platform in the shade. I only had a short swim (with a bar of soap) in the reservoir because it was absolutely freezing. The water had come from the snowmelt in the mountains and it took my breath away when I first got in. It was great to cool down properly and swimming in cold water is the only way to do so in a climate like this. It is impossible to describe how refreshed you feel afterwards. After another siesta, I climbed up a beautiful gorge in the desert landscape. It felt very remote, with the exception of the Soviet-built hydroelectric dams every few miles with large reservoirs behind them. I camped at a town called Kara-Kol and shared a paddock with a horse. Laura called my Kyrgyzstan mobile and we had a great chat, which really picked my spirits up. It had been a while since we had last talked. The dogs annoyed me that night until I remembered Paul had given me some earplugs.

The next day I cycled around Toktogol Reservoir, a huge lake behind another Soviet dam. I had to cycle all the way to the end of the reservoir and back along the other side to a point I could see, not far away on the other side. It would have been good to have a boat. I climbed for a few hours as the road passed over the hills surrounding the lake, but it was cooler higher up in the mountains and so I didn't mind. I cycled all day until, arriving at the town on the other side of the lake, I was invited to stay by a shopkeeper. It was unusual to be invited in by a lady. Muslim women were usually quite reserved when they talked to me and often didn't have the 'authority' to invite guests inside; it would usually have to be run past the man of the house. This lady wasn't covering her head so I imagine that she wasn't particularly religious. I was led to her beautiful house and taken to a stream in the garden to have a wash. The shopkeeper's husband was a vet and he showed me his Soviet textbooks. He then got out a photo album from when he fought in the Soviet Army. There was a picture of his regiment in front of a statue of Lenin, and he did some quite alarming acting of the position he held in the army; he was the gunner in a tank. It was fascinating to see photographs of the Soviet soldiers. I looked through the entire album and saw pictures of his squadron on their time off, playing cards, drinking, smoking and laughing. There were holiday pictures of the family visiting Alma-Ata (now Almaty in Kazakhstan) and their trip to the nearby mountains. This album was a window into life in another world, an extraordinary thing to have seen: *the personal life of an ex-Soviet soldier.*

I had an enormous dinner. Thinking at first that the bread, cream and jam was the full meal, I ate loads, then the lady brought in potato stew. It was probably the best meal that I had in Central Asia but unfortunately I was full from the 'starter'. Having eaten as much as I could and not wanting to insult them. I sneaked the rest into a bag for the next day, It would make for a great lunch.

The next day I was shattered and my morale was low. I hadn't slept well for some reason, possibly due to the huge amount of food eaten the previous evening. My knees were hurting too from my exertions over the past weeks; I hadn't had a day off for a while so decided to take it easy and to treat myself to a short day. I cycled fifteen miles in the morning and stopped at a beautiful café where I slept on a platform in the middle of a river, shaded by trees. It was great to relax. I read and chilled out until late afternoon, then started climbing up another large pass. I had to ascend about 2,200 metres of altitude gain, up to 3,175 metres. This would be the second-to-last pass of the Tian-Shan mountain range. The height gain took place over a monster fifty mile climb. I climbed for an hour or so that evening, camped, then climbed all of the next day arriving at a yurt near the top in the early evening. They gave me biscuits and Koosmoos, which is an absolutely disgusting drink. It is gone-off horse milk, which is allowed to go fizzy through fermentation and is slightly alcoholic. They loved it, but I certainly didn't! The first mouthful made me gag, but I managed to finish a single cup. It was so horrible. I left the yurt refusing a second cup, but thanking them for their delicious drink.

I made it to the top of the pass just before sunset and camped with a nomad family just after the summit. There were three generations of women living there but the men were working away from their yurt. I had a go on one of the nearby shepherd's horses, which made me think that I had definitely chosen the right form of transport, not feeling anything like as safe on the horse. I pitched my tent by a river, on top of the soft grass. The pastures covered the mountains, with streams flowing through the fertile land. I fell asleep in the safe haven of my tent, which had been a brilliant and comfortable shelter in so many different places now, warm in my sleeping bag as the snow started falling outside. I could hear the yaks mooing as I fell asleep. This was one of my favourite campsites of the trip.

I woke up to find the old lady (probably in her eighties) pumping milk through a contraption connected to a wheel. It separated the milk into a thick creamy liquid and a much runnier one. I assumed the thicker one was for the koosmoos. Her daughter was milking a cow, and I was given a glass of fresh milk before I left. This was the second time in Kyrgyzstan that I had been invited to stay by women. Perhaps it is a more liberal country than the other former Soviet states that I had visited and women have more freedom here. I thought about the old lady. She would have lived through the Second World War, the time of the Soviet Union and its break-up. *What an interesting story she could have told.*

The following day's ride started with a quick descent into a valley. To begin with it was more of the same beautiful and remote scenery, as the road took me through pastures dotted with yurts, but then the yurts became shops aimed at truck drivers and it felt a bit artificial. I managed to refill my fuel bottle with some very cheap petrol for my stove. By lunchtime I had reached the bottom of the final pass before Bishkek, the capital city of Kyrgyzstan. Once climbing, I looked up to work out which way the road went. The weather was closing in at the top of the mountains; an intimidating sight.

Sure enough, after a few miles it started raining, which became snow after I got high enough for the temperature to decrease sufficiently. I could see lightning coming from the clouds on the mountain tops in what was a pretty serious storm. Feeling cold, I stopped for a while in a yurt and bought some cheese balls from the family who lived there. They were very salty but nice, probably made from horse milk. The snow stopped after an hour or so and I carried on climbing. Not long afterwards, the wind picked up and the snow started again. It was being blown into my face horizontally and I was getting really cold this time.

Not having the equipment to be riding in these freezing and dangerous conditions and concerned about being struck by lightning on the top of the mountain; I stopped at the next yurt and was welcomed in with a chai and a tasty stew. At one point the entire extended family, who were passing by car, came in. There were fourteen of us in one small yurt, sat around the central wood burning stove and drinking chai while the snow carried on falling outside.

In the morning the snow had stopped and I climbed up the pass into the clouds. Around an inch of snow had fallen during the night and it had changed the view entirely. I was now cycling in a wintery mountainous landscape, which the previous day had been a view of sunny green meadows. At the top of the pass there is a tunnel to save climbing the remaining three hundred metres of mountain, so I went through it, a bit nervous. A few years ago someone broke down in this tunnel and lorry drivers, waiting in the queue didn't turn their engines off. The tunnel filled with smoke and four people died from carbon monoxide poisoning. I got through without incident though to find an astonishing sight on the other side.

I looked down from the top of the huge mountain into the wide valley disappearing into the distance. There was snow on the first few hundred metres of descent then below this, grass, trees, a river and towering cliffs. The road snaked down and down into the distance and a smile appeared on my face at the thought of at least fifty very easy miles! I zoomed down the road, taking the 'racing line' around the hairpin bends until I reached the bottom, where I followed the valley towards Bishkek. I covered eighty miles in a few hours and arrived at Bishkek at around seven o'clock. I found a cheap dormitory for two dollars, and then headed out to get some food. I decided not to stay in Bishkek long As there didn't seem to be much to see and I wanted to get to China as quickly as possible. Having been in Central Asia for a long time, I was ready for a change, most importantly in the cuisine. I ate bread and real cheese that night, bought from an overpriced supermarket. The cheese was a treat that I hadn't had in a long time. The next morning I had a quick look round, bought some scissors from a market to trim my beard, got breakfast, and then headed to the nearby border with Kazakhstan, which I crossed easily. Unfortunately, the Kazakh border guards wouldn't stamp my OVIR registration paper, which meant I had to either cross the country in five days or register in Almaty, which could take a while. I would try to find out what the registration process involved and then make a decision on what to do.

I had absolutely loved Kyrgyzstan. The main road route through the country had been picturesque and varied, but I would like to come back one day to see some of the more remote areas. It is such a beautiful country, and I met some of the friendliest people of the entire trip. I wasn't particularly looking forward to Kazakhstan. From what I had read in my guidebook, it would be little more than a ride through monotonous scenery for a few days, with the city of Almaty to break it up. There was the possibility of a detour to Charyn Canyon, which is supposed to be impressive. However, China was less than a week away, and having been in Central Asia for so long it sounded like the 'Promised Land' to me.

17. A dash through Kazakhstan

Bureaucracy is a giant mechanism operated by pygmies
- Balzac, Honore De

Having arrived in Kazakhstan for the second time, I felt welcome straight away; the people were very friendly. I was given a free drink by a lady at a roadside stall, who had asked me where I was going, and then went to a police station to try to get my visa registered. They said that it wasn't possible there, even though they had told me at the border that it was and advised me to go to Taraz, which was over two hundred miles away in the wrong direction; *great advice for a cyclist in a hurry*. I cycled out of the border town of Korday, into the desert. Not expecting desert so soon so I hadn't bought enough food and water. I was annoyed with myself for my complacency because if this leg had been planned properly I would have stocked up in Bishkek. As a result, I was forced to buy snacks from very expensive petrol stations and asking for water at houses, before purifying it with chlorine pills.

I met an Australian cyclist, heading in the opposite direction to me. He had some bad news. The OVIR office (where you get your visa registered) in Almaty was closed at weekends. It was Thursday and I was over a full day's ride from Almaty, so would arrive on Friday evening at the earliest. The process would take a full day meaning a stay in Almaty until Tuesday morning. Three nights in a pricey hotel was not affordable as it is a very expensive city. The alternative was to dash through Kazakhstan in five days. I had already wasted most of one of them and had about 350 miles still to go, which I would have to cover in four days. The headwind was very strong and I was making hardly any progress. *I was in trouble!*

I camped in some trees on the side of the road and the next morning woke up very early, determined to get a big day in. The wind hadn't started yet; it usually picked up at about eleven o'clock, so I had almost a full morning cycling without wind and the benefit of a long downhill. Sure enough the strong wind arrived, but the afternoon's ride was sheltered on a good road with trees on either side. I stopped at a café for a big lunch, which fuelled me through until the evening and managed to get to Almaty ahead of schedule that night (Friday), covering 110 miles; my biggest day for a long time. I checked in to the cheapest hotel available. It was way over-budget, about fifteen dollars a night for a rubbish twin room, which I shared with a Norwegian tourist. We went to a café together and had a drink. He bought food but I couldn't afford to eat out, so I ate bread in the room later on. Almaty seemed to be a pleasant city. There wasn't a huge amount for tourists to see but the night life looked good and it seemed a lot richer than anywhere else that I had seen in Central Asia. The nearby Tian-Shan Mountains are apparently great for trekking and skiing too. Kazakhstan's oil wealth is centred here and there were a lot of expensive cars around. I headed back to the hotel quite early and got some rest, preparing for another big day.

The road out of Almaty was bad quality and boring. I was just trying to put in as many miles as possible. This was not fun cycling, and not what the trip was about. If I wasn't so hell-bent on making it around the world on an unbroken chain, I could have taken public transport to get through the country in time to avoid paying a fine for not getting my visa registered. I managed ninety miles on the first day out of Almaty and slept behind some trees on the side of the road again. In the middle of the night, a car crashed right next to my camp. It was a minor accident, but it gave me a shock and I couldn't sleep for about two hours while the recovery crew cleaned up, oblivious to my presence about ten metres away.

The scenery got slightly more interesting after Almaty. I passed through a hilly desert and then a gorge followed by a wide plateau, where the strong headwind was blowing once more. After finally crossing the plateau, I descended to the Charyn River. There was no time to make the detour to the canyon as I focussed on getting to China and having a decent meal. The climb out of the river gorge was steep, but I got up it quickly, and made it to a town that night, where I found a shop, bought some food for dinner, including two ice creams and a beer, then cycled out, settling for a horrible swampy campsite which was teeming with mosquitoes.

With loads of new bites to add to my collection, I got going the next day at sunrise. It was about sixty miles to China and I wanted to get to the border at a reasonable time to make sure of crossing it that day. If not, I had heard it was a two hundred dollar fine for not having the OVIR registration. Despite being tired I managed to drag myself out of bed before sunrise. Persuading my aching legs to push the pedals around, I got the miles done in the morning, arriving at the border at lunchtime.

I was delighted to have crossed the country in time having thought it to be an almost impossible task on the afternoon four days ago when hearing about the OVIR office closure. I had pushed myself as hard as I could, overcome another challenge and was planning to have a good rest in Korgas, the Chinese border town and to gorge myself on noodles and stir fry. I had one more obstacle to cross though. The Kazakh border guards don't usually allow cyclists to cross the border, but apparently force you to take a bus for a ridiculous fee for the one mile ride. I had heard that cyclists had crossed the border by bike recently though. I wanted to cycle around the world, not the world minus one mile. After a lot of explaining, negotiating and stubborn behaviour on my part, they let me through on the bike, more to get rid of me than anything else, I think. I was delighted, and let out a whoop in no man's land. I was finally let into China after about ten passport checks, and was welcomed by some delighted looking Chinese police, who must have known that I had managed to persuade the Kazakhs to let me through.

Everything was in a new language that I couldn't read, and I was nervous of entering this new world. I had absolutely loved Central Asia and by the end of my time there had felt at home and comfortable. I was sick of plov however, and eager, more than anything else, to eat some decent food. Where better to do this than China? I wondered how I would cope in the world outside the former Soviet Union…

Photographs of Turkey, the Caucuses and Central Asia

The spectacular Black Sea coastal road

One of the many tea stops!

Tortoises on the road

Sumela Monastery near Trabzon

Laura at Sumela Monastery

Zaza's lounge in Gori, Georgia

Jvari Monastery in Mtsketa

Party in Mtsketa park!

Tblisi

Party on the Caspian Sea ferry! Rashad is standing up, the guy to my left is the Georgian, the rest are Kazakhs.

GPS reading on deck while on the Caspian Sea ferry

Aktau sunset

Disembarking the 'Professor Gül' in Aktau Port

The 'Dangerous Section' in the Kazakh desert

A choice of tracks and galloping horses in the distance

I slept in culverts like this throughout the desert crossing

Mark and Camille on the beautiful tarmac raod

Camping in the desert

Deteriorating road

Beer in Bukhara in front of the "Minaret of Death"

119

The wonderful Registan in Samarkand

Eating plov in Tajikistan

It's a long way down on the Pamir Highway!

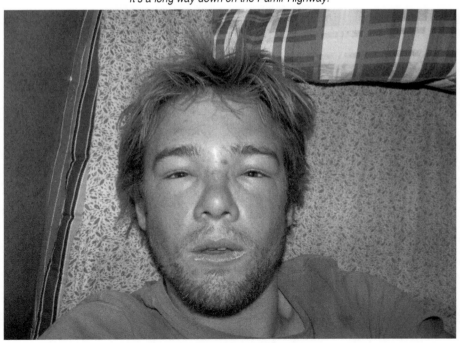

Stung by a bee in Khorog

The spectacular Wakhan Valley

Leaving the Wakhan valley on the Khargush Pass (4344 metres)

The high point of the trip: The White Horse Pass on the Pamir Highway

Not a bad spot to live!

123

Old man living in Karakol in the Eastern Pamirs

The climb up from Karakol

The descent in no-man's land between Tajikistan and Krygyzstan

Looking back into Tajikistan from the Kyrgyzstan border

Sunburnt nomad kids

More friendly hosts

Camping with nomads in the Tian-Shan

The start of an 80 mile descent to Bishkek

PART 3: CHINA

From Korgas to the Pacific Ocean

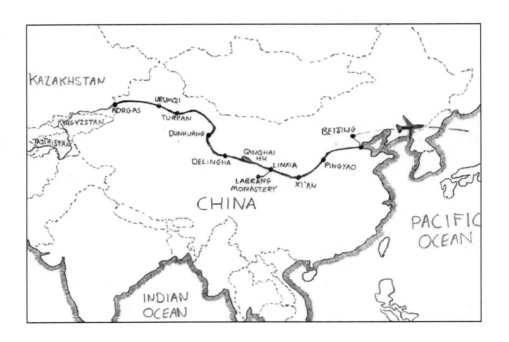

18. A new world

China is a big country, inhabited by many Chinese
- Charles de Gaulle

China was immediately different, not just because of the new alphabet, language and people's appearance but because I was back in civilisation for the first time in months. Korgas, the border town, was developed, clean, had lots of food choices in the supermarkets and offered excellent restaurants. Having checked into a hotel after searching for ages for the cheapest in town, I went to explore and had a delicious noodle stir fry enjoying the sensation of finally eating some good food again. I had forgotten what it tasted like. I found an internet café, Skyped Laura and my family and then went to bed. The hotel room was a ridiculous luxury for me. It cost about seven dollars, had a big double bed, a TV and air conditioning. I savoured the comfort for the night and had a rare lie-in in the morning.

For breakfast, I had an enormous pile of delicious meat dumplings for eight yuan (about eighty pence). I left Korgas in the early afternoon and cycled down a road built especially for bikes, next to a dual carriageway. Gliding along the tarmac was a wonderful experience, having been bumped around on poor roads for so long. Chinese people on bikes and electric scooters waved, pointed and smiled at me. I found an apple tree covered in juicy red apples. The first one I ate was delicious so I devoured two more, and then stuffed my panniers full of them. I decided to take a break in a dense wood, where I was hidden from view about ten metres away from the road, I sat down and started reading. Three hours later, I woke up! It was quite late by that stage, so I took a well-deserved evening off and put the tent up. I obviously had some sleep to catch up on.

After a big breakfast, I got going early. Early was now nine o'clock instead of seven as I was two hours ahead of Kazakhstan time. The whole of China operates on Beijing time, which meant shorter mornings but longer evenings in this western part of the country. I was given some boiled water at a shop and bought some snacks. Now that I was in the countryside, there wasn't as much choice: lots of disgusting processed meat, pickles and some pot noodles. I settled on some stale looking biscuits and a pot noodle, which the shop prepared for me, then joined a brand new dual carriageway and cycled up the hard shoulder. The road was half finished, so a lot of the time there was an empty carriageway which I could simply lift my bike on to and use as my own private bike track.

The road started climbing into the mountains and I got my first glimpse of the unbelievable scale of development in China. The new road that they were building was a massive undertaking. There was a series of long tunnels followed by an absolutely gigantic new motorway bridge spanning a wide valley. The bridge wasn't open at that stage so I had to climb the old dusty and bumpy road, to a high pass. On the other side of the pass was Sahram Hu, a large high-altitude lake, surrounded by Kazakh nomads living in yurts.

This part of China, Xinjiang Province, is historically not Chinese. The people who live there are mainly Uighur Muslims, who look Kazakh, eat Central Asian food and speak Arabic. All the road signs have two languages on them but this didn't help me, because both alphabets were completely incomprehensible to me. There were Chinese character place names on the photocopied maps I'd acquired in Samarkand however, so I could match the shapes of the Chinese characters on the signs to the place names on my maps. This worked quite well. Xinjiang's capital, Urumqi, was where I was heading. It had the Chinese characters "乌鲁木齐". I looked for the second symbol, which looked a bit like a ladder and the third symbol, which was a three legged person.

I found it difficult to connect with the people in Xinjiang Province. Although they were very friendly, it didn't seem possible to stay with families in this part of China. I asked a couple of times for places to camp or stay but they always pointed me towards expensive tourist hotels. Unfortunately, tourists aren't allowed to stay in cheap hotels in this part of China, so I mainly camped or slept in tunnels under the motorway. The tunnels were a convenient place to sleep; made from concrete and usually very clean, they had a flat floor, a roof, and were out of view of the drivers on the road. This made them were a perfect shelter for the night and saved me having to put the tent up.

From the lake, I enjoyed a forty mile descent past herds of camels, with views over the desert at the foot of the mountain range as I glided along at thirty miles an hour, overtaking lorries on the perfect road. Having reached the plain at the bottom, I tried to mentally prepare myself for more days in the desert but was not feeling particularly excited about the prospect. I stopped at a village for lunch and got a plate of excellent hand pulled noodles. I watched the chef make them; he started with one short, fat noodle then passed the end from hand to hand, stretching it out by bashing it on a steel worktop. He repeated this until he had a pile of long and thin noodles. The process was done with incredible energy and speed. It took me a long time to eat my meal due to my appalling chopstick skills. About halfway through my bowl of noodles, a coach load of Chinese tourists, who were heading to Sahram Hu, pulled up and ordered food. The restaurant went crazy. All the staff were worked off their feet preparing fifty different orders for very demanding customers. The new arrivals' table manners were absolutely appalling as they spat on the floor and slurped the soup and noodles unbelievably loudly. People were shouting, the atmosphere was crazy, and I loved it. I had been flung into another world again. My chopstick skills improved considerably over the course of that meal. I practised them by observing what the locals did and tried to copy them. I thought that next time I had a meal in a restaurant I might be able to finish my food before it got cold.

After a night spent surreptitiously camping in a wood by the roadside, I cycled for a couple of tired miles, and then found a restaurant for breakfast. It was cheaper to eat in restaurants than to cook for myself in China. A good meal cost about five yuan (fifty pence). To buy the raw ingredients would cost at least that, and I wouldn't be able to cook them anything like as well. Not sure if it was open, I entering the large dining room feeling uneasy, but worries were brushed aside by a group of six nineteen to twenty year olds, who ushered me inside and invited me to sit with them. One girl could speak English pretty well and translated for me. I had tofu and pumpkin soup, which was pretty bland. When I had finished, the girl asked her parents how much I should pay for it. She was upset that they charged me ten yuan (about one pound) for the food. Actually this was a pretty steep charge for the meal; I imagine that locals would pay considerably less. She thought that they should have given it to me for free so she went off to buy me some Pepsi to make up for it. I tried to pay her for it, but she wouldn't take the money and said that she was sad her parents had charged me. It was a lovely gesture, very touching. It seemed that the younger generation in China were generally very friendly.

I was struggling to connect with the older generation. For some reason, the sign language and the pointing at pictures that had worked so well in Central Asia didn't work at all here. It seemed that when the local people saw a Westerner approach, they instantly shut down didn't try to communicate. It was a shame because I don't think they were being rude: maybe they are shy or maybe it was just a vast cultural difference that I didn't understand. In the past, Chinese people weren't allowed to approach Westerners; perhaps this behaviour was a hangover from that time, or perhaps it is still frowned upon in certain areas. I hoped that it would be limited to this part of China. Over the next few days, I tried to ask directions a few times and was completely blanked. This happened even when I pointed at my Chinese character map. The people seemed to be afraid of me, or possibly of being seen talking to me. Another odd thing was that on the rare occasion that I did manage to start communicating with a Chinese person and I didn't understand what they were saying, they wrote it down in Chinese characters and were surprised I couldn't read it. I learnt later that the Chinese learn written English very well at school, but are not as good at speaking it. Maybe they assumed our system was the same. All this contributed to a pretty lonely first week in China so I was very much looking forward to meeting my cousin Phil in a few days' time.

For a couple of days before reaching Urumqi, I just got through the miles, riding on the motorway hard shoulder. I was back in the desert, but it was more populated than the Kazakh and Uzbek deserts, with large cities breaking up the remote stretches, so it wasn't much of a challenge. I listened to music and audiobooks to try to entertain myself and made good progress, eating great food. Each night I slept in a tunnel under the motorway; they were present every mile or so. One morning I woke up in one of the tunnels to a thunder storm outside and the tunnel slowly filling up with water. I quickly packed up, rode about three miles to a petrol station and entered it completely soaked. I went into the shop and they let me share their gigantic breakfast until the rain stopped. It consisted of different varieties of very spicy noodle stir-fries. The pressure was on because a critical audience watched as I ate the food with some chopsticks. I did okay though and only got laughed at once. A couple of days later at a restaurant; I tried to pay for the food, but was told to put my money away. I was absolutely loving eating well again and the people in Xinjiang Province were turning out to be hospitable, despite the initial difficulties communicating with them.

Eventually I chose to leave the motorway for a couple of days because I was so bored with its monotony. Progress was slower on the parallel country roads and it was more difficult to find places to sleep because I was almost constantly riding through populated areas. One night, I was forced to find a cheap hotel in a big town, which I have no idea how to pronounce or write down. I wasn't too bothered about having to pay for a night's sleep because it was very cheap. I used the opportunity to wash my clothes and to get clean. When I woke up in the morning needing, needed the toilet rather urgently, probably due to the new food having an effect on my digestive system. Grabbing my money and passport, I rushed downstairs to where the bathroom was. When I got back to my room, my phone had been stolen. This was annoying, mainly because of the disappearance of my musical entertainment for the next couple of boring days before I reached Urumqi. I was so relieved that I had thought to grab my other valuables though. I couldn't report the theft to the police because I was staying in the hotel illegally. These rules are so stupid; the Chinese Government must think that if tourists stay in expensive hotels they will somehow not notice the poverty that is on display all over the place. Being banned from staying in cheap hotels wasn't great for me. I usually got turned away but the odd hotel owner was prepared to break the rules as long as I didn't make it obvious that I was staying there. This was probably a small risk on their part, but the cash I was paying for the room must have made it worthwhile for them.

Finally I reached the city in the centre of the Earth; Urumqi is at the location on the planet's surface that is furthest from any sea. It had certainly been a while since I last saw an ocean or sea. The riding through the desert had been uneventful that morning and afternoon, until the city appeared on the horizon at about five o'clock. I gradually descended into the sprawling metropolis of over two million people and tried to follow a map to the hotel that my guidebook recommended. It turned out to be impossible, so I just cruised in and stopped on a random street at a random cheap hotel in a neighbourhood I liked the look of. It was a good choice; this part of the city was buzzing, although, again, I had no idea what it was called. Walking around the area that I was staying in that evening and visiting the many street stalls selling food, I ate forty-four kebab sticks with meat, seafood and vegetables on them. It was a huge meal and it cost twenty yuan (about two pounds).

A rest day in Urumqi was spent sorting stuff out, buying a cheap replacement phone and eating delicious food. I had planned to visit the SOS Children's Village there but unfortunately the Government permission for me to visit hadn't arrived. I hoped that I would be able to visit the one in Beijing. The following morning, I packed up and cycled off to the airport to meet Phil, guided out by a guy on a fancy road bike. He didn't talk to me but stared directly into my eyes at every red traffic light. At the airport, I waited for Phil to arrive. He appeared looking tired but (unlike me) normal, and I think he was a bit shocked by my appearance. I hadn't had a haircut for six months and needed a shave.

We put his bike together at the airport entrance, abandoning the cardboard box he had it packed up in. We hit a café for lunch before heading back into Urumqi because our route continued on the other side of the city. Phil's rear disc brake broke after a couple of miles; maybe something had happened to it on the flight. We stopped at a bike shop to buy a new one. It was great to be able to pick up decent components again; the bike shops in China are comparable to European ones. Heading out of the city, we stopped at a restaurant, where we accidentally ordered a plate of chicken organs for dinner. It was actually quite tasty, but a bit too garlicky, and the slimy texture meant we didn't finish it. We discussed Phil's mechanical problem. Phil and I have been on a few biking holidays with my Dad. We developed a game where the person who has the most mechanical problems has to buy beers at the end. This was no exception, so Phil had to take a point for his broken disk brake. We argued about the rules of the game and decided how many points certain mechanical failures were worth.

That night we camped in a large grassy area off the side of the motorway which was very pleasant and safely isolated. I blocked the end of a sprinkler with a bit of plastic so that it didn't squirt us in the night. It was ridiculous that the grassy area on the side of the motorway was irrigated. They had an extensive sprinkler system to make a completely unused area look pretty. We were in the middle of an enormous desert, and a lot of people who lived nearby probably don't even have a water supply to their home.

Phil and I caught up over a cup of green tea and I was delighted to have some company again. Phil had been on a long journey, flying from London to Moscow then to Beijing before flying back on himself to Urumqi, in the west of China. It was strange to think that he had crossed to Urumqi in a matter of hours, a journey that would take us a couple of months. I was really looking forward to cycling as a team for the rest of China, a country in which (from my initial experiences at least) company would be very valuable.

19. One becomes two

You never have the wind with you - either it is against you or you're having a good day
- Daniel Behrman

Our first morning together was spent cycling along a flat desert road, without anything to look at. In the afternoon we started descending into the Turpan Depression; the second lowest point on the planet after the Dead Sea. Phil bought a pea flavoured ice cream, which was as disgusting as it sounds. Mine wasn't much better, an orange flavoured one which didn't taste remotely like orange and was brown. The descent went on and on and there was a roaring tailwind, which sped us up even more. We were travelling at thirty miles an hour, alongside another incredible Chinese engineering project; a high speed railway line. It was completely raised off the floor on stilts, climbing up and tunnelling through mountains. Apparently they are building this railway from one side of the country to the other. The scale of development was mind-boggling.

Like me, Phil was riding a mountain bike converted into a touring bike. His was lighter, made from aluminium, and not as heavy-duty, but it didn't need to be as strong because we would be on tarmac roads for most of the time in China. Mine was chosen to take a battering in Kazakhstan and Tajikistan, but we weren't expecting that here. He didn't have front panniers but had all he needed in his rear ones. A lot of the kit I had was good for both of us; we shared the stove for example, and my toolkit would fix both bikes. I was planning to use Phil's new Ortlieb waterproof panniers for America, but for now I was still using my original non-waterproof ones.

The tailwind blew us through an enormous wind farm; one of the largest in the world. China's wind energy industry has expanded exponentially in recent years and they have leapfrogged the rest of the world; jumping from 2,500 Mega Watts (MW) of installed capacity in 2006 to over 62,000 MW at the end of 2011. Eventually, the road changed direction, and the tailwind became a crosswind coming from diagonally behind us. We were leaning into it at about twenty degrees and getting blown along at about twenty-five miles per hour without pedalling at all which was great fun, but pretty dangerous when a truck came past and blocked the wind, sucking us towards it. We ended up riding on the hard shoulder on the wrong side of the motorway to prevent this from happening. On the other side of the road, the wind hit us before the passing trucks so there was no suction effect. There was no way the tents would have survived that wind so we retreated into a tunnel under the road for the night not getting much sleep because of the wind rushing down it. We made a barricade with our panniers and bikes, which helped deflect the wind a bit and eventually I got about four hours of sleep.

The next day, we arrived at the ancient Silk Road city of Turpan, which was a lovely place, although very hot. It is statistically the hottest place in China due to its very low altitude; Turpan is below sea level. Temperatures were back up into the forties and progress was tough. I felt sorry for Phil as he had come straight from English temperatures into this while I had the chance to build up to it. On the way into Turpan, we stopped at an irrigation canal for a refreshing swim and I washed my clothes in it. I was reminded about what a refreshing feeling it is to completely submerge yourself in cool water after spending days in the beating sun. After cooling down, we went straight to the market and ate a huge amount of food. We could barely cycle afterwards, but managed to visit the Emin Minaret, an impressive forty-four metre tower joined to a mosque made from clay. Once we'd digested our ridiculously big lunch, we climbed out of Turpan and passed the famous flaming mountains, so called because their orange colour and the many snaking gorges running down their sides, making it look like they are on fire. After turning away from the main valley we climbed past some Buddhist caves and a large cemetery then reached another road tunnel, where we slept for the night. Phil was settling into the pace of the riding very well; he was slightly faster than me with my extra luggage and we were making good progress. I was carrying a lot of stuff I didn't need, like the various souvenirs that I had acquired and decided that I would try to post them home when I could.

The houses in this part of the region were really strange, made from clay bricks, with lots of gaps to keep them cool. They are all the same rectangular shape and have no windows, but plenty of light enters through the gaps in the bricks. It looked as though they had plastic sheets that could be positioned along the walls to deflect rain when it came, but I imagine it doesn't rain very often in this part of China. There were hundreds of these houses and they made a weird but impressive sight as the lines of identical rectangular buildings stretched away into the distance. We descended again, to the city of Shanshan for lunch. At a shop, we bought what we thought was coke flavoured ice cream. It turned out to be frozen coke syrup; the highly concentrated stuff which pubs dilute to make coke on tap. On a massive sugar rush, we headed out via a wash in another very fast flowing irrigation canal. A short evening ride took us to a small town, where we stocked up on supplies, preparing for a couple of days in the desert before the next town; we were both carrying a heavy load.

The next day the wind changed direction and became the strongest headwind I've ever ridden into. It was also a hot wind, which made things really uncomfortable. We limped on for twenty miles, which took us about seven hours. It was pointless carrying on into the evening because we were both shattered and making negligible progress and Phil was also ill with stomach problems and short of energy. We stopped at a tunnel under the road and were surprised to discover that there were some Chinese road workers living there while constructing the new motorway. They were living in an underground concrete tunnel without toilet facilities having to cook all their own food, which I assumed must have been delivered to them. They were very nice, jolly people and we took up their invitation to stay there for the night. They cooked us delicious bean noodles and one super-strong guy carried our fully laden bikes down a very steep slope into the tunnel on his own. There is no way I could have done that. *I fell asleep praying for a change in the wind direction.*

After a good rest and a great breakfast made for us by the road team, we headed out into the headwind again. After a while, we reached a climb that was sheltered and made pretty good progress. We found a truckers café for lunch, which was dirty, surrounded by rubbish and human poo, but served very tasty food. We had stewed pork, which had been boiled for hours over a coal fire. The desert riding was tough and the headwind lasted for a few days which wasn't much fun, so having Phil's company was very valuable. I thought that I had probably done enough solo desert riding for one lifetime. Eventually, we reached the city of Hami, where we went to a restaurant for dinner and a few beers.

Phil felt worse in the evening and threw up his dinner, so the next day we had a late start and a good rest. We headed out after stocking up on food from one of the very rare, decent Chinese food shops. I got blanked when asking for directions again, but then a truck driver chucked a couple of bottles of mineral water to us then drove off. This is typical of China; contradictions and odd behaviour, but also very kind and friendly people. Phil was still ill the next day so we took our time and plodded along against the ever present headwind. The only places to buy food were more disgusting trucker's cafés, with unbelievable hocking up and phlegm spitting going on all around us. I nearly got hit by a big melon that some idiotic trucker threw at me for absolutely no reason. That night I watched James Bond on Phil's iPod, which was amazing having been deprived of technology for so long. We spent the next few days speaking like Sean Connery!

More desert and truckers cafés followed and the days became repetitive, merging into one in my memory. Whenever we stopped to eat at one of the cafés, groups of Chinese people came over and grabbed our stuff, took our maps out of their cases and walked off to read them with friends. They kept touching the bikes and checking the tyres were hard, then nodded to their friends approvingly. It is a different culture completely, and at home their behaviour would seem rude. Here it was perfectly acceptable. We had to keep an eye on our valuables, and the behaviour was annoying, but we knew that they meant well. Phil's map case was already showing signs of wearing out, with rips appearing down the sides. The food at the cafés was often pretty good but, oddly, every table had a bowl full of garlic cloves. We didn't understand what to do with them until we saw the truck drivers on the next table. They were peeling whole cloves of garlic and eating them, one after another; disgusting! I tried to eat one and managed a little nibble, which was horrible. The taste stayed in my mouth for the next few hours. How can they enjoy eating raw garlic? I wondered whether they didn't enjoy it, and it was a macho thing, akin to a British person ordering a vindaloo or eating raw chilli peppers, or maybe it was for health reasons.

We were really looking forward to reaching the town of Xingxingxia that evening for a decent meal and a wash. After a massive day spent fighting the headwind again, we arrived and were thoroughly disappointed. It was basically a big rubbish tip, toilet and truckers stop. There was a tunnel under the road that was used as a public toilet because there was no other facility in town. Truckers used it very regularly by the looks of things and it was a large space with an average spacing between poos of about six inches. It was the most disgusting thing I have ever seen and it still haunts me in my dreams! Just imagine the logistics of going for a number two in view of everyone else. After getting a hasty meal at a grimy café and doing a runner to a camping spot behind a sand dune a few miles down the road, we vowed never to mention that town again. It was a low point.

Things didn't improve the next day. After a morning of cycling along a half-finished, dusty road, we spent the afternoon fighting yet another headwind. The highlight of the day was the fake plastic policemen on podiums directing traffic! At last we finally left the motorway, and with it the horrible truckers cafés, human poo and piles of rubbish. We cycled down a quiet road through a beautiful desert landscape and found a place to sleep behind a wall. The night sky was amazing, with many shooting stars. China was beginning to get exciting, the desert was mostly behind us and the Tibetan Plateau in Qinghai Province lay ahead.

We woke early and headed out into the desert again. Suddenly we saw the great wall. It wasn't like the tourist-restored sections you see on photographs. It was crumbling and only present in patches, but great to see. It looked like there had been a number of parallel walls at one point and they must have been virtually impenetrable when they were first constructed. We had some lunch then got back onto the small desert road. On the horizon, I could make out some vegetation that we eventually reached. It turned out to be a substantial oasis, and it was refreshing to see fields and agriculture again. There was a large swamp in the desert, with a town in the centre, where thousands of melons were grown, packaged and taken away on trucks. The melon growers each gave us a free sample, and by the time we had cycled through the town I was seriously sick of eating melon. For some reason the melons were packed in boxes with dolphin pictures on them. We were still pretty close to the point on the planet that is furthest away from the sea. Why on earth were there dolphins on the melon boxes? *Another unanswered question to add to the list of unanswered questions that China was providing!*

By late afternoon, we reached the city of Dunhuang, where we found a hotel. I sent home four kilograms of gear that I didn't need any more, for the modest price of twenty pounds, and then we headed out to eat at the night market. It was a fascinating place, very modern and spotlessly clean. We saw an opera being performed on the streets by a woman with a beautiful voice. Foreigners were banned from using the internet in any internet café, which was odd. Every internet café that we tried was full of teenage boys playing online games. This had been the case in every city we had been to so far. It seemed to be a national pastime for males, and some females of that age group. It was sad to see so many young people spending hours and hours in front of computer screens.

Anyway, we had a great evening, completely going to town on the food stalls in the market. We ate a lamb burger, sheep entrails stew (which was nicer than it sounds) and a pizza made from greasy bread and toppings. The food in China was so much better than in Central Asia. The chefs were proud of what they were cooking and I started asking them to write down the name of meals that I liked so I could ask for it again. I wrote my own description of the food next to the characters and ended up with a list of food that I could order by pointing at what previous chefs had written.

Dunhuang was the town at the end of the desert. Next we would be climbing up into the mountains to the Tibetan Plateau in Qinghai Province, which is the same culturally as Tibet, is high altitude, full of monasteries, and should be stunning. I also thought there would be less human poo around! We had a rest day planned to visit some Buddhist caves and were both looking forward to getting off the bikes and out of the bloody headwind!

20. Buddhists, soldiers and a massive farce

The world is a book, and those who do not travel read only one page
- St. Augustine

We left our bikes in the hotel in Dunhuang and got a bus to the Mogau caves. There are over two hundred Buddhist caves there, full of paintings, statues and sculptures. Apparently it is one of the best examples of Buddhist art in the world, and it was absolutely spectacular. We saw a gigantic statue of Buddha, the third biggest in China, and the library cave with a hidden chamber that has only recently been uncovered. The monks hid their priceless books, art and manuscripts in there, then walled up the entrance to hide the contents from the Muslims who raided the caves and defaced many of the sculptures. By defaced, I mean literally de-faced; they chiselled the faces off. The Mogau caves are one of the most important Buddhist sites in China and have been a place of pilgrimage and shelter on the Silk Road since the Fourth Century. They are built into the side of a mountain, and although we were only shown a few of them, it gave us a feel of the enormous scale of the place.

Back in Dunhuang, we ate in the market once more, before getting ripped off in a few shops for rice and other supplies and then left the city. We cycled back into a desert landscape, towards the mountains on the horizon. They were slowly getting bigger; soon we'd have a mother of a climb. We camped amongst trees next to the original site of Dunhuang. There is an ancient walled town there, which was being restored, and it looks like you would imagine an ancient Chinese fortress to look: huge, thick battlements and curved temple-like towers. It was an impressive sight as the sun set over the ancient walls.

I was woken up the next morning by a toad croaking on my fleece that I was using as a pillow. I had only slept under a mosquito net that night and it must have climbed in somehow. After a quick breakfast of pineapple jam, onion bread and dates, we carried on to a strange city at the foothills of the mountains. It was a modern 'model' town, and was spotlessly clean; with fake trees and a huge, empty mosque. There were even shaded covered walkways linking the city together. There weren't many inhabitants and we weren't sure why it was there or what it was for, but it had a good restaurant where we had lunch, and a few shops, which allowed us to resupply.

Apparently, the Chinese Government is trying to move people into Western China in a bid to populate the region with native Han Chinese rather than the Uighur Muslims, who look Kazakh and don't consider themselves to be part of the country. They have lived in what is now Xinjiang Province for centuries and it has been in and out of Chinese rule many times, so they are not native to China. The Government is apparently not happy with this situation. We thought that perhaps this city was part of the Government's repopulation plan. If so, I didn't think the plan was going very. I can see why; if I lived in the wealthy East, I wouldn't want to move to a desert.

Every Inch of the Way

We left in the early evening and began the long climb to Qinghai Province. Qinghai was once part of the country of Tibet. The Mongol empire then conquered it before China claimed the region in 1720. It is on a high altitude plateau and is full of Buddhist monasteries and Tibetans. It is a good way of seeing Tibetan life, without the need to jump through visa hoops and risk getting into trouble with the police in Tibet proper. Although I would love to visit Tibet, it was well off my route and unfortunately not possible on this trip. We climbed out of the desert through towering sand dunes and then a more fertile landscape, on a brand new road with a perfect road surface. It was fantastic cycling, the best in China so far, and it would have been road biking heaven with a lightweight racing bike. Sweets fuelled us up countless switchbacks, to the top of the pass at 3,665 metres. It took us four hours to climb 1,500 metres; pretty good going considering our hefty loads!

A long descent led down to a high altitude desert plain, which we quickly crossed with the help of a strong tailwind. I felt sorry for the Chinese cyclists whom we saw heading in the opposite direction. I also felt slightly vindicated however, because (with the exception of a couple of days) I had been fighting a headwind for about a month now and felt that I was due a tailwind. On the other side of the plain, we arrived at an isolated desert village next to a power station in the middle of nowhere. It looked like a bombsite, but there was a well hidden restaurant where we had dinner. One thing I learned about Phil on this trip is that he can eat a lot of rice. For most people, rice is stodgy and filling, not so for Phil. He will eat and eat and eat it and enjoy every second. He was gutted that for most of the trip it was difficult to get rice. Northern Chinese people eat more noodles, whilst their southern compatriots are the rice eaters. Every time we found a place selling rice, Phil was sure to order a bowl or two.

More miles through barren desert followed, on a completely straight road with absolutely nothing to look at and a constantly unchanging horizon. It was seriously boring riding and pretty demoralising. Eventually we reached a corner, which took us up an interesting climb through dark coloured and rocky mountains, to the top of one of the best descents of the trip. A perfect road surrounded by Pamir-like scenery, with snow-capped peaks dominating the horizon. The road descended steeply through more dunes into an enormous bowl, surrounded by the giant mountains. A short climb took us out of the bowl and we reached the town of Iqe. Again, we were disappointed. From our map, I was expecting a bit more than a half-finished toll gate, with no facilities at all. The road workers gave us bread dumplings and water so we managed to refuel. Ten miles later we were in another tunnel under the road. It was a cold night but my sleeping bag was still working well, so I was warm. Phil only had a thin one however, so he was wearing everything he had and was inside my survival bag.

Back on the road in the morning, we were pulled over by a couple of very unprofessional soldiers in an army truck. They looked excited to see us but tried to remain calm. They shouted "*No photos*" and demanded to look through the ones on Phil's camera. They didn't ask to look at mine for some reason; perhaps Phil looks suspicious! There was an endless convoy of army trucks full of soldiers heading west;

we could see hundreds. We wondered what they were doing. It looked like more than a training exercise. It must have involved thousands and thousands of infantry soldiers. They all waved at us as they passed, with incredulous smiles on their faces, and they must have thought us a very odd sight.

Other than meeting the army, the morning was pretty uneventful until we reached a decent sized town. Phil bought a balaclava in an attempt to stay warm at night time, and then we headed out into another strong tailwind which blew us uphill for forty miles. We climbed to an altitude of 3,700 metres and stayed in another very clean and totally hidden tunnel under the road. I took a picture of Phil pretending to be a terrorist in his new balaclava. We then sorted through our food and found that we had accumulated quite a lot of stuff we weren't going to eat. Shopping in China was always a bit of a gamble because the pictures of the food on the packaging have absolutely nothing to do with what is inside the packets. An appetizing looking pack of custard creams could contain stale biscuits with a luminous green filling, for example. Due to this, we acquired loads of terrible biscuits and other snacks, which we had a great time disposing of by lobbing them down the tunnel, trying to smash them into as many pieces as possible. We also tried putting root ginger in our green tea, which was delicious.

The morning began with a short climb, before a long descent against a freezing headwind to a forgotten-looking town by a lake. Back on the search for good food, an out-of-the-way café served us some delicious pork, boiled in broth for an early lunch. In the afternoon, we discussed inventions that would improve touring bikes, which I can't mention here because they aren't patented yet. After redesigning the bicycle, we reached our first city for days; Delingha.

When we arrived; we tried checking into about ten different cheap hotels, but no-one would take us. They all pointed us to the same big official, expensive looking tourist hotel. In the end we went to see how much it was, just in case we could afford it. It was cheaper than we expected, about seventy yuan (seven pounds) each, which was well over budget, but okay for a single night. The receptionist told us that we had to wait in the lobby for a while because we had to register with the police. They took about an hour to show up. When they did, the police chief himself told us that Delingha is closed to foreigners. Imagine that; a city of about a hundred thousand people closed to foreigners. What would happen in the UK if we made a city the size of Oxford exclusive to British people? Human rights groups would be up in arms. How can the Chinese Government get away with it?

Anyway, the whole city was closed to us and we were only allowed to stay in the expensive hotel. We were not allowed out without a police escort. The police chief seemed to have decided that we weren't a threat. I was worried that he would change his mind when he demanded to look at Phil's photos. The first one was of Phil pretending to be a terrorist in the balaclava! We were given permission to spend one night in Delingha with a constant police escort. This was another example of Chinese logic which was very odd. Officials didn't seem to think independently and followed the

141

rules to the letter, even if they made no sense. So providing two policemen as free tourist guides, along with free transport seemed like a good use of police resources!

After a wash we met the two young policemen who had been given the job of taking two foreigners around for the evening. We were driven around in an electric milk float style police car. It was so funny. They could speak okay English, so we could communicate with them. They soon forgot their orders to take us to the nearest shop and café and took us on a grand tour of Delingha. It was a lovely place, very clean with bustling streets and markets, with views of the nearby mountain range to the north. We were taken to two great restaurants and we didn't get ripped off at all thanks to our two police escorts. We realised how cheap China actually was for locals. They had been given orders not to let us go to an internet café, but one of them let me use his phone to check my emails. He then showed us his pistol and took the magazine out in a full restaurant. We asked them to put the siren on to clear the traffic for us, which they happily did and eventually we ended up back at the police station, waiting in a minibus for them to come out to go out for a beer. We were taken to a dance club in a hotel and sat at the bar on the top floor with beers we had bought from a shop because they wouldn't serve foreigners.

So we were illegally sat in a Chinese night club and illegally drinking with the police. One of them wouldn't drink on duty and the other, *"Only one shot of beer"*, which was actually about ten. For some reason, the Chinese drink lots of shots of beer rather than drinking out of a glass at their own pace. We watched the Chinese dancing, which was much better than in an English nightclub. The dance routines looked well practiced; it was more like ballroom dancing than anything else. About half an hour into the night, the police chief turned up. He was off duty and one of our guides wasn't, he was at risk of getting into serious trouble. We all did a runner out the back exit, but I reckon they were seen and probably got into trouble the next day. They took us back to the hotel and on the way back pointed at some ladies of the night who they referred to as *"Bitches"*. They told us that they cost 300 yuan for a night, or thirty pounds. Back at the hotel, a maid took us up to our room to ensure we were safely hidden away and that the strange foreigners couldn't put themselves or anyone else in danger. It was an excellent but unbelievably ridiculous night.

21. Amazing cycling

I want to ride my bicycle,
I want to ride my bike,
I want to ride my bicycle,
I want to ride it where I like.
- Queen

We left the deserted hotel after the worst buffet breakfast in history; soggy, cold and spicy vegetables and tepid dumplings. There were fifteen cooks for four guests and of course they needed to eat too. They ate all the fresh food, leaving the soggy stuff for the guests (just Phil, a couple of Chinese businessmen and me). Employment seems to be provided in certain places in China, probably a relic of the communist era. Some people are doing entirely pointless jobs. I imagined a normal day at breakfast in the hotel. The cooks made a huge and disgusting buffet; no guests ate it so the cooks did: repeat... We hit a couple of food shops, and then I went to use the internet in a 'China Telecom' shop to book a flight to America from Beijing. I was breaking the law by using the internet, and sure enough more police found us after about half an hour. Phil was outside with the bikes and they spotted him as they passed. I had successfully booked the flight though for the eighteenth of October, which gave us about five weeks to complete the 1,600 miles to the end of Asia. This was very possible, but wouldn't give us much time to relax. Anyway, the police removed us and we were escorted out of the city, after the pleasure of their company for lunch. On the edge of the city, we waved goodbye to our escort and they watched us cycle away from Delingha. What a crazy experience; we'd been chucked out of a city because we look different from the rest of the inhabitants.

On the road out of Delingha, we noticed that we were being followed by a guy on an electric scooter. We kept ahead of him for a while then tried slowing down; he did too. We cycled faster; he did too: *very strange*. We stopped, waved at him and he came over. We swapped bikes and Phil and I both had a go on his electric scooter (although I went back to continue on my bike from the place I left it... *every inch of the way and all that*.). The scooter was slow but eco-friendly. I wouldn't want one, a racing bike would be quicker! It was a funny experience; he wanted our autographs so we signed a piece of paper: *"From Russia with love, Roger Moore and Sean Connery"*. He couldn't read it anyway and it amused us greatly. Phil then tagged his scooter with some stickers that we had acquired from the melon village in the desert a few days earlier. We found a great campsite that night in an old river bed and had a coal-fuelled fire from lumps of coal that we collected on the road (there is a lot of coal in China and a fair amount of it is spilled on the road by overloaded lorries).

After a morning's ride the next day we arrived at a non-descript Chinese town and had decent lunch in a Muslim restaurant. It got a bit fiery: a load of firecrackers went off across the road then the chef had a fight with a customer who wouldn't pay for his food. I bought a *'Red Oxen'* energy drink (*possibly a copy of Red Bull?!*). The cycling wasn't very interesting as we passed through barren landscapes broken up by towns like Ulan that we reached that evening. They are nice enough places and have good markets, but are almost identical and have no defining features. In Ulan we bought an entire cooked duck (including the head and feet), which we ate while sitting on a wall, feeding the scraps to a kitten. It was very fatty but delicious (the duck not the kitten!).

Having camped in the woods on the outskirts of Ulan, we were back in the mountains, and the road took us up another mountain pass. We stopped at a shop where a lovely old couple sat us down in their living room. Communication was limited but they seemed pleased to have us there. They had wide smiles on their faces as they passed over bottles of mineral water. I imagined them laughing and telling their friends about the strange white men who had called into their tiny shop that morning. We climbed up a beautiful green valley all morning, saw a Buddhist Monastery covered in gold leaf and then, in stark contrast reached a massive coal refinery. It was so big that there was a large town built in high rise buildings just for the thousands of workers on the factory site. We had lunch in truckers' café; delicious chicken noodles. After lunch, a great descent led us to a high plateau, away from the mountain peaks. We crossed a river and couldn't resist having a wash in the freezing water; the urge to be clean was stronger than the urge to be warm. The road was built alongside a railway line, which we followed uphill. It was late in the day so we were on the lookout for a place to camp. There was loads of coal and a big bundle of straw on the road, so we made a massive pyromaniac fire in another dry river bed, next to where we pitched our tents. My speedo told me it was a one hundred mile day.

The next morning disaster struck. I checked the tension of the spokes in my back wheel and found that my Rohloff hub was damaged. I could feel panic building inside me. One of the eyelets where the spokes attach to the hub was snapped and another cracked. Two spokes weren't doing anything so my wheel was basically dead. It would last a little longer, but it was a time bomb waiting to break. The hub has internal gears, so replacing the wheel with one I could have got in China wasn't an option and nobody sells Rohloff components there. I would have to fix it, which would involve getting a replacement hub body sent from home. We had a think about what to do and decided to try to get to the next town. After about an hour my wheel was wobbling horribly so we did a bodge job on it, wrapping a length of chain around the hub, connecting it to itself and wedging a bit of metal cable between the spokes to hold it in place. Then we bent two new spokes into the chain and connected them to the rim. It seemed to be a decent bodge and I reckoned it would hold for a while.

We continued through the beautiful scenery, which was getting more fertile, and vegetation was returning. I went to use the internet in a petrol station, pretending I had an emergency (which I suppose I did). I emailed Rohloff, sending them pictures of the damage and asking their advice. I had no choice but to continue and to wait for their response. Despite having the worry of my damaged wheel hanging over me, the rest of the day was fantastic. We climbed to a new record for China, an altitude of 3,817 metres. There were colourful Buddhist prayer flags on the top of the pass and a shrine.

A man stood at the shrine throwing confetti into the wind. We descended down a winding, sweeping road, past herds of yaks to Qinghai Hu, an enormous high altitude lake. In the early evening we reached a town on the lake shore; my wheel bodge seemed to be working for now.

After dinner, I searched for the internet again and was allowed to use it in a police station. This was a massive contrast to Delingha, where we were chucked out of the town for using the internet. I got a fantastic response from Rohloff; they promised to replace the broken parts for free and send me the tools that I needed to fix it. I am certain that it was not even their fault that it broke. I think that the blame lies with the bike shop that built the wheel because to begin with I had experienced far too many broken spokes, and the unbalanced forces of a poorly built wheel had probably overstressed the hub. While I had been in the police station, Phil had been integrating with the local community and managed to get us some dinner. We were offered food by a lovely Tibetan lady, delicious soupy stew with dumplings. Although very welcoming, she didn't understand our hints when we asked for a place to stay for the night, so we left the town and slept in a tunnel a couple of miles down the road.

The next morning it was raining heavily so we slept in for an extra hour and got going at about nine o'clock. We rode a very fast seventeen miles and reached a small village, where we were invited into a monk's home to shelter from the rain. He was wearing a maroon robe and a huge smile as he opened his door to us. We were served noodles and yak meat soup. It was absolutely delicious so I had three helpings; they were very filling. A woman sat outside winding the handle of a machine which separated yak milk into thick cream and a thinner liquid. I remembered seeing one of these machines in Kyrgyzstan on the night that I camped with nomads.

Ten miles further along the lake, we spent two hours trying to find food in the shops. It was very touristy, due to its location on the shore of the famous Qinghai Hu. There were no Western tourists there, but there were a few coach loads of Chinese visitors. The shops all had very extravagant names, which described their contents in a non-too-accurate way. From the outside, the shops looked like they sold local produce, but in reality there was almost nothing in the town that wasn't mass-produced and two months or more past its sell-by date. Eventually, we stocked up on just-about-acceptable supplies and continued to the end of Qinghai Hu, arguing about how many points a broken Rohloff Hub was worth on the point accumulation game. We settled on two, maybe rising to more if it led to further problems. That put the score at four to one and a half, which wasn't looking good for me. We camped around the back of a shop that night. The owner spoke perfect English because he used to live in Manchester. He told us that he had liked England but preferred life in China because his family were there. He led us to a courtyard, where we pitched our tents. From where we were camping, we could see a Buddhist monastery with a giant golden statue of the 'future Buddha' looking down on us.

Back in England, Mum packaged up the Rohloff components and gave them to Oli to take to the DHL office in Crewe. I was about 600 miles from Xi'an and that was where the spare parts were heading. I needed to arrive in time to pick them up before the national holiday, which lasted for the whole of the first week of October. This gave us ten days to cross a giant mountain range. Also, my bike had to make it that far with the damaged wheel. Completing the ride now depended a lot on chance, which was a worrying feeling. All I could do was carry on, ride slowly over bumps and pray that the wheel would hold out until Xi'an.

The next day, we climbed over a beautiful 3,500 metre pass before descending to a small town just off the motorway. We were offered food by a very friendly guy and were invited into his beautiful house. He was a trucker; they must get paid well judging by his giant wide-screen television and bright purple sound system. His family sat with us and we tried to communicate over endless portions of noodles. Eventually, we said goodbye and climbed another beautiful green valley to a lovely campsite by a stream. It reminded me of the Highlands in Scotland (with the exception of the yaks). We set up camp next to the stream on a flat viewpoint looking out over the valley. My gear crisis continued when my tent ripped as I put it up. One of the corners split where the peg strap attaches to the fly sheet. It took me an hour to sew it up again, using part of a ratchet strap to reinforce it. I thought that it was as good as new once I was finished though. Phil made tea as I repaired the tent, and then it started snowing.

In the morning the tents were covered in a couple of centimetres of snow, which started falling again as we left the campsite. It was very cold; I was wearing everything I had except for my overshoes, which I gave to Phil after a couple of hours when he was worried about his toes falling off! Phil's coat wasn't very waterproof so he was wearing a plastic sheet tied around him like an apron. He looked hilarious, but it seemed to keep the wind off. When Phil's toes got really cold, we stopped to warm them up. My Jamaican coloured walking socks were keeping mine warm but Phil's were freezing. We took it in turns to rub them, and after about twenty minutes the colour came back. I checked the temperature gauge on my speedo and it was minus ten degrees; the coldest weather of the trip.

We reached the top of a pass and did a clockwise lap of the Buddhist shrine, which apparently brings you good luck. We needed good karma; I thought *'No more broken equipment and good weather would be excellent please!'* The descent on the other side of the pass took us to a small town, where it was warmer; maybe karma was on our side. We stopped at a shop, had pot noodles there and watched Mongolian archery on the TV. In Mongolian archery, a horse rider gallops at full speed past an archery target; he grips the horse with his legs and fires an arrow at the target. The most points scored after three shots wins. When more than one archer has the same number of points, the time taken to ride the distance is taken into account. It was pretty spectacular and those archers are seriously skilled.

We were doing well and were aiming to get to a town called Zebar that evening, around sixty miles away. If we could make it, I planned to talk to Laura on Skype for what would be the first time in over a month. We climbed another massive pass into the cold mist, and then we cycled into dream China: tree covered peaks in the mist, monasteries dotting the mountains and a winding descent, dropping around 1,000 metres in height. This is what China looks like in the tourist brochures.

We cycled straight through the town at the bottom and started up yet another gigantic climb on a road which wound back and forwards up a steep slope. A man was stuffing a squealing piglet into a cloth sack on the back of a rickety old motorbike. A group of teenagers in a jeep stopped when they saw us, giggling as they showed us a huge bag of marihuana that they'd picked somewhere nearby. We continued up the pass to gobsmacking views over the rolling mountains, dotted with fields and monasteries. Over the top, we crossed a series of smaller passes, got to a shop and gorged about 2,000 calories each. A number of smaller passes disappeared under our wheels, each one with Buddhist prayer flags decorating the top of the climb. This continued until it got dark; the scenery had been incredible all day. There was a spectacular sunset over the hills, each of which had a Buddhist shrine on its summit. We climbed for over an hour in the dark which was confusing because we had no idea of the gradient, or of the direction of the road. Eventually, we reached the summit of the final pass and cycled six miles downhill into the town of Zebar, arriving at about half past nine. I got to a computer with Skype in an internet café, talked to Laura for an hour, and then went back to the hotel, where Phil was asleep. I was absolutely shattered but felt great to have been able to chat to Laura again, after so long without spoken communication.

In contrast, the next day we only covered seven miles. We were tired after our strenuous previous day and it was raining again, so sheltered under a bridge and decided to take the afternoon off, a decision that the weather probably influenced. Phil went off to get wood for a fire; I spent the time reinforcing the rip in my tent. It was the shortest day of the entire trip but it was lovely to have a rest. We lounged around under the bridge, chatting and reading. I fixed the holes that had appeared in almost every item of clothing I had with a needle and some yellow thread that I found in the bottom of one of my panniers. I aired my sleeping bag while I caught up on my diary, and napped then got an early night. In the morning my stove took twenty minutes to get going. The fuel tube was getting blocked and it was very difficult to clean out, but eventually I got it going again. *The gear crisis continued.*

Feeling refreshed the next day, we set off up a short climb, which led to a reservoir at the top of a spectacular gorge. The descent followed the gorge, which was full of giant sandstone formations and towering rock pillars on both sides of the road. We descended to a town at the bottom, where a Muslim community lived. The mosques were very different from any that I had seen so far; the main towers were multi-level pagodas, which extended from colourfully painted and ornately carved wooden roofs. We could see into many of the gardens, which were walled and colourful. In front of most houses there were solar kettles. These clever devices use a large concave mirror to focus sunlight onto the kettle, which is held on a stand in the middle. This area was very different from the Tibetan culture we had just left; we were back in a populated area, people were hanging around on the street again and the shops were better stocked.

147

The road took us down to the Yellow River and into a large town where we stuffed ourselves with delicious juicy dates. We passed through a village that mass produces chilli powder. All the houses were drying chilli, which were then crushed by machines on the roadside. There were plenty of new things to look at and there was never a dull moment with shouting kids, adults staring and people operating the chilli crushing machines on every corner. We passed through the town, back into the countryside and camped in the giant Yellow River Gorge. My stove finally packed up; bread and dates for dinner then.

After a similar breakfast the next day, we followed the Yellow River in the rain. A Belgian guy stopped his taxi, gave us directions and told us that he was terrified by his driver's driving. As he was driven off, I could see his point! We followed the dirt track along the gorge, then through a series of tunnels. It was raining again, so we sheltered in a tunnel for lunch. As we sat there we were passed by a digger with a terrible driver who kept nearly crashing into the tunnel walls.

All afternoon, we climbed in the rain on a dirt road until dark, climbing a number of small passes that led us over the forested hills and then completed another huge night ride along terrible roads. A layer of wet mud lay on top of a hard-packed surface and made the riding very slippery and dangerous. I fell off twice as the road got wetter. We were completely caked in mud and resembled Glastonbury Festival goers after diving in the mud pits. Eventually, after hours of hazardous night riding, we reached the city of Linxia in a complete state. By Chinese standards, Linxia is fairly small (it has a population of 250,000), but it took us a long time to navigate into the city centre. We eventually found a reasonably priced hotel, but we thought we could probably find somewhere cheaper. Around the corner there was one, but when we went inside we were put off by the horrible assistant behind the reception and the naked man sleeping in the foyer. We didn't ask why he was there, this was China and there was no need to ask the question; we had learnt by this stage that some questions couldn't be answered! We returned to the first hotel that we had found. They let us stay despite our appearance and told us that we could store our bikes in their boiler room. Finally, in the bedroom, we had a much-needed wash. It took a long time to scrub all the dry mud from my legs, arms and face. Who knows what the staff on the reception desk thought when we turned up. It was good of them to let us in. We were planning to visit Labrang Monastery the following day, in the nearby mountain town of Xiahe. It is the second most important Tibetan Buddhist monastery in the world, after the one in Lhasa, the capital of Tibet.

22. I don't eat meat unless the Muslims kill it

It is better to travel well than to arrive
- Buddha

We got up early to catch a bus that took us into the mountains and the town of Xiahe; the location of Labrang Monastery. There were bus stops in the middle of nowhere with queues of people waiting to board the bus; I wondered where they lived. The bus stopped for a toilet break at one point, but there was no toilet. A monk got off the bus and did a poo on the side of the road. He squatted down with his robe touching the floor around him, did his business in full view of the entire bus, and then got up, leaving a neat little pile behind him. *Unbelievable!* We had a quick meal of Tibetan soup and large dumplings on a café balcony overlooking the main street. As we sat there, I watched the Tibetan monks in their maroon robes going about their daily lives, on trips out of the monastery to buy supplies from the shops on the high street.

At the monastery we saw Western tourist faces for the first time since Dunhuang. The monastery is an expansive complex of beautifully ornate buildings in mountainous scenery. We saw gold leaf covered rooftops with carvings of dragons projecting from each corner, Buddhist artwork, sculptures and bizarrely, yak butter carvings. The yak butter carvings are a traditional gift from local Buddhist families to the monastery. They are kept in a specially designed room to keep them cool and to stop them melting. There was an odd smell but the carvings were very detailed and colourful and must take a huge amount of skill to create.

We found out that Labrang Monastery is one of the six great monasteries of the Yellow Hat School of Buddhism. The Yellow Hat School follows the teachings of Je Tsongkhapa, who lived in the fourteenth and fifteenth centuries. He taught that there are three principal aspects to the path of enlightenment: compassion, insight into wisdom, and a 'whole-hearted wish for liberation'. The monastery was founded in 1709 and is still a very important spiritual site of Tibetan Buddhism that is currently inhabited by around 1,000 monks.

Our tour guide, Tin Jin, was a maniac. There is no other word to describe him. He had been a monk since the age of thirteen and had been at Labrang for the last five years, studying a Philosophy degree. The degree takes twenty-five years to complete! It involves debating and discussing ideas with the teachers. A degree in traditional Chinese medicine at the monastery takes fifteen years; they have to learn how to collect ingredients and how to manufacture the medicine as well as how to prescribe it. Some of the traditional remedies are very effective, some aren't. I spoke to Tin Jin and had the following conversation:

"You don't believe in killing animals, but I've seen monks eating meat at restaurants. Are you a vegetarian?"

"Naaa, I likey eating meat!"

"So you don't mind killing animals? I thought Buddhists don't believe that is right?"

149

"I don't kill animals. I don't eat meat unless the Muslims kill it!"

I looked at Phil incredulously. That seems to be a slightly odd way around the rule to me. Tin Jin laughed and smiled; his innocence and immaturity for a twenty-three year old was quite amazing. He was a very likeable guy but behaved like a child.

Tin Jin took us into halls containing beautiful tombs of previous monastery leaders, carved from dark wood, and then into a large prayer hall that can hold all 1,000 monks at a time. Unfortunately, we didn't have much time because the last bus back to Linxia was at five o'clock. We had absorbed the atmosphere of the place and I left having experienced how different life was there. The bus got us back to Linxia in time for a great dinner in a restaurant which had hotplates in the middle of each table. Customers are given a wok to put on it, and then have a choice of soupy broths to boil. Once the broth is hot, it is used to cook seafood, meat and vegetables, which are then fished out with a large spoon. It was excellent fun and the food was delicious.

We had a long lie in the next day and left the room covered in mud; there wasn't much we could do about it unfortunately. We had to argue our way out of being charged for a chipped mug in the room, which we were pretty sure we hadn't damaged. After getting very annoyed, they allowed us to use their boiler room to wash our bikes; more contradictions! I discovered that my headset (what the handlebars rotate round) was disintegrating, so I took it apart, greased it and had to replace the ball bearings individually. Phil had to fix his gears and clean them out because they were full of dirt and not working properly. We cleaned the bikes using a hosepipe that the hotel provided, and toothbrushes from the hotel room. After fixing these problems, the point score was five to two and a half; it was still not looking good for me.

With significantly healthier bikes, we left Linxia via a wonderful bike shop; a large workshop with bits of bike lying around everywhere. This is what my future garage will look like. I bought four bolts to fix my panniers, which were coming apart, and some ball bearings to top up the broken headset bearing, which was missing a few. That evening we reached a motorway, which we powered through some miles on before arriving at an excellent grassy campsite just off the roadside. Two Muslim boys came over and 'helped' Phil erect his tent. I put mine up much more quickly without their help and gave them sweets for their trouble. We made a fire and cooked dinner on it using Phil's mess tin; it was a brilliant end to a great day.

Heavy rain greeted us again when we woke up so we had breakfast in a tunnel under the motorway, hoping that the rain would stop. Leaving the tunnel, we cycled along the motorway for ten miles, before reaching reached a town where I spotted a workshop and got the pipe from my stove blasted with a compressor, which unblocked it. The cause of the problem was diesel rather than unleaded petrol being given to me at the last petrol station and it was blocking the pipe. We bought some unleaded and that evening we got the stove burning again alongside another fire, which we cooked marshmallows on.

China's industry greeted us again on the outskirts of Huichan and I was reminded that we were in the fastest growing economy in the world, which isn't all ancient Tibetan monasteries and mountains. High-rise flats were half built in every direction and the skyline was dominated by cranes. We went to a bakery where the baker tried to overcharge us by about 300 percent compared to his previous customer because we aren't Chinese, so we left that town quickly. During the evening we passed along a peaceful, pretty road that took us through villages and fields. We stopped to buy supplies and saw a group of old men, still wearing the communist-style blue suits from the time of Mao. They were sat in a circle outside a shop, playing a card game with some complicated looking symbols and gambling; *a window into another age.*

After a few more miles we came across a very friendly little village surrounded by hills. We bought some delicious muffins from the kindly lady in the village bakery, who didn't overcharge us, and then ate them and drank a beer on the side of a hill where we pitched our tents. That night, I lay awake for a couple of hours, reflecting on the tour so far, replaying the journey in my head and looking through the thousands of photographs that I had taken. It seemed like I had been cycling for a lot longer than half a year. All of the places and cultures I had been through felt like a dream. I had seen so much but still had such a long way to go although the end of Asia didn't seem that far away. I couldn't imagine what was ahead of me in the USA, which seemed like a world away.

In the morning, we sat on the hillside and had a decent breakfast, finished the muffins and had jasmine tea, as we did every morning. Before we had risen that morning, a man with a herd of goats and sheep was snooping around the tents. I thought it was Phil, so I said hello and he scarpered, followed by his animals. We left our campsite, then descended for a while and followed a reasonable road for a few miles.

On the road, we were deafened once again by the bus and truck horns. In China it is apparently a legal requirement for drivers to honk their horns at cyclists to 'warn' them that they are coming. This seems a bit ridiculous because heavy lorries bumping around and revving their engines on the poorly surfaced country roads are difficult to not hear. Unfortunately, in China the horn on a lorry is the main modification drivers seem to make to their vehicle. Huge air horns are mounted on the roof of the lorries, sometimes with several on each one. They are unbelievably loud and the drivers absolutely love using them. Some of them enjoy honking as close as possible to the unwary cyclist, which made me jump out of my skin every time. I would ride along, hear a lorry approaching then tense up, waiting for deluge on my ear drums to begin. Sure enough, when a lorry got close; HOOOOOONNNNNK! The driver laughed in the mirror and the passenger leant out the window with a huge smile. Repeat one hundred times a day.

We tried to get onto the motorway at lunchtime but the toll gate guard wouldn't let us through so we cycled along a country road for a while then lifted the bikes onto the motorway at a bridge. We spent the rest of the day just getting the miles done. There were numerous tunnels and we got shouted at in one by a lady on the PA system. I remembered Turkey and the tunnels after Trabzon where the same thing had

151

happened. That was the last time I had seen Laura. I couldn't wait to see her again. We were trying to plan a time to meet up, either in Beijing, or possibly San Francisco, I was really hoping that it would work out.

It wasn't a particularly interesting afternoon, but the tunnels saved us a lot of time that we would have spent crossing mountain passes. Eventually the police stopped us and told us to leave at the next junction; we told them that of course we would... we didn't. I looked down at my speedo and noticed that I was approaching 10,000 miles. When the moment came, I took some photos of the occasion. It wasn't a beautiful place to hit the milestone, but it felt great to get to five figures. That is a bloody long way by anyone's standards. After a few boring hours of motorway riding we had made good progress, so stopped at a service station and were given permission to put our tents up in a field around the back.

We were allowed to use their sparkling new bathroom to have a wash (a huge contrast to the-town-that-should-not-be-named; Xingxingxia... oops!). We continued along the motorway all morning. The ride included a five mile long tunnel, which was pitch black in the middle and terrifying when traffic passed us. My wheel was holding out well but I was keen to get to Xi'an as soon as possible, where I would hopefully be able to fix it. Riding on the good road surface of the motorway presented the best chance of getting there without wheel failure, so we tried to do so as much as possible. At the city of Tianshul, however, we were chucked off the motorway by the police, so we rode along back roads through beautiful hills. It was much more interesting cycling, but slow. It was raining AGAIN, so we stopped at a garage to shelter and were given coffee. When the rain eased, we spent the evening cycling along the Yellow River valley then camped under a railway bridge, which was fairly sheltered. My tent zip broke but I managed to fix it after about an hour of trying, using the zipper from my wallet. We hadn't been able to find any food that evening so had our emergency pot noodles for dinner that had been stored in a pannier for a few days for just such an occasion. The rain was getting frustrating and we both wanted to reach Xi'an to have a proper rest. It was tiring, and the cycling wasn't great.

There was yet more rain the next day. The railway bridge had done a good job of keeping us mostly dry during the night, but unfortunately trains woke us up about once an hour because they honked their horn before crossing the bridge. Despite being knackered that morning, we made good progress along the Yellow River Gorge because the road was either flat or downhill, with no climbs as it followed the river. A man waved us over for a coffee. He had two seats under a parasol on his drive. It reminded me of Turkey once more, and the much more frequent invitations for tea that I had received there. China wasn't as open or friendly as Turkey, but this was a refreshing display of hospitality and now and again we did have an experience like this.

We passed a small town, ate wonton dumplings and fried bread - which was really tasty, full of energy and, most importantly, very cheap. We were managing to live on about three pounds per day at that stage. As we cycled out of the town, Phil got three punctures from a broken glass bottle. He had to fix the two on the front wheel but left the slow one on the rear for later on. We had now reached flat land and the mountains and river valleys were behind us. A few boring days of riding through an industrial, heavily populated area separated us from Xi'an. After hours of monotonous scenery, we reached the large city of Boaji in the early evening. As we entered Boaji, we saw a gigantic statue of Chairman Mao in the middle of a roundabout. A large proportion of the Chinese population still worships him, despite all the deaths and misery that he caused. He was built up to be a God in China, and the older generation find it hard to let that idea go. I wondered how many of the people knew about the deaths of millions caused by the famine that Mao's ridiculous ideals and his 'Great Leap Forward' led to. We did some urban camping that night in an industrial wasteland next to the motorway and it finally stopped raining.

That night I read about Mao's *'Great Leap Forward'*, in an excellent book called *'Wild Swans'*. During this time, the whole population were forced to produce steel. Everyone became obsessed with steel and they melted down any metal that they could spare or find. Backyard furnaces were set up in villages, schools and hospitals. Businesses turned into steel production facilities. Critically, farmers stopped producing food in the quest for steel production. Lies that were common place in the communist society became deadly and farms were encouraged to boast about what they were producing and massively over-exaggerated their food production levels. Impossibly high food supplies were reported on the news and the country was under the impression that levels were at an all-time high. Newspaper reports about vegetables the size of vans were circulated. Why then did no-one have anything to eat? Amongst other things, people resorted to eating an edible alga that grows in urine. Tragically, the steel that was produced was of terrible quality and therefore completely useless. During this time, millions of people starved to death and Mao resigned as the head of state, but was still head of the communist party. He took a back seat for a number of years and wrote the *'Little Red Book'*. He later returned with the *'Cultural Revolution'*, a terrifying period of time where people spied on each other, children became weapons and attacked teachers, former officials with too much power were killed or imprisoned and many intellectuals were sent to the countryside to labour on farms as Mao considered them a threat. In conclusion, Mao was a power-mad and immensely selfish person who somehow managed to persuade a nation that he was a God-like leader. How people can still adore him amazes me, but the years of propaganda have set Mao's status in people's minds. Until Mao's generation is gone, there will still be people who love the man.

We left Baoji and spent the morning on the motorway, which gave us time to recalculate the points tally after Phil had fixed his punctures. The score was now five points to four in Phil's favour. It was looking better for me; I stood a chance now. That day, I had to contact DHL because the parcel with the replacement parts for my hub had now reached Xi'an. Apparently, there was a problem with the delivery address and it was very important that I got the parcel on the day we arrived in Xi'an, otherwise it would be delayed by the weeklong October national holiday.

For the next couple of days we moved quickly and followed the motorway into Xi'an. The night before we reached the city, we were on schedule to pick up my parcel in time. We camped in a maize field, where I saw a huge tarantula,. I was paranoid that it had got into my tent so I kept checking the corners and my bags. I had no idea if it was dangerous, but it wasn't a chance I wanted to take. The ride into Xi'an was easy enough the next day and we reached the ancient city in the centre of the large city, passing through the old city walls via the West gate. We found a cheap hotel for about forty yuan (four pounds) per night on the ninth floor of a grimy looking building. I called DHL straight away, to get them to deliver my parcel to the hotel that day. They said "*No problem*", so Phil and I headed to the bus station to go to see the Terracotta Army.

23. Illness and a spot of tourism

Diarrhoea is hereditary. It runs in your jeans...
- Unknown

The Terracotta Army was incredible. The amount of work that must have gone into making each of the life-size warriors would have been immense. It is 2,200 years old and was created to be buried with the first emperor of China, to protect him in the afterlife. Archaeologists reckon that in the three pits containing the Terracotta Army there were over 8,000 soldiers, 130 chariots, 520 horses and 150 cavalry on horses, the majority of which are still buried in the pits. It was an amazing thing to see.

We took the bus back to Xi'an to hopefully return to my DHL parcel and an evening of bike maintenance. My heart was beating fast as we approached the hotel; a great deal was riding on the parcel being there. I asked at the reception and it hadn't been delivered. *Why can't things just be easy!* After about an hour on the phone, I eventually tracked it down to the DHL warehouse on the outskirts of Xi'an, but was told that it was too late for their delivery drivers to bring it to the hotel, and that the reason that it couldn't be delivered earlier was that I hadn't paid the *'import tax'* on it (about seventeen pounds), which I knew nothing about until then.

This was a double blow; that was a lot of money for me compared to my five pounds per day allowance and I didn't know how I could get the parcel. Luckily, after finding an operator who could speak good English, I was told that I could go to pick up the parcel directly from their warehouse that night. The hotel phoned a taxi for me, and Phil and I were driven there. The taxi driver didn't disappoint us with his driving speed, and he made sure that we arrived before the warehouse shut. I picked up the parcel, paid the *'import tax'*, and headed back to the hotel, thoroughly relieved. This was the start of getting my bike fixed. Next I had to rebuild the hub, then the wheel; two things that I had never done before. I couldn't afford to pay a bike shop to do it, and anyway I doubt they would ever have seen a Rohloff hub here.

The next morning I got up early and followed the instructions in the Rohloff manual, which explained how to take the hub apart, fit new seals, put the new casing on, change the oil bath and reassemble it. Once I had finished, it looked like it had gone together well, and seemed to work okay. Next I used my bike as a wheel jig and attached a cut off cable tie onto the frame, positioned next to the rim of the wheel. This showed me how close to straight the wheel was as I rotated it. I followed instructions on which order to put each spoke into the wheel and eventually got them all in the right positions. Next I tightened the spokes to a tension which pinged at the same note as the ones on the front wheel and put it on the bike. It worked!

Very pleased with myself, I chilled out for the rest of the day. Phil and I found a roadside barbecue that night, and we celebrated reaching Xi'an; it was the beginning of the last leg of China. The next morning, I spent some more time fixing my bike and ordered a few replacement bits for Laura to bring to San Francisco. Laura had now booked her flights and we were going to spend a week together in San Francisco. I was so excited about seeing her, and it was only two weeks away. This added to my motivation to reach Beijing and I had no doubts now that we would make it. We left the hotel, and headed to a bike shop on the way out of Xi'an. They let us use their tools and hydraulic fluid to re-bleed Phil's rear brake, which wasn't working. They were really kind people and wouldn't take any money for their help. They even gave Phil a free bell! It started raining heavily again that afternoon. We cycled out of the city limits, and found a sheltered and well-hidden spot under a railway bridge to stay for the night.

The next morning I woke up to find that Phil was really ill with a tummy bug and had thrown up a few times in the night. We stayed there and rested for the morning, hoping that Phil would feel well enough to move on in the afternoon. A local guy walked past at around eleven o'clock and looked concerned when he saw Phil. He returned about an hour later with two policemen; *not good!* They asked us for our passports. While Phil was looking for his, his illness caught up with him! He had a bit of an accident in his pants. Apparently he thought it was a fart: it wasn't! Ever the joker, Phil said: *"Tom, I'm going to need some more nappy pants!"*

Nappy pants are what my Mum calls padded lycra shorts to tease my Dad when he goes road biking in all his gear. We had been wearing them every day, but the pair that Phil was holding was now, without a shadow of a doubt, completely unwearable!

"What literally? Okay, I'll deal with the policemen!" I replied.

I passed Phil a clean set of boxers shorts from his bag and he went off with the poo bag, a bag which contained all of the essentials; bog roll, hand sanitizer and a cigarette lighter to burn the paper. Phil sorted himself out while I entertained the policemen. They were so annoying, asking for all of our details. They wouldn't leave us alone. Phil returned wearing only a dirty white T-shirt and boxers, then started talking to the policemen with an incredulous smile on his face. He was a bit delirious with tiredness, but also very aware of how funny the situation was. Eventually, we followed them away from the bridge and back to the road, then were allowed to cycle away. Phil was still very ill so we stopped at the first hotel we saw and got a room. I went to an internet café to update my blog.

We were both feeling the pressure a bit. We had to get to Beijing by the sixteenth of October to see both the Great Wall and the Forbidden City before our flights. We still had about six hundred miles to cover in the next nine days. This was very possible, but with Phil being sick he would find it very difficult unless he could recover quickly. Phil was very slightly better the next day so we continued on through some pretty average scenery. There were a few scenic hills and some small gorges to look at, but it was mostly boring. It was a huge achievement of Phil's to manage to cycle sixty-three miles that day, despite being very weak; I could tell he was struggling. Luckily, that night we were given a back room in a Shell garage to sleep in and the use of the staff kitchen. This show of hospitality came at an excellent time, because we really needed the comfort that night.

Phil told me later that he was close to stopping and hitching a ride to catch up with me during this illness. It wasn't an option to stop for any more rest days or we wouldn't make the coast in time. Thankfully, over the next couple of days, Phil got his strength back and recovered. We cycled through some boring scenery and expansive areas of industry. Massive coal power stations spurted out pollution and coal dust, which we got covered in. Every day finished with us looking like we'd been working in a coal mine, covered in soot. I couldn't believe that millions of people lived in this environment. Their life expectancy must have been massively reduced because of the constant exposure to dangerous particles caused by the pollution. We spent three days in this atmosphere; about two hundred miles of coal power plants and smog. We reached the Yellow River again, which we couldn't see across because of the haze. It was considerably bigger than when we had left it a few hundred miles ago. Our route had taken us in a straight line east. The river had run over five hundred miles north into Inner Mongolia and back south again to where we were now.

We tried staying in a SINOPEC petrol station, after our success at the Shell service station. To our delight they gave us a large cupboard to sleep in. Unfortunately, after about an hour, the night shift manager came along and wasn't so welcoming, telling us that we had to leave. After arguing for a while (we'd been given permission by the other manager and had unpacked everything, brushed our teeth and were about to go to bed) we realised there was no way we could stay there. The manager called his son, who could speak English, and told us that he would put us up in a hotel in the next town. A nice gesture, but unfortunately it meant packing everything up and cycling another five miles in the dark. With hindsight, the hotel turned out to be pretty good. It was useful to have got that extra bit of distance done, and very kind of the manager to pay for a room for us.

At lunchtime the next day we were given a free lunch; really tasty boiled chicken stew. This was in exchange for photos of us with the restaurant staff. They were planning to put them on the wall. I would love to go back there one day to see if they did. After more flat roads, with not much to look at, we found a place to sleep in a wood. We found out pretty quickly that it was home to a colony of huge black and yellow spiders that sat in the centre of giant webs strung between trees. They looked pretty nasty. Phil walked through one of the webs by accident at one point, and he jumped a mile, while I checked his back for the spider. We cooked a tasty vegetable rice dish, while keeping one eye out for spiders, and then got a good night's sleep. In the morning, a spider had made a web on my bike. I brushed it off and we escaped the wood without any spider bites. We lifted the bikes onto another motorway, which we managed stay on all day without being chucked off by the police. We ate in service stations that were gradually improving as we approached the rich cities of the East.

Before we left the motorway, China threw up another treat. Imagine the scene; a hill on the motorway, a bridge crossing the road, a huge banner spanning the bridge with a message in ten foot high letters. The banner would not have been cheap; it was in English so the people who would read it would be businessmen travelling along the motorway between the large cities. You would have thought that before spending thousands of yuan on getting the banner printed, the designers would have got an English speaker to check it and ensure it made sense. Apparently not... The banner read:

"The expressway builders with rich fruits are the van of Shanxi."

It stopped raining when we eventually left the motorway, at the ancient walled city of Pingyao. The walls were impressive, tall and very wide, with pagoda style towers on the gates and corners. Pingyao is a world heritage site and is a beautiful place to visit. It is a traditional city, with a lived-in city centre. If you can look past the souvenir shops, seeing the traditional houses in ancient surroundings is like looking back in time. There were people going about their everyday lives in the ancient town centre. We had a look round, chilled out, and stuffed our faces with delicious local food. Some of the dishes on the menu looked interesting; God knows how they mistranslated it so badly:

- *'Fried mushrooms with rape'*
- *'Pull the rotten son'*
- *'Cold vegetable in sauce cow tendons'*

Perhaps unadventurously, we stayed away from these exotic cuisine options and opted for the more standard, but delicious, dim sun pork dumplings and noodle stir fry. We wandered around the town centre where I bought a fan as a present for Laura and tried to negotiate a good price for a replica *'Little Red Book'* but failed. All of the stall owners claimed that they had an original version, despite the fact that it was very obvious that the books that they were selling were brand new. In the evening we chilled out and played pool at the hostel. Neither of us got seven-balled, which was a good job because the forfeit was to run around the table with no trousers!

After the pool session, we sat down in the hostel and planned our final few days, as well as the location of our arrival at the coast. Neither of us were too bothered about a glorious finishing point, such as in Tianjin, or at the end of the Great Wall. We just wanted to reach the coast as quickly as possible to give ourselves a couple of days in Beijing for sightseeing. We settled on Huanghau Port as the best place to finish. It looked like a fairly decent sized city on the map. We would be able to get a bus from there to Beijing once we had reached the coast. *We weren't far off now!*

24. The end of Asia

To travel is to discover that everyone is wrong about other countries
- Aldous Huxley

So this was it, the last leg of the biggest landmass on the planet; Eurasia. I had left from my home in Cheshire nearly seven months ago and in less than a week would reach the other side of China. I couldn't believe it.

On the way out of Pingyao we had dumplings in a little family-run café for breakfast. After eating, we cycled along the G108, the road that we would be following for the next few days, in the ever-present heavy rain. By lunchtime we were completely drenched and sheltered in the only restaurant we could find. It was very expensive compared to what we were used to, and had an unusual way of presenting the menu. Along the whole of one of the sides of the restaurant was a large, long and thin open kitchen. All of the dishes that the restaurant cooked were on display on the counter spanning the whole length of the building. There were some delicious looking options, beautifully presented but very expensive. Of course, we had the cheapest food available; a sort of dumpling broth and some bread, which was actually pretty good.

The rain continued all afternoon, as we passed pretty villages in the countryside. All my kit was wet again, but it was good cycling, except for the constant deafening refrain of car horns. The rain finally stopped in the evening and we found a wood next to a motorway to camp in. I wished that I had waterproof rear panniers; I had just dried all my kit out in Pingyao. We pitched the tents and started cooking. After a few minutes, a queue of lorries began to form. There must have been an accident and it looked like we would have company for a while. We turned off our torches and sat inside our tents. It would be hard for anyone to spot us unless they ventured into the wood to go to the toilet. Chinese truckers seemed to go on the roadside so this didn't worry us too much. It was difficult to sleep with the headlights and noise until the queue cleared a couple of hours later.

The next morning it was my birthday; I was a quarter of a century old on October the eleventh 2011. It wasn't a particularly memorable day of cycling; we spent most of the day riding on the motorway. We had covered fifty miles by lunch, which we had in the large city of Yangquan. An English speaking headmistress, whom we met at some traffic lights, took us to a cheap restaurant with a large outdoor seating area. On the other side of the city, we carried our bikes back onto the motorway, trying to avoid the numerous human poos left by the truck drivers who must have been stuck in the traffic jam the previous night. It was seriously disgusting. We dodged our way through a queue of trucks waiting to pass through a tollgate and darted between them stealthily, to avoid being seen by the police. We managed to ride through the toll gate and got past a police car by cycling on the other side of a moving lorry, which blocked their view. They didn't see us and we laughed happily as we sped off away from the tollgate, singing the James Bond theme!

Every Inch of the Way

The motorway was a good place to ride, away from the manic horns, the hard shoulder was a place of relative peace and safety compared with most of the back roads in this overpopulated part of China. We spent the afternoon riding on the scenic motorway, covering a distance of forty-five miles, and we came across the Great Wall again. We didn't know it was going to be visible from this road but although it was foggy, we could see it snaking up into the hills. It really is an incredible piece of engineering. We had been cycling for around a month and a half since we had last seen it and we still hadn't reached the end. Shortly after seeing this spectacular scene, we left the motorway at the small town of Janxing where we found a great shop and bought frozen stuffed dumplings for dinner, loads of snacks, rice wine, beer and candles to celebrate my birthday.

We started looking for a place to camp, and around the first corner were rewarded with the best sleeping spot of the entire trip. Carved into a cliff by the side of road, was a ruined Buddhist temple a short climb up the cliff face. We managed to scramble up to it and lift our bikes into the cave. There were statues in there; their faces had been chiselled off, possibly by Muslims raiding the temples, as had been the case in the caves we saw in Dunhuang. We cooked dinner, lit the candles and drank the rice wine. It was one of the best and certainly the most unusual birthday evening I've had.

In the morning I spent a while readjusting the spokes in my back wheel which wasn't quite right after I had rebuilt it in Xi'an and was slightly off centre. It had rained all night so it was good to have slept in the cave. What wasn't good was that the road was now covered in a thick layer of wet coal dust, which we got covered in very quickly as we raced downhill to Shijiazhung, a city with a population of over ten million and a name that is very hard to pronounce when asking for directions. It is enormous, covered in smog, and was not a place we wanted to cycle through, so we decided to join the motorway ring road, which we cycled on for the rest of the day and the next morning.

The following evening, we joined the G307; *the last road in Asia*, which would lead us all the way to the coast. The road was lined with beautiful orchards so we camped in one of them that night, hidden from the world. It was wonderful to relax and chill out. Phil had now fully recovered from his illness and we were on the home stretch. For the next couple of days we followed the G307 wasn't particularly memorable, but perfectly pleasant cycling. It wasn't too busy and the towns were okay, with good shops and cafés. I had experienced enough of China now and was ready for a change of scenery. America began to excite me. When I wasn't planning ahead to my next continent, I spent a lot of the time reflecting on Asia, mentally replaying every stage in my head; Turkey, Georgia, the ferry, the desert, Samarkand, the Pamirs, Kyrgyzstan, the Kazakhstan dash and China. I wanted to remember every moment of it, and as I got closer to the coast, my achievements up to that point began to dawn on me. Asia hadn't been easy. All those rainy days and headwinds, the snow, the beating sun, the illnesses, the mechanical problems, the huge mountains... *America would be a piece of cake after this!*

On the last afternoon, the road followed the motorway again. We passed endless sand flats and tidal channels and could smell the sea. We had fun blocking the narrow road to see how long it took to get honked at (not long)! It was satisfying getting our own back for the appalling driving we had experienced in China. We passed harbours and boats then arrived at the port of Hunhuang, cycling east to try to find a way to the sea. A wrong turning took us to a dead-end at a power plant and the guards wouldn't let us through to the coast. We struggled back five miles against a strong headwind, which was very demoralising. I realised it was possible we weren't going to be able to get to the sea, which would have been a massive shame.

We asked around, using a picture of the sea to indicate where we wanted to go, but nobody understood. Eventually we managed to explain to a couple of guys that we had crossed the whole country and we wanted to get the coast. They smiled and told us to follow them. They got into a van and drove at bike pace for six miles until we finally arrived at the sea. It was an unbelievable feeling of achievement! I put my bike wheel in the water; I had made it all the way from England to the other side of China on Sandy! It isn't just a bike. It is the best bike in the world. Phil had his own achievement: cycling from Urumqi, the city furthest away from any ocean in the world, to the sea.

We didn't have long to celebrate because we wanted to get a bus to Beijing. We got into the back of the van with the bikes. Phil's was half sticking out of the back door so we were holding on to it from inside. There was no point in cycling back to Hunhuang now. We had done enough of that. I was all for being lazy and accepting a lift this time. They drove us to the bus station. It turned out that there were no buses to Beijing that day, but there was one very early in the morning, which would get us there at about eleven o'clock. That was fine; we would chill out and get to Beijing for a decent time the following day. We went to look for a hotel, but China wasn't finished with its restrictions and crazy rules yet. It turned out that we were in another city that was closed to foreigners. No hotel would take us except an official tourist one, which cost about forty quid a night. We were taken to the police and we explained to an English speaking policeman:

"We have just cycled here and we needed a place to stay, but we can't afford to stay in the expensive official hotel."
"You must stay in the official hotel," he replied
"Can we stay in the police station?" we asked.
"No no no," he said.
"Why can't tourists stay in cheap hotels?"
"That is the rule," he replied.
"Why is that the rule?"

He didn't know. In China you don't ask these questions, the rule book is concrete. He never questioned the rules and took them as gospel. Common sense had gone completely out of the window. Mao's legacy was still going strong and his influence had spread to this young ambitious policeman. It was clear that despite China's massive recent development, some things would take a long time to change. In the end we were offered a place to stay by one of the guys who had guided us to the coast for about eighty yuan (about eight pounds). It was strange to agree to pay for a room in someone's house after all of the amazing hospitality in Eastern Europe, Turkey, the Caucasus, Central Asia and Qinghai, but we were happy to have a place to rest and the family cooked us a tasty meal.

The next day we took a bus to Beijing and found a cheap hostel near Tiananmen Square. Mao's face still looks down on the square from a giant portrait hanging from the gate of the Forbidden City. I thought back to the statue of Stalin in Gori, and pondered why it was that past tyrants are still worshipped by so many. Apart from this portrait, I was really impressed by Beijing. It had a lovely atmosphere and was much greener than I had expected. It was brilliant to cycle around too, due to the large network of bike lanes. We saw the Forbidden City, ate Peking duck, packed our bikes away into boxes for the flights, and took a bus out to a popular part of the Great Wall, which was even more spectacular than in the photographs. We bought tea, knives and meat cleavers as presents and before we knew it, it was time to leave China. Phil was flying back to Blighty, I was heading to the USA, to San Francisco. I felt like I was nearly home now; just the small matter of crossing North America. First, a week off in San Francisco with Laura; I hadn't seen her for about five months, which was far too long.

China still hadn't finished making things difficult. We paid a guy twenty yuan to take our stuff to a metro station on the back of a motorised trailer thing. He wouldn't take us all the way for some reason so we struggled with the bikes down to the metro. They wouldn't let us on, but a girl and a man who worked there helped us to carry our bikes back outside, and to get a taxi that wasn't a complete tourist rip-off. We loaded the bikes into the back and realised there was only room for one of us with the seats down, so I got in and Phil took the metro. As soon as Phil left, the taxi driver could see that I was stuck unless I took his car so increased his price by twenty yuan.

I was pleased to be leaving and looking forward to the next challenge, but China had been fantastic. Having spent over two months cycling there, I had more of a chance to get to know it than the other countries I had been to. I saw different people, different religions, very varied landscapes and climates and I probably learned more and gained more than in the other countries. I had loved China, but despite spending so long there, I still don't understand the country. It is so different from the other countries I have been to. The language barrier had made things very difficult but the crazy rules more so. It was at these times that I valued Phil's company the most. Alone, all of these challenges would have been hard to deal with, but with Phil they were just funny. We made a great team, so thanks for coming Phil. *Two continents down, one to go.*

Photographs of China

The new road near Sahram Hu

Sahram Hu

163

Tofu and pumpkin soup with local teenagers

The very convenient tunnels under the motorway

Camping in irrigated woodland in the middle of the desert near Urumqi

Cooling off in an irrigation channel

Phil on a very boring desert road

Remains of the Great Wall

Finally out of the monotonous scenery

A Buddhist shrine in the mountains

Making friends in Delingha

The perfect road?

Chillies drying outside a typical Muslim house

Labrang Monastery

Old men playing cards in standard-issue communist suits

The Terracotta Army

Rebuilding my wheel

Pingyao

Nasty-looking spider!

The end of Asia!

The Forbidden City

The Great Wall near Beijing

PART 4: AMERICA

From San Francisco to Flagler Beach

25. Culture shock and a week with Laura

San Francisco has only one drawback - 'tis hard to leave.
- Rudyard Kipling

I was given a free meal at the airport gate and then two more on the plane, where my seat was by an emergency exit over one of the wings so had extra legroom. A great start to my flight was improved by a fair amount of red wine. I hadn't had any for a long time! I even had a whisky for a night cap. The air stewardesses seemed a bit annoyed that I was treating their free drinks policy a bit too liberally, but this didn't concern me; it was luxury beyond comprehension compared to my life during the past few months. We landed smoothly in San Francisco Airport where I eventually passed through security after a lot of questioning. The visas from the 'Stans' caused suspicion with the American border guard, who asked:

"Do you have a flight booked out of the country?"
"No, it said it wasn't necessary on the visa application," I truthfully replied.
"That isn't true; you have to have a return flight booked."
"That's not what it said on the ESTA website," I told him.

He looked at me annoyed but obviously doubting his own knowledge on the subject.

"What will happen if you run out of money?" he asked.
"I won't," I replied (not as truthfully this time)!
"What happens if you do?"
"My family will get me home," I told him.

I hadn't asked them if that was the case, but assumed that if I was stuck I wouldn't be left and forgotten in America. I was planning to not run out of money though, and thought I could make it for two more months with what I had.

Eventually, after being aggressively and suspiciously interrogated for another ten minutes, he let me through. I was amazed that because I had visited some countries that he didn't know much about and had 'stan' in the name, I was treated like a threat to America. A bit shaken up, I collected my bike and bags and rushed up to the BART train station to board a train before rush hour, during which bikes aren't allowed on board. The BART took me to a Caltrain station, where I boarded another train to Palo Alto, to meet an old school friend; Sam.

In the station car park I rebuilt my bike and was relieved to find that the baggage handlers hadn't damaged it. I cycled off to meet Sam on the beautiful Stanford University campus. We caught up in a campus restaurant; Sam was shocked that I had been sleeping in drainage tunnels but very interested in my stories. He helped me plan the first part of the route through the USA, before I cycled to Sam's house where I met his landlady, had some food and caught up on emails. I reflected on how different life was here in the USA, having a kind of reverse culture shock. Getting back into living in a developed world was strange, having been out of it for so long. The first things I noticed as odd were:

Every Inch of the Way

1. Drivers giving way to bikes, something I hadn't experienced since Western Europe.
2. No honking horns.
3. Water in toilet bowls, and always a western style toilet, with paper and soap provided.
4. Being able to speak to people again, and hear their conversations. It makes a massive difference.
5. Cleanliness.
6. Not being stared at and blending in.
7. Politeness.
8. No blocked internet sites (I could get my news from the BBC rather than the Sun tabloid website)
9. Having a ridiculous amount of choice in shops. *Why do you need ten brands of peanut butter?*

Sam got back from university and kindly gave me a San Francisco guidebook and an American phone to get me started. I went to bed in the spare room, which had a tank with turtles inside. In China they would have been for eating, but these were family pets! The next day I went back into the city, checked into a hotel that Laura had booked for us, and then went to the airport to meet her. I hadn't had time for a haircut, but otherwise was looking (and smelling) the best I had in months.

It was wonderful to see her after five months. We took the train back into the city and bought a takeaway pizza and a bottle of wine. We spent the next three days in San Francisco; ate well, went to a diner with a brilliant jazz band, cycled over the Golden Gate Bridge, looked around Union Square and Fisherman's Wharf, took a ride on one of San Fran's famous street cable cars and visited Chinatown. Laura was having a much deserved break from working the crazy hours of a recently qualified doctor and I was shattered. For my birthday present, Laura hired us a car and we went for a drive down *Route 1* on the Pacific Coast. It is a spectacularly beautiful road, with perfect beaches every couple of miles. We saw sea lions in Santa Cruz, then drove up to Henry Cowell State Forest Park and camped there for two nights under the giant pine trees. We walked around the forest on a trail and had a barbecue on an open fire. It was such a peaceful place.

We drove back to San Francisco via one of the perfect Pacific beaches, where we had a picnic. California would be such a pleasant place to live; the climate is great, and to be able to go to one of the Pacific beaches whenever you wanted to would be fantastic. Back in the city, we saw Alcatraz, which is a really interesting place. The stories of the prisoners who tried to escape were incredible. The second best attempt was by a prisoner who worked in the laundry room. He washed army uniforms, and over a period of a few years he stole an entire uniform bit by bit. Eventually, he had everything he needed and managed to hide it under a pier where the boats landed. One day he was working down by the pier and a boat was due to leave Alcatraz. He jumped under the pier, put the uniform on, and then casually strolled onto the boat. Nobody asked any questions. He was the first prisoner to escape from Alcatraz Island. Unfortunately for him, the boat wasn't going to San Francisco, but another island in the bay, Angel Island. He was noticed missing during an unscheduled head count and was swiftly recaptured. If the boat had gone to San Francisco, he may well have escaped.

The most successful escape attempt was by a group of three men who chiselled through the three foot thick concrete wall in the back of their cells, using sharpened spoons. They covered the noise by playing the accordion during the 'music hour' and made panels to hide the holes during the day, which fooled the guards, and left papier-mâché heads in the beds when they left their cells. Once they had crawled through the holes they had made, they reached a corridor that led to an air vent and took the rivets out, replacing them with soap, shaped into rivets to disguise their route. Floats made from stolen rain coats allowed them to enter the water in San Francisco Bay at around ten o'clock at night. They were never seen again. Whether the escapees made it to land drowned remains a mystery. The story goes that after this escape, the prison warden received a blank postcard every year, with a Mexican stamp from on it.

On our last night in San Francisco we ate in an upmarket French restaurant, which was a million miles away from what I was used to. I felt completely out of place. It was really hard to say goodbye again the next day, but this was the last time I would have to. Laura's flight was delayed, which meant she would miss her connection in Chicago, so they put her on an earlier one, which gave us twenty minutes to change terminal and check in. We just made it and there was no time to say goodbye properly. I was really sad heading back into San Francisco but luckily Harry, my flatmate from fifth year at Edinburgh University, was arriving that afternoon.

I spent the afternoon fixing my bike and checked into a cheap(ish) hostel. I felt terrible thinking about how long it would be before I saw Laura again. I had known for a while that I would ask her to marry me one day, but it was then that I decided I was sure and it would be time to propose soon. It wouldn't be straight away when I got back, but when I could afford a ring, I would do.

I had to get my mind back on the journey though and set off to meet Harry at Powell Street station where we caught up over a giant burger. Seeing a good friend helped my mind-set and I was soon excited about the prospect of getting back on the road. We discussed routes, put his bike together, and then got an early night, ready to leave the next day.

So we began a new continent as a new team; Harry on a lightweight drop handlebar road bike, me on Sandy, my trusty steel framed mountain bike. Mine was considerably heavier, but I was hoping that I'd be able to keep up, having done 11,100 miles of training!

26. It's downhill all the way to Yosemite, man

For my part, I travel not to go anywhere, but to go. I travel for travel's sake. The great affair is to move.
- Robert Louis Stevenson

It was good to be back on the road again. Harry was very excited about starting and his enthusiasm was infectious. Soon I was as excited as he was and once again hit by the spirit of adventure. We left the *'Backpacker's Hostel'* and cycled through San Francisco, via Fisherman's Wharf and the south end of the Golden Gate Bridge. From there, we headed south down Highway 1, the breathtakingly beautiful Pacific Coast highway that I had driven down with Laura, passing the town of Pacific, climbing and descending with great views of the sea cliffs and beaches until we reached Half Moon Bay, where we had lunch sitting on the sand. We turned inland; *heading east once more*, climbed a long hill and then raced down through wooded countryside. This part of California was lush, green and picturesque. As we rode down a long hill, Harry almost hit a fawn that ran out in front of him. At a junction, we went the wrong way and I only noticed the mistake after about four miles of cycling in the wrong direction. This was the first time I had made a notable navigation error on the entire trip. The other times I had been lost were not as a result of my poor map reading. It must have been Harry's fault; that was the only explanation!

Our first campsite together was on a grassy field, behind some trees near the freeway. I started pitching my tent as normal, not thinking twice about camping so close to the motorway. Harry wasn't used to this and I think he was a bit wary on the first night. I thought back to my first wild-camping night in the UK; it had taken me ages to find a spot I was happy with. Once we started cooking, we relaxed and planned our route. We decided to try to pass through Yosemite National Park. It would be spectacular, but there was a chance that the road would close in the next few days if snow fell. Tioga Pass shuts for the winter at the first heavy snowfall of the year. It was open at that moment, but if snow arrived within the next week, we would have to backtrack and cycle a different pass over the Sierra Nevada Mountains. The chance to see Yosemite's scenery made the risk worthwhile, but I had my fingers tightly crossed!

We had peanut butter sandwiches for breakfast, something I had really missed for the last six months. Back at home, every day starts with peanut butter on toast for me. We cycled downhill to the Dumbarton Bridge, which took us to the other side of San Francisco Bay. We found a bike shop in Livermore where I bought a new pump. Harry 'pimped his ride' with a horn and a squeaking tortoise! Back in the countryside, we climbed through a quiet valley alongside a beautiful clear stream, which I had a wash in at lunchtime. After a pretty afternoon's ride, we found a place to camp on the outside of a bend in the road. Our campsite was so different from the one the previous night. We were further inland now and the ground was very dry. It seemed a world away from the green fields and woodland on the coast. We were heading back into a desert environment.

In the morning, we entered the desert and cycled over some small hills where we met a couple of Swedish guys who had cycled from New York and were heading to Los Angeles. They were a father and son team, which made me think that I would like to do a tour with my Dad in the future. Over the hills was a completely flat plain, where we passed through fertile farmland on quiet back roads, before reaching a dead-end where the road met the Interstate. We had to lift our bikes onto the ten-lane motorway and rode along it for a few miles. Ten minutes into our motorway adventure, the police came and chucked us off. They were much more efficient than their Chinese equivalents. It didn't matter because the next junction took us to Manteca, which was where we had planned to get to for lunch. We reached Yosemite Avenue, the road that we would follow for the next couple of days, all the way to Yosemite National Park. In the afternoon we passed through dense woodland and then that evening we finished in a forested plantation.

Life was easy here; the cycling was good, the quality of the roads was great and the scenery was beautiful. We weren't doing huge days as Harry eased into the ride, and everyday tasks were so simple compared to in Asia. In the USA, you can go to a shop, find food within its sell-by-date and easily get enough calories by buying some of the many snack foods on offer. If you are lost, asking for directions is easy and the locals are only too happy to help. Mine was a good life in America, but it seemed almost too simple. I missed the adventure of Asia and the unknown. Still, this was California. I was sure the expansive deserts and large mountains that lay ahead would spice things up a bit.

I cooked bacon butties for breakfast at sunrise. Someone was hunting in the plantation so we made a quick getaway and started climbing into the foothills of the Sierra Nevada Mountains. It was great riding, the best since the Chinese mountains. The scenery was beautiful as we climbed and descended a series of small desert hills. We stopped to fill our water bottles up at a Motel with *'girls girls girls'* advertised on a sign outside. The lovely old lady who ran the place, gave us soup and said we would need the energy to get up the hill to Yosemite. Her sons were really tough looking guys covered in tattoos, and I was a bit uneasy as they came over to talk to us. To my surprise they were really nice gentle people who respected the UK because: *"You guys have sensible sized cars!"*

After lunch we climbed *'Old Priest Grade'*, which has a reputation as an incredibly difficult cycling hill climb. It was the steepest long hill of the bike ride and has an average incline of fifteen percent over a distance of one mile. Its reputation is well deserved! I set myself the challenge of climbing it without stopping. I made it in one go, standing up and straining the pedals round, pushing down with one foot and pulling up on my SPD cleats with the other. As I sprinted the final few metres to the top, I felt great. It was tough, but I dragged my heavy bike up it pretty quickly. The training miles had definitely paid off. I waited for Harry at the top and talked to a guy on a Harley Davidson about the road to Yosemite;

"It's downhill all the way to Yosemite from here, man", he told me.

Every Inch of the Way

1,000 metres of altitude gain later, we arrived at Yosemite. It was frustrating to be told that we had an easy ride coming up, only for it to be uphill all the way. People who ride motorbikes or drive cars just don't see the gradients of the roads and are unable to judge distances. They are very happy to whole-heartedly and very confidently tell you these facts though. It is very demoralising to spend a day going uphill if you're expecting a few hours of descent.

After an afternoon of climbing, we picked up a rack of spare ribs from a supermarket to cook on a fire later that evening. As it got dark, we came across a campsite that had been closed for the season, in a beautiful pine forest. We had the whole place to ourselves along with running water and an enormous pile of firewood. Bears were a worry, so we put our food inside a bear locker and camped on the other side of the site. The ribs were delicious, cooked on our giant campfire, and no bears disturbed us, which was slightly disappointing because I really wanted to see one, but also a relief.

I woke up wet in the morning, because there was a lot of condensation in the tent; it was cold at night at the higher altitudes that we had now reached. Harry went for a wild poo and started a forest fire while burning the paper. We only noticed after it had been smouldering for a few minutes. Panicking, we ran back and forwards to the tap with our water bottles and managed to put it out. We were both very careful about burning bog roll from then on.

Most of the morning, we climbed through a beautiful pine forest. I saw a diner where I had eaten with my friend Ed when we came here a few years ago on a road trip. It was beyond my budget this time so we cycled straight past. and entered Yosemite at around lunchtime, where we spoke to the ranger at the park entrance. Tioga Pass, the 3,031 metre high point of the road going through Yosemite, was still open. This was great news. The forecast was good for the next couple of days so it looked like we were in luck. The ranger told us that all of the campsites were shut on Tioga Pass Road and that we weren't allowed to wild-camp. We assured him that we would get the sixty-seven miles of climbing done that afternoon, and that we wouldn't wild-camp. He seemed to believe us! For the entire afternoon, we passed through the unique scenery of Yosemite National Park: thick forests, huge rounded granite peaks, cathedral-like cliffs, mirror-like lakes and beautiful rivers; we found a wonderful wild-camp site on one of the rocky peaks. A tall dead tree provided a good place to hang our food to keep it safe from bears (although we later learned first-hand that a bear would have had no problem climbing the tree to get the bag). After a feast consisting of pasta and energy bars, we slept outside under a blanket of twinkling stars on a smooth rock.

On Halloween, we woke up to a glorious Yosemite sunrise and walked up to the summit of the granite dome, to experience it in all its glory. After retrieving our bag, we ate breakfast on the peak, with an incredible panoramic view of the sun rising over one of the most spectacular landscapes in the world. That morning, we rode through more thick pine forests and saw giant elk running through the trees, but unfortunately no bears still. We climbed the last few hundred metres to Tioga Pass in the early afternoon. Yosemite had been one of the highlights of the entire trip for me. The

180

descent from the pass was brilliant too. It hugged the side of the mountain and was steep enough to build up some serious speed. We passed two beautiful lakes and I reached a speed of 51.5 miles per hour on the perfect downhill road; a new trip record. We descended to Lee Vining, a remote little town in the middle of nowhere with a massively overpriced shop and a big salt lake. After stocking up, the road led us towards Death Valley. We found another great campsite in the desert that night and were treated to a shooting star display as we drifted off to sleep. That morning we had woken to the grand splendour of Yosemite National Park. By the evening we were in the remote, barren, dry desert; *a vast contrast.*

We woke up the next morning with frost on the sleeping bags because we hadn't used the tents. For the first few miles, we climbed over a small pass then started a long descent, during which we lost over 1,000 metres in altitude. I got another new speed record of 53.9 mph. I looked back when I reached the bottom and looked back Harry wasn't there. In the meantime I had a conversation with two really nice women, Diana and Tabatha, who had stopped to see if I was okay. I told them what we were doing and they were concerned about Harry, so they went back to see if he was alright. They came back to report he was fine and was fixing a rear wheel puncture. Diane put her hand on my shoulder and said a prayer for me out loud. It was a very awkward experience but a nice gesture.

That night was brilliant. We found some natural hot springs. There was a series of open-air pools at bath temperature, we swam for ages in the dark and washed all our clothes. It was great to get clean and warm, until we emerged into the freezing night air. We slept out in the open next to one of the springs. In the morning, we were woken by a beautiful sunrise over the mountains, but Harry was feeling ill; he had a migraine. After a couple of hours with a towel over his head, he felt better and we left. While he was resting, I swam in the hot springs and was probably the cleanest I had been on the whole trip by the time I got out. It's a great way to start the day, swimming in water at bath-temperature. When he felt well enough, Harry walked to the nearby thermal spa building to ask to use the 'Restroom'. He was told:

"We don't like your type around here, you're a freeloader. Get out of here and f off!". What a lovely chap!

The desert continued as we cycled to the isolated town of Lone Pine. We saw Mt Whitney, the highest mountain in continental USA, as well as many other snow-capped peaks. At Lone Pine we stocked up on supplies of food and water for Death Valley before climbing up past a tiny settlement called 'Owen's Lake'. We found a dry river bed to sleep in for the night and set up camp. My culinary camping skills reached a new level and I cooked delicious fajitas while Harry built a massive fire. Within about fifteen minutes of stopping most days, Harry had a huge fire burning, and so we were rarely cold at night-time. Harry had downloaded Blackadder onto his phone, which we listened to. Lord Flashheart is hilarious. I still loved nights in the desert as much as I had the first time that I slept out in one in Kazakhstan. *Just a fire, the stars, some food and nature.*

The next morning we climbed a 1,800 metre pass into Death Valley National Park, followed by a long descent to Panamint Springs, where we stopped at the diner for lunch. We asked the barmaid what life was like in such an isolated place:

"I kinda like how simple life is out here, but it can get kinda boring."
We sat down and ate a tasty burger for lunch, then I heard a guy say:
"You know it's time to quit when you get a bullet in your head!"

I have no idea what he was referring to…

We left Panamint Springs on a dead straight road that looked to curve up into mountains about two miles away. Fifteen miles later we reached the foot of the mountains. The horizon takes a lot longer to reach in the desert. Harry raced up the climb and I could see he was really getting into the ride now and getting fitter. With my extra weight, I couldn't keep up so we met at the top. I had to stop halfway up for a peanut butter calorie boost. Harry was buzzing; he was loving the scenery and getting the same kicks out of climbing mountain passes as I did.

Another great descent took us into the main valley of the national park, containing Badwater; the lowest point in the USA at eighty-six metres below sea level. We camped at Stovepipe Wells that night with a Lithuanian couple who were driving around the country, having won US citizenship in a 'green card prize draw', and a Dutch couple on a motorbike tour of the national parks. They were trying to visit every one in the USA. We shared a campsite, some crisps and beers and talked about our trips.

Bacon butties got us going again the next morning and we needed the energy to fight one of the strongest headwinds that I had faced on the entire trip. We took it in turns to ride at the front and made steady progress, swapping positions every mile. The wind was as strong as the one in the Chinese desert where Phil and I had spent an entire day struggling to cycle twenty miles. There were impressive views of sand dunes, canyons and mountains before we reached the park headquarters at Furnace Creek. We got some food there, and then climbed up another pass out of Death Valley, which was sheltered from the howling wind by mountains either side. We camped in an old abandoned campsite, both very tired. It was freezing cold that night and we had only managed forty-six miles against the headwind. It is seriously demoralising putting in so much effort for so little reward. *I hate headwinds!*

California had been just awesome. San Francisco has to be one of the best cities in the world. After that had come the spectacular Pacific Coast, Yosemite, then Death Valley. It had made for ten days of the most stunning and varied riding imaginable. Where else in the world could you find that mixture of world class places to visit? To be able to cycle between them is amazing. Anyone got a spare two week holiday? Fly to San Francisco, cycle this route in spring or autumn and fly back from Las Vegas. It would be one of the best short holidays ever. For us, Nevada was waiting just a few miles away; we would get there early the next day.

27. The house doesn't always win

Man, I really like Vegas
- Elvis Presley

We crossed into Nevada just after the tiny settlement of Death Valley Junction on a pleasant desert road, which climbed up and over a small pass to Pahrump. At the first Wal Mart supermarket of the trip we ate a roast chicken each! Back in the desert, a dual carriageway took us up to the final pass before Las Vegas. It was a long climb and the hour was late, but we wanted to get to Vegas as early as possible the following morning to have a full day off. We cycled into the night and climbed to about 1,700 metres, where a layer of snow coated the ground. Near the top of the pass, there was a low tunnel under the road which was surprisingly warm compared to the temperature outside. It felt like a heater was on in there. I am not sure why it was hot; maybe the concrete bridge had stored the sun's heat. We cooked pasta, lying on our fronts in the very low tunnel, and then settled down for the night.

It was an eventful night. Harry went out for a wee at about two in the morning and climbed up onto the bridge to look at the stars. For some reason he fainted and fell about two metres. He bashed his leg, arm and more worrying, his head. I heard him cursing when he came back round, obviously in pain. We didn't think that he had been unconscious for long, but he was bleeding a great deal and shivering in the cold. I helped him back into the tunnel then cleaned and bandaged the head wound. It wasn't bleeding too badly so we decided to see how it was in the morning rather than calling an ambulance; fully appreciating the importance of medical insurance at this point. Without medical insurance, this could have been very expensive injury.

Harry could ride okay when we got moving, so we rode down to Vegas passing other cyclists coming up the hill, presumably inhabitants of Las Vegas on short day rides in the desert hills. We descended in the falling snow towards the city, which loomed ahead of us; a beacon in the desert. It was a great feeling to arrive there on bikes. We cycled into the centre along Las Vegas Boulevard, a.k.a. 'The Strip'. The massive, ridiculously over the top but hugely impressive casinos flashed past; Mandalay Bay, Luxor, New York New York, MGM Grand, Venetian, Bellagio, Paris, Caesar's Palace, the Stratosphere and many more. We found a cheap motel near the Stratosphere and relaxed before heading out. Harry's head seemed to be okay and he decided not to get it checked out, after talking with my parents, who are both doctors.

We looked round the casinos on the strip; saw flamingos at the Flamingo Casino and lions at the MGM Grand. We saw someone screaming with delight after winning a jackpot on a slot machine, and old lady gambling addicts feeding coin after coin into them. Poker, roulette, black jack, and other games that I don't know covered the casino floors. There is incredible theming all over Vegas; a replica Manhattan skyline with a roller coaster, an Eiffel Tower, Venetian gondolas, a giant pyramid, and the spectacular Bellagio fountain water music show. In the evening, we went to Downtown Vegas and had a tasty all-you-can-eat buffet involving a lot of meat. We then tried our luck on the casino floor, starting with twenty dollars to gamble with on the roulette table. We got up to thirty and a couple of free drinks then tried black jack. This wasn't a good move; we lost twenty-one dollars and were down to nine. Back to roulette, we eventually got up to thirty-five dollars then lost a bit. We left on twenty-six dollars with winnings of three dollars each. More importantly we had left 'up on the bank'; we had beaten Sin City and not lost any money. Vegas was a great place to visit, but cycling through some of the non-touristy parts was alarming. There were dozens of homeless people and drug addicts sleeping on benches. Sin City has destroyed a lot of people's lives.

We left Vegas on an excellent bike trail to Lake Mead via Boulder City. Boulder City is an interesting place because it was built for the workers who constructed the Hoover Dam. The trail wove up and down hills in the desert, and then into a storm drainage channel, which was great fun because it had banked corners that we raced around. We reached Lake Mead, and then descended all the way to the Hoover Dam. It was seriously impressive to see; the scale was incredible. It was hard to believe that it was seventy-five years old. We spoke to a lady who worked there; she told us that ninety-five people had died building the dam. She also said that there is a big problem with suicides there. As it is on the state border, depending on where they jump, either the Nevada or Arizona police have to come to sort it out. This is more difficult for the Arizona police because the nearest city, Kingman, is seventy-five miles away. *Between the dam and Kingman there was only desert.*

We had to backtrack up the hill to cross the gorge on the new bridge that had recently been built. The aerial view of the dam from the bridge was spectacular as we crossed it into Arizona. We changed our clocks forward an hour then cycled back into the desert, climbing up from the Colorado River. On the side of the road there was a stunning viewpoint looking down to the winding river in the gorge below. We stopped there for some lunch. A crazy guy from Chicago came to speak to us; he had Sicilian relatives who'd been in Chicago for years. I wondered if they had known Al Capone... The guy was driving an old Dodge car from San Francisco to Chicago to sell it for a profit; apparently he would be able to get a lot more in Chicago than he had paid for it in San Francisco. He was impressed but perplexed at what we were doing and couldn't understand why we were doing it.

We had a tailwind all afternoon, and the seventy miles through the desert to Kingman were very easy. At Kingman we joined the famous Route 66 and headed out of the city in the early evening. There were lots of great looking diners and motels with the Route 66 logo. Route 66, also known as the 'Mother Road', is 2,448 miles long, and stretches from Chicago to Los Angeles. A major route used from 1926 by people who migrated west until it was closed in 1985; there are a number of sections remain open and it is still possible to follow the majority of the old route using other roads. It is an historic road and I thought about all those people who had used it to seek their fortunes in the 'Wild West', hence the famous quote, *"Go west young man..."*. We went east, and slept in a tunnel under the road at the end of a 101 mile day. Harry was definitely getting into the ride now.

184

The Mother Road was beautiful the next day. We cycled north through some very isolated towns in the Indian reservations, had a delicious lunch in a Route 66 diner and were served coffee after coffee by the friendly and motherly waitress. I left on a caffeine high, back into the Arizona desert. Cycling up a short hill covered in cacti, we saw a native Indian man with long straight black hair standing on a cliff with the sun behind him. It felt like a scene straight out of a Western film. We went to a bar that evening and bought a beer, then were presented with another *'on the house'*. It was a tiny little town where everyone knew each other. We listened in to conversations about the locals' everyday lives. An old lady got gradually more tipsy before she came to speak to us, calling us *antisocial* because we hadn't joined them for a drink. We explained that we were tired because we had been cycling all day. She didn't seem to think that this was a very good excuse for not wanting to get drunk with the people at the bar. We retreated into the pool room and had a game of doubles with a couple of local guys. The bar owners let us use their empty aircraft hangar that night to sleep in. It was freezing outside and the ground was covered in ice and snow. A corrugated iron panel kept banging against the side of the hanger until I blocked it with a piece of wood. Eventually, I got to sleep.

The next day we rode the rest of the Route 66 loop to the town of Seligman, before joining the Interstate 40. We saw our first American civilian carrying a gun. He had a pistol attached to his belt and was wearing camouflage gear. He looked dangerous. The whole day was spent on the motorway, which is legal on the I-40. Apparently, if there are no alternative roads to take, cyclists can ride on the motorways in America. We cycled on the hard shoulder, which had a terribly cut-up surface. It was also covered in wire shards from exploded lorry tyres. We both got a few punctures but made good progress and continued into the dark, climbing around 700 metres in altitude pretty quickly and arriving at Williams, the town forty miles south of the Grand Canyon. At Safeway we ate another roast chicken, and then completed ten more miles before camping under a bridge in the middle of a dual carriageway, where we ate an entire family-sized caramel tart. We were absolutely whizzing through the miles at this stage and both loving the riding, which was varied, exciting, spectacular and remote. Harry was proving to be another great riding partner.

By sunrise the next day we were back on the bikes and had ridden the thirty miles to Flagstaff by half past ten. We went to a car hire shop to get a vehicle to drive to the Grand Canyon because we didn't have time to cycle the detour. The smallest vehicle that they had was a Chevrolet Silverado pick-up truck. It was without a doubt, the most remarkable vehicle that I have ever driven. For a start it was massive; far bigger than any car in the UK. It had a huge bonnet that would have made the driver very safe but would crush any normal sized car or person that it hit. To counter this, most Americans buy a car the same size so they are also safer. This is like a country having nuclear weapons to defend themselves from another country's nuclear weapons. It was terrible to drive, only having four gears but a massive V8 engine so gear changes where a crashing, high revving and jolting experience. This goes someway to explaining how we managed to get an incredible twelve miles to the gallon out of it. I couldn't help thinking that attempts to adopt low carbon transport and renewable energy sources were happening in another galaxy than the makers of this plastic-lined cockpit my Silverado inhabited.

I have since done some work about sustainability in America and learnt (assume my maths is correct) that if America swapped their cars for British cars, they would save more energy in one year than their entire wind industry has done in the last decade. That is calculated simply by replacing their average fuel consumption (twenty-two mpg) for an average British car's (thirty-eight mpg) doing the same mileage. This illustrates pretty well that America has got its environmental priorities massively wrong. I am all for wind energy, I work in the industry now but it isn't going to save the planet unless people change their habits.

Anyway; apart from the *'Chevy'* pick-up, the drive to the Grand Canyon was great. We drove through the high-altitude desert plain, past a smaller canyon formed by one of the Colorado's tributaries arriving at the Grand Canyon late in the afternoon. It was Veterans' Weekend (America's version of Remembrance Day in the UK) and we were happy to find that entry to the national park was free because of this. We cycled around the canyon rim and sat down to watch the sunset. It was the most incredible view. The colours of the canyon changed as the sunlight cast shadows, highlighting different rocks as the sun sank behind the horizon. The higher altitude north rim was white with snow, the orange rocks stretched in ridges and gorges as far as the eye could see, and at the bottom was the main gorge, with the Colorado River snaking its way along, gradually cutting away at the rocks and deepening the canyon. It really is one of the wonders of the world.

We slept in the back of the pick-up truck that night in the car park at the National Park visitor centre. Being able to sleep in the back was the only good thing about it! We got up for the spectacular sunrise over the canyon and then drove back through the snow, to Flagstaff. After returning our horrible vehicle, we left Flagstaff on the I-40 and made up some good mileage as we descended with a tailwind. Harry got two more punctures, but we still did over fifty miles and got to Winslow, a town made famous by the Eagles song *'Take it Easy'*. There is a crossroads there, covered in pictures of the Eagles, a big Route 66 logo on the road, and the song line, *'Standin' on a corner (In Winslow, Arizona, what a fine sight to see...)'* painted on a building. We treated ourselves to a burger in a restaurant that evening then did another twenty miles in the dark and cooked a second dinner of spaghetti in a tunnel under the road.

The next day we reached Petrified Forest National Park. The fossilised trees look exactly like fallen tree trunks, but they are made from rock. Apparently the logs were brought here by ancient rivers and were then buried in volcanic ash. Quartz crystals formed and replaced the wood, creating perfect fossils of ancient trees. There is a book of letters from people who had stolen rocks and returned them because they believe that their lives have been cursed ever since. The trees and the letters, however, were outshone by the cat on a lead being taken for a walk around the national park trail. It was hilarious; the owners said that they loved their cat but not as much as the late

Arnold, which they had trained to behave like a dog. They said that the new cat could sit, roll over and walk just like Arnold! He tried to make it do these things but it just stared at him looking annoyed. It wouldn't walk either; it just stood still until the owner dragged it along. I thought; *"Why didn't you just get a dog!"*

The next day we saw an old guy with a long walking stick walking backwards for the twenty plus miles between two towns. Harry shouted:

"Why are you walking backwards?"
"Something different," he replied, and left it at that…

We cycled through some spectacular rock formations in the remote desert then I saw a bit of twisted metal on the roadside. It was an Arizona number plate. I picked it up with the plan to attach it to my bike at some point. American plates are much more interesting than our British ones. It had a desert landscape on the bottom with a sunset and the slogan *'The Grand Canyon State'*. Soon after that, I found a California one and decided that I would start collecting them, despite the fact that they were fairly heavy.

Arizona left us with another shooting star display as we camped out in the desert eating steak with pesto pasta. The state had been great, with stunning scenery, fantastic cycling, and some crazy but, more importantly, very friendly people.

28. Billy the Kid and aliens

Whoever invented the bicycle deserves the thanks of humanity
- Lord Charles Beresford

New Mexico greeted us with a long climb into the Rocky Mountains. We rewarded ourselves at the top with a massive burger followed by the biggest brownie I have ever seen at another diner. The waitress didn't think we'd eat it, but we proved her wrong. A couple of guys at a petrol station were really interested in our trip, so we chatted to them for a while. The conversation turned to the Afghan war and America's military. They assured us that if it wasn't for America, we would be speaking German. They were very nice guys, if a little too patriotic!

We continued climbing through the Rocky Mountains and reached Pie Town, a little village in the middle of nowhere. We were told about The Toaster House, a great place owned by a lady called Nita. She had recently moved out of the village to a nearby town, but has left her house open for passing travellers; what a nice thing to do! She had left many of her possessions in there, including a sound system with a great music collection. The house is kept well stocked with food and bathroom stuff, so we gratefully tucked into some pasta and had showers. We lit a fire in the wood burning stove and listened to Bruce Springsteen, the Eagles and Pink Floyd while we drank a bottle of wine. It was a great spot and it once again demonstrated the kindness of strangers, which is alive and well all over the world. I definitely wouldn't have got this far without it. Every time I listen to *'Take it Easy'* by The Eagles now, memories of Arizona and New Mexico come flooding back; it will always be a special song for me.

We left the Toaster House after leaving a donation in the donation box and writing in the guest book. Back on the road, we were helped by another strong tailwind as we passed through the remote New Mexico desert. We saw the 'Trinity Site', where the first nuclear bomb was tested in July 1945. Three weeks later, the USA dropped the atom bomb 'Little Boy' on Hiroshima...

A bit further down the road was the 'Very Large Array' radio telescope observatory. It has an array of twenty-seven giant satellite dishes, which work together to look into the depths of the universe. We descended to Socorro during a beautiful sunset and headed to a supermarket to get some food. We had bought some and were about to start eating it at a table in the supermarket, when a lady called Kate Burleigh approached us. She said that she had seen our bikes outside, and asked us if we were hungry and needed a place to stay. We said that we were hungry and that we would love to stay, so she went back around the supermarket to double the amount of food she'd bought. We had a lovely evening with the family. The eldest daughter, Erika, had just been cycle touring herself, along the Pacific Coast, so we shared stories. The father, David, told us the history of New Mexico; this part of it used to be Mexican, and then was owned by Texas when Texas was an independent country. Texas gave New Mexico to the USA and it became a state. I was asked to show the family where I had been on their globe and David was delighted that I could use a globe to point out the route of a bike ride that I had been on!

After Kate fed us syrup pancakes for breakfast, Erika guided us out of the town. We started climbing over the final mountain range of the trip. As I climbed, I thought about our latest wonderful hosts. The Burleighs were a lovely family; bright, sociable and very kind. They didn't have a TV, so maybe this made them more outgoing? Not one of the Burleighs was in the slightest bit surprised by having two strangers sleeping in their living room. Wouldn't the world be better if everybody had this attitude? I vowed that when I returned home I would try to behave in this manner. Kate Burleigh had said that we may find them strange, being the only family in America without a TV. I respected this massively and thought about how strange it was that the same society can create such vastly different groups of people...

New Mexico continued in this friendly way. It is a very sparsely populated state, but the people there were the friendliest that we met in America. The mountains were very remote and we cycled long stretches without passing a shop. We had to carry more water than normal, but I was used to cycling through remote areas by this stage. I wasn't worried about surviving in remote places any longer. America wasn't difficult compared to Kazakhstan. I was enjoying myself, felt completely at ease and was beginning to think about returning home. At that stage, there was no doubt in my mind that I would make it. I was ready to go home, and would be back in around a month but would concentrate on enjoying my last few weeks of this amazing freedom though. *How would I cope in a nine to five job on the other side?*

The next day we tackled the last big climb of the trip. It was a memorable moment and I was emotional as I passed the final summit. Climbing large mountains on a bike is a unique experience. I thought about all the climbs that I had completed; Wales, the Black Forest, Bulgaria, Turkey, Georgia, the Pamirs, the Tian-Sian, the Tibetan Plateau, Yosemite, Death Valley and now the Rocky Mountains. The mountains seemed to divide the ride in my mind. They were enormous physical barriers that split the ride into sections. They were the most spectacular parts of my trip and I had enjoyed being in the mountains the most. There is something so pure and simple about a man on a bike verses a mountain pass. The feeling of achievement while whizzing down the other side of a long climb is a feeling that is incomparable to anything else in the world. I can see how people get addicted to climbing cols in the Alps.

With all these thoughts in my head, we descended to Lincoln and saw the courthouse where Billy the Kid had been captured, imprisoned, and then escaped after killing a group of policemen. There is a hole in the wall still, where his shotgun shell hit when he fired it inside the courthouse. He was later caught and shot by a policeman in nearby Fort Summer.

We made great progress that evening and reached Roswell, a city famous for the supposed crash landing of a UFO just after the Second World War. As we entered Roswell, we noticed people giving out free pizza so went to get some. They turned out to be the Salvation Army and kindly offered to put us up in a motel for the night. We had

Every Inch of the Way

to go to the police station to get their permission first though. Sergeant Sharpe, a striking looking guy with a big knife scar down his cheek, very aggressively interviewed us. We explained that we were short of cash and had been offered a room for the night. He was messing around with us though and eventually broke into a smile and gave us the bit of paper we needed for a free night in the motel. I think he respected our cheek for asking in the first place! On the way to the motel, we went to a pub to try and meet Alien fanatics. We cycled along the high street, which had glowing alien heads instead of street lights. Unfortunately we didn't find anyone who *'believed'* in the bar, but were advised to go to the UFO Museum the next day. Apparently we definitely would meet believers there.

So on the way out of Roswell we popped into the UFO museum. It was quite expensive to visit, so we went to the free library instead. It was full of documents 'proving' the existence of aliens. The librarian was a 'believer'. She told us five different types of alien had been seen in Roswell, all with different skin colours; one had lived in Roswell after crash landing a UFO in 1947 and the government covered the whole thing up. They can apparently communicate through telepathy with humans. *Maybe Josep, the Croatian I met near Trabzon in Turkey, would be able to explain this better.* It was so strange to see someone believing in something so far-fetched. Something odd did happen in Roswell in 1947, but most people think that a US Army weather balloon was being tested and crash-landed there. Lots of new technology was being tested after the Second World War.

One day's ride across the desert after Roswell took us to Texas. It was a fairly uneventful stretch apart from the cowboys. We saw a group of them training for a rodeo, lassoing cows and galloping around an enclosure. It was seriously impressive. They galloped after a young bull at full speed whilst spinning the lasso over their heads before finally throwing it over the bull's horns and catching it, then dragging the bull into a pen. They let us watch them for a while. New Mexico had been great, but next up was the largest state in Continental USA; Texas.

29. Thanksgiving, guns and McDonalds

Travel is glamorous only in retrospect
- Paul Theroux

The first thing I noticed about Texas was that there were oil pumps everywhere. The air even smelled of oil. This state is rich because of its oil reserves, and a lot of Texans have jobs in the industry. It is no wonder that petrol is so cheap and that they all drive big trucks; it keeps their economy rolling. The first town of note in Texas was called Plains; a suitable name! We went to a small supermarket to buy dinner. An old lady approached us and asked us what we were doing. She invited us to the Thanksgiving church service and the after service meal that evening. We were both very keen to experience a Texan church service and keener to eat some Thanksgiving food, so we accepted straight away. The very kind and friendly lady, Estelle, was married to a really gentle and kind guy called Everett. We met their son Michael and his family.

Michael was a very friendly and talkative guy, but unique. He and his wife had renounced their US citizenship and didn't use money. They believed that Western society is bad; that people are becoming far too reliant on imports, and can no longer look after themselves. They were trying to become self-sufficient on their small farm and believed that sooner or later there will be a war that ends society as we know it. When this happens they wanted to be prepared, so while that didn't mean they couldn't use modern technology, they tried to not rely on it. It is an interesting idea, and while I definitely think people in the West are becoming too reliant on technology and on other people, I'm not sure how the family will benefit by removing themselves from it. The kids, for example, are home-schooled and have almost no interaction with other children. Interestingly, although devout Christians, they follow the laws of the Torah, for example circumcision and not eating pork.

Estelle's husband Everett was very knowledgeable on American history and told us about Texas, the civil war and slavery. He was a strong Republican and had some very sensible arguments supporting George Bush and against Obama, and although I didn't agree with them I could see his point of view. He also told us about the current drought in Texas, which was ruining farmers' crops and had resulted in many animals being shot because there wasn't enough food for them. He and Estelle were great hosts and we really enjoyed our night there. The church service was pretty standard and similar to British churches. I was a bit disappointed because I wanted to see a rocking Evangelical church. After the service, the Thanksgiving buffet-style meal was excellent and we ate about ten courses each. As we sat down to eat, we met lots of people from the parish. One guy had a gun and carried it with him wherever he went. We were at a church event and he felt he needed protection. We asked him if he'd ever used it.

"Only on wild dogs, it is fun chasing them in the pick-up and shooting them dead," he replied with dead-pan face....

Rain! The next morning we experienced the first rainfall for three months in Texas. The family were delighted, as was the rest of the state. We weren't, and couldn't help being a little bit annoyed by the rain's timing. As we left, Michael gave us a letter to read later on that day, saying it contained some thoughts and advice for us. We cycled through the plains to Brownfield, where we got out of the cold and the rain in a Mexican restaurant. It was really cheap and the fajitas were delicious. Dave, the friendly waiter gave us unlimited hot drinks and dessert on the house. He also told us that he would be in Austin at the weekend. And if we were there then, we should meet up.

We read Michael's letter. It was very odd and contained a lot of animosity towards US society, including the phrase *"I hate the world's money"*. Also it told me that he and his friend Dallas had been praying and had detected *pain and suffering* in my heart. I was a bit shocked at this and very confused because I was very happy. Harry was told that Michael appreciated his honest faith in Jesus and urged him to continue on his journey. I wondered whether my lack of faith had caused him to write this but was very glad we had met him. He was a unique, very kind, but in my opinion, misled. I emailed Michael regarding the letter and asked him what he meant, but never got a reply.

With a lot to think about, we cycled on through the never-ending desert. The cycling was boring, and the only thing of note that happened was being chased by some large dogs guarding a house. I picked up some stones and threw them at the dogs. The owner sped past in his pick-up truck, swearing at me. I shouted that they were trying to bite us; he said we better move on before he started throwing rocks at us! An afternoon of very average riding brought us to the town of Samesa, where we looked for a place to stay. We met a guy called Arthur, who phoned his church. They offered to put us up in a motel, which was really kind. I told the pastor we only needed a place to pitch the tents. He said he loved what we were doing and wanted to give us a comfortable night out of the wet and cold. It was great to have some privacy and to have a night of completely worry-free sleep. Wild-camping is great, but can never be one-hundred percent free from concern.

In the morning, we headed over the road to a burrito café where Arthur had told us that he would buy us a couple of burritos for breakfast. The people in Texas had been amazingly generous so far. We cycled on and arrived at Big Springs, a thoroughly average place full of fast food restaurants. As a farmer, Harry was very interested by the irrigation systems used for the giant fields of crops in Texas. They have so much land that the shape of the fields doesn't matter. The irrigation systems are on long arms, with water sprayers along their length. They rotate around a central point, irrigating huge circles of land on which the crops are grown. All afternoon, we passed though pleasant farmland full of deer, and that night we asked permission to camp on a ranch. It was massive and, judging by the owner's house, they were doing very well.

After a slow start the next day, we cycled eighteen miles to Sterling City. There were so many pick-up trucks. A lot of drivers in Texas genuinely don't believe that bikes should be allowed on the road. As a result we got a few honks and shouts and a lot of trucks passed very close to us at full speed, in a bid to put us off. There was a huge number of dead deer on the road too. Every hundred metres or so, we came across the carcass of a deer that had met a nasty end to its days. This reminded me constantly that the road was not a safe place to be and I was extra-cautious. It was not much fun on the Texan main roads, so we decided to take a scenic route via Austin since we had heard it is a cool place and we could meet up with Dave from the Mexican restaurant there.

Advertising some Americans' lack of geographical awareness, a man who I asking where a good place to eat was, told me to go to Sterling City. I pointed out that was where we were, there was a big sign saying so behind us! We had an utterly appalling burger at Dairy Queen, and then spent the afternoon cycling to San Angelo and playing twenty questions to pass the time, the cycling was so boring. I got a puncture from some more wire that had come out of an exploded lorry tyre. We went to a supermarket for dinner, then left the town shouting Alan Partridge quotes. Texas was very monotonous by this stage and I was definitely going slightly mad!

The next day was Thanksgiving Day. We made signs out of cardboard and attached them to the back of our bikes. Mine said, *'Happy Thanksgiving'*; Harry's said, *'Got any spare turkey'*. The morning was uneventful, but we got a fair distance under our wheels and a lot of appreciative waves for our signs from the passing traffic. We arrived at the town of Eden around midday and were invited to a motel for lunch. The lovely family who owns it put on a huge thanksgiving lunch each year for anyone who wants to turn up and has nowhere else to go. We were welcomed in and ate turkey with about twenty other people. A girl who'd been on American Idol sang, and we were educated in the rules of American Football. The mother owned a caravan in the next town, about thirty miles away, so we cycled there in the afternoon and stayed that night in the caravan. En-route, our signs worked! We were handed a bag full of leftover turkey and gravy that we ate as a snack, to fuel us through the afternoon.

Finally, the following afternoon Texas delivered some pretty countryside in the form of hills and woods. We enjoyed the riding for the first time in a few days, despite the headwind. It was great to be enjoying the cycling again and the time began to pass quickly again. At a town, we got talking to a Jehovah's Witness family outside McDonalds, who forced twenty dollars into our pockets (again, despite our protests) to *'buy a good meal'*. Situations like this were difficult because we didn't desperately need the money and felt bad taking it, although it definitely helped us. It was also rude to turn the offers down, so in general, I accepted almost every offer of help that I was offered on the trip. I want to make it clear how grateful I am for all the help, and to make sure that I come across as thankful to everybody who supported myself, Nino, Paul, Phil and Harry, from this family in Texas to the villagers who gave us melons in Uzbekistan and in China.

That night we found our good meal. In fact, it was the best meal I had on the entire trip. We had been recommended a pit barbecue called Coopers in the town of Llano. We found it, and enjoyed gigantic pork chops, barbecued jacket potatoes and salads. The tables were long and communal so we sat next to locals and got talking to them. A family next to us had been hunting that day; the favourite pastime of the locals in the area. They pay money to a landowner then are allowed to hunt deer. They are taught as kids how to track and shoot the animals and to prepare and cook the meat. The father used a bow and arrow to shoot, which I imagine takes a lot of skill. I think this is a great thing to do. The state has laws limiting the number of animals allowed to be hunted so the deer population is maintained and the hunters can take any animals they shoot home to eat. We talked about our trip and another twenty dollars was donated to our food fund. As we left, we were given a massive steak each by the smiling chef; *'for the road'*. It might not have been the most exciting state, but the people were so kind.

That night, we slept in a tunnel under the road again. Unfortunately, at about eleven o'clock it started raining very heavily. The tunnel started filling up fast and everything was in danger of getting soaked. We rushed out, pitched our tents, and moved everything into them. The only casualty was a corner of my sleeping bag, which fell into a puddle. This was annoying, but on the whole not bad considering the interior of the tunnel now resembled a lake. It was great being in the tent with the thunder and lightning outside. I was warm, and I felt safe in the tent that had been my home for nearly nine months.

The next day, we cycled into Austin. Dave contacted us and told us where he was staying; the *Doubletree Hotel* in the north of the city. We cycled in from the south, so saw a lot of Austin. It looked like a nice place, with a large river flowing through the city centre and interesting modern buildings. When we finally arrived at the hotel it turned out to be a Hilton! Dave let us stay in his room, which had a spare double bed. We pushed our dirty bikes through the sparkling reception and, amazingly, were allowed to take them up into the room. We had a quick wash and found the most respectable of our clothes, half of which were damp after the thunder storm the previous night and headed out into Austin with Dave and a group of his friends and visited a few bars on the famous Sixth Street. It was a good night and great to get off the bikes for an evening. It turned out that Dave was a very successful bank manager and, as a result, had plenty of spare cash, which he was delighted to spend on booze for the group.

The less said about the next couple of days, the better. It was incredibly boring cycling around the outskirts of Houston, the third biggest US city. I think we must have seen over one hundred McDonalds in one continuous shopping centre. There was a drive-thru or drive-in for everything: restaurants, banks, pharmacies, churches, cinemas, liquor stores, post offices and even a place which sold alcoholic drinks. I just don't understand where evolution decided that it would be a good idea to be so lazy that getting out of your car was an inconvenience. You can even get married in a drive-thru wedding chapel in Vegas. It means that life can be conducted with almost no contact with other people. I compared it to the close village societies in Tajikistan, where the elders of the village are respected by everyone and all the people know each other. I know where I would rather live.

We were so bored that we tried to work out how much packaging McDonalds gets through in Houston. We guessed there were about 500 restaurants in the city area. Most are open for twenty-four hours and probably average at least thirty people being served a meal every hour so that's 360,000 per day in Houston. If an average meal has packaging that weighs around one hundred grams, that's thirty-six tons of rubbish per day and 13,140 tonnes per year. Very approximate and probably incorrect mental arithmetic, but very wasteful in any case! I should point out at this point that this isn't just a criticism of the USA; many other developed nations are very wasteful too. This was just the time that it seemed most obvious to me.

The gas-guzzling trucks were more present than ever and then I saw the worst thing of the entire trip: a church flashing the following message in LED lights on a sign outside:

"Christ has risen
Christ is the Son of God
Therefore Islam is false"

There was a mosque down the road; I wondered what they thought of that sign. I never experienced any animosity towards Christianity in Asia, but here in America a house of god is flashing that message past millions of commuters every day. This made me so angry that I wrote an email to the church asking for an explanation, with no reply yet. I'm not holding my breath. I was becoming disillusioned with American society but reminded myself how important the good memories from this country and the wonderful people I had met were to me and my overall journey. The majority of my time so far in America had been brilliant but unfortunately a small minority of people can misinterpret religious or political leadership.

The final night in Texas restored my faith in America. We were invited into a young guy's house who was barbecuing a deer that he and his mates had shot with a bow earlier that day. It tasted delicious. We had venison steaks wrapped in bacon, hunks of meat stuffed with cheese, and no part of the animal was wasted. We talked to the hunting group about stalking deer and whether they preferred shooting with a bow or a rifle; opinion was divided. There were a lot of weapons around but I have no problem with people owning guns for hunting animals; it is only when they own them for 'self-defence' that I don't think that it is justified.

One more day's ride brought us into the swamps near the Gulf of Mexico and finally the Louisiana State border. We cheered as we left Texas! It wasn't the most exciting part of the ride, but was very important to have experienced. The main positive to take from Texas was the Texans, who were almost all very kind and friendly people.

30. 'Gators and paranoid police

It is good to have an end to journey toward; but it is the journey that matters, in the end.
- Ursula K. LeGuin

Finally out of Texas, the first thing to notice about Louisiana was the mosquitoes. Every time we stopped, a swarm appeared around us and started biting us. We crossed into Louisiana on the interstate and then followed a country lane, *'Old Road 90'*, through the swamps. The swamps were thick with undergrowth and had a thick canopy so were dark at ground level, where giant storks nested in the murky pools on giant straw nests on islands in the water. At an information office, we acquired a couple of maps which would guide us to New Orleans. We cycled late into the evening because we needed to get some big days in, in order to make it to the end of America in time for our flight home. We had to average about seventy miles per day and the headwind was making things difficult.

We illegally crossed a motorway bridge to avoid a long detour around Lake Charles. It had a lane closed for road-works, which was safe to ride on, so we made a break for it, hoping not to be spotted. We reached the top of the huge bridge and descended the other side into the city of Lake Charles, an intimidating place with some nasty-looking neighbourhoods that we cycled through as fast as possible. On the search for some good food, we found a Cajun restaurant and ordered gumbo, which is a delicious spicy stew served with rice. The people in the restaurant couldn't believe what we had done and how far we had come, so we got extra big portions. *"Damn, that's far! You guys must be hungry, you gonna need some more food!"*. I didn't mention that I had also cycled across Europe and Asia.

That night, we asked a couple of dog walkers for a place to stay and they gave us their workshop in the garden to sleep in for the night. The relative comfort and shelter meant that it took us a while to get going the next morning. We were both getting tired, and trying to get big miles in every day was taking it out of us. We hadn't had a day off for ages and it felt like we were just fighting to the end without having any time to relax. I was enjoying the physical challenge and we had the motivation of Christmas to keep us going; if everything went to plan, we would be back in time. The fatigue was making me irritable though and I probably wasn't great company. Harry was also very tired and he needed a good night's sleep. Unfortunately, in situations like this it is difficult to be in a team. We were both knackered and wanted a day off. I was pushing us because, having come so far, not finishing was not an option. I was getting us up early in the morning and pushing late into the evenings. It is hard, when you're tired, to get up and ride into a headwind all day. Maybe I was being selfish, but I think that we both knew that the miles had to be done.

As we crossed Louisiana, the riding got more exciting and we started joking around again and enjoying ourselves. We cycled along a small back road in Cajun country which was beautiful; very flat, and with historic towns and peaceful countryside. Many people spoke Cajun French and the whole area had a unique feel to it. It was much more interesting than Texas and had a lovely atmosphere. Children played in the gardens as we rode through quiet villages. At lunchtime, a friendly restaurant owner gave us alligator meat to try. It was delicious, tasting a bit like chicken with the texture of fish.

We reached Franklin that evening, keeping to our difficult schedule well. We camped in an RV park for free because the owners weren't around to pay. A drunk guy called David who lived there 'helped' Harry to pitch his tent. It reminded me of the time the Muslim boys had 'helped' Phil put up his when we were camping in the forest just off the motorway in China. It seemed like an age ago. David was a nice guy and very lonely, so we talked to him for a while as we cooked. I felt very sorry for him; he had tried to make his way in life but had hit a dead-end and he knew it. I think he had a good evening telling us his story though.

The headwind was still blowing the next morning so we were destined for another struggle. Most of the day was spent on the US 90 dual carriageway. It mainly passed through swamps again, but we had a great day. We saw a group of alligators sunning themselves on a rock and then swimming through a swamp. In the same pool there was a large turtle, seemingly unaware of the alligator's presence. The scenery was unique and there was always something to look at. In another repeat of China, we found a good place to camp around the back of a petrol station near a wood. The cashier in the petrol station said we were welcome to camp there but seriously asked:

"Aint you afraid of the possums?"

The next morning we set off for New Orleans on the US 90. The heavens opened and we got absolutely soaked within a couple of minutes. A few minutes later we were dry again thanks to the powerful sun. We arrived at a bridge that led into the city to be told we couldn't ride over it by a policeman. It was monitored both ends so there was really no way around it. The other option was to take a ferry across the river further east. We reasoned that getting a lift over a bridge was no different from taking a ferry and that this wasn't cheating as long as we cycled from the other end of the bridge.

We cycled to the traffic lights at the southern end of the bridge and asked a guy, who looked like a gangster rapper, if we could throw the bikes in the back of the truck and get a lift over. He said:

"Yeah, cool man. Get in!"

We put the bikes in the back of the truck, standing there as we lifted them up. The lights changed, he revved the engine and shot off with us standing up in the back of the truck... *nutter!* We lay down, trying to hide from the police as he drove very fast over the bridge. He stopped at the lights on the other side and we jumped out, thanking him. It was very funny but scary! I hadn't expected to have to lie in the back of the truck, and thought he was planning to give us a ride in the cabin *'up front'!*

Every Inch of the Way

The best way into the city centre was on the bike track along the top of the storm levees that protect New Orleans from storm surges. The huge pumping stations along the levees show the engineering effort it takes to protect the city from flooding. We asked which defences had failed when Hurricane Katrina flooded the city. Apparently it had been the flood protection system in the north, where there is a sea lake. The water came around the back of the city's main defences. The levees we were cycling on had not failed. The bike track took us into the French Quarter and we had a drink at a Parisian style café on the side of the main street. It is a beautiful city, with a very chilled out atmosphere.

We cycled north through the city to Louis' house, a guy we met through www.warmshowers.com. It is a very useful website where cycle tourists offer each other free accommodation. I wished that I'd known about it earlier in the trip. As we rode through the north of New Orleans, I didn't notice any effects of the hurricane, except for the damaged road surfaces. Some neighbourhoods didn't look very welcoming though so we passed through them particularly quickly. We met Louis, had a beer and some excellent homemade pizzas, and then drove around the city in his vintage BMW. He showed us the neighbourhoods that hadn't been redeveloped since the hurricane. There were whole blocks with ruined and abandoned houses and some plots of land with no remnants of a house at all; they were simply washed away. Some neighbourhoods had been forgotten about, some had people living there still and some were being redeveloped with fantastic new eco-homes, which were architecturally very interesting.

In the evening, Louis took us to a bar with a live blues band, which is what New Orleans is famous for. They were very talented, and we enjoyed a few local beers before heading back to Louis'. As part of his job, Louis designates cycle lanes in New Orleans. We followed one of them out of the city the next morning, over a series of bridges through the swamps. We passed houses on high stilts, which protect them from high water levels during the hurricane season. After a few hours of riding, we reached the state of Mississippi. Despite only being in Louisiana for a few days, I had really liked it and would love to go back. New Orleans is a fascinating place and well worth a visit. The local French-influenced Cajun food is delicious and the blues music is the beating heart of the place.

We arrived in Mississippi late in the day and it was almost dark. I had stupidly forgotten to charge my bike light up in New Orleans so I followed Harry's rear light along the side of the road, dodging potholes and bumps by trying to follow his line exactly. We entered a Wal Mart, ate a roast chicken on a bench in the entrance and had a chat with a complete nutcase who worked there and had obviously taken a few too many chemicals in his lifetime! He wasn't interested in talking to us about our trip but loved British rock bands, and so we chatted about Pink Floyd and David Bowie. He suggested we could camp around the back of Wal Mart where there was a grassy area. He bode us farewell, waving his infrared barcode reader saying:

"I've got Ziggy Stardust's ray-gun!"

The next morning Harry had a really bad migraine and couldn't cycle. The police turned up to try and move us on but let us stay when they saw what state he was in. We managed to pack up and cycle over to a nearby McDonalds at around one o'clock, where stayed there until about three. If there had been more time available, we would have taken the day off and found a hotel room where Harry could recover. Unfortunately, time wasn't on our side. We only had a week or so to get to the other side of Florida, so set off at three and managed almost forty miles that evening. Harry had done amazingly well to get the miles done after being so ill.

About thirty miles into our evening ride, we reached Biloxi, which is Mississippi's answer to Las Vegas. There were loads of massive floating casinos in the ocean. If they're offshore, they get around the Mississippi gambling laws and so are legal. They were huge, very impressive buildings, but not quite as ridiculously extravagant as the casinos in Las Vegas. We cycled straight past them and over a long bridge across an estuary to the town of Ocean Springs. At a small wood, we decided to set up camp and pitched our tents. Unfortunately, somebody had seen our torches and called the police. It was an abandoned bit of land so it was very strange that the police responded to a call about two torches in a wood. Anyway, they found us and were very suspicious. We saw that they were looking for us so we shouted out to them, to let them know we were there. They warned us to keep our hands where they could see them and made us tell them where our ID were in our bags because they didn't trust us to get them out ourselves. We were being treated like suspects to a crime; it was way over the top. Anyway, after they had run a criminal record check on our driving licenses, they started treating us like humans and let us stay in the wood, assuring us that if any crimes happened in the local area we would be prime suspects.

We had breakfast in a Burger King the next morning and the cheap syrup pancakes were actually pretty good. The manager looked up the ferry timetable for a boat that we needed to take later on that day. We headed out of Ocean Springs and stopped at a shop to pick up some food. A guy pulled up on a bicycle which had been converted to be driven by a petrol engine. It went about thirty miles per hour and did 150 miles to the gallon! He zoomed off, pedalling to begin with to turn the engine over and get it started. Once it had kicked in, he shot off, accelerating fast. It was an amazing machine.

As we were approaching the Alabama border, we found a huge scrap yard; a number plate goldmine. On various roads so far, I had found number plates for every state we'd been through except for Nevada. I had also found a Florida one so I only needed Mississippi, Alabama and Nevada to complete the collection. Harry asked the owner if we could have a couple but he told us that he wouldn't give us any. We took that as an invitation to help ourselves, so we left with a Mississippi and Alabama plate each, feeling guilty, but delighted to have acquired plates for two states. I was on the lookout for a Nevada plate for the rest of the trip.

We fled into Alabama with our stolen number plates. It was a beautiful state to pass through with coastal swampland and houses on stilts in the water. People were fishing in the swamp and we saw sea birds and lots of jumping fish, leaping out of the water. *It was so peaceful.* After a pizza, we cycled out into the sea along a series of long bridges linking a chain of islands. The last was Dauphin Island, a large bird sanctuary. We arrived there just in time to get the last ferry of the day over to Fort Morgan, on the other side of a river estuary. From the ferry, we watched a beautiful sunset over the island as we were piloted between the huge oil rigs in the estuary, lit up in the dark.

There was nowhere to buy food when we got off the ferry. We found ourselves on a long spit of land that sticks out across the estuary. After a few miles, we reached the only open place for miles around; an overpriced and tacky restaurant. I ordered the cheapest thing on the menu, which was a terrible cheese burger. We started chatting to the locals, and a lovely couple said that we could stay in their holiday home. They usually rent it out at this time of year, but luckily for us it was empty that night. We cycled ahead and they met us at the house, three miles down the road. It was a beautiful house; the guy who owned it had built it himself. It was on stilts for flood protection, and triangular shaped with a glass front and a giant homemade ship's steering wheel for decoration on the front of the house. There was a gigantic TV with surround sound and really comfy sofas. It was a bit different from what we were used to. The couple let us stay in their lovely house, full of expensive gadgets, with no idea of who we were other than what we had told them. *Yet another kind gesture from wonderful people.*

In the morning we got going at a good time. It was hard to drag ourselves away from the house but the clock was ticking. We emerged onto the Gulf Coast once more and, if possible, it was even more beautiful; with white sandy beaches, sea marshes, estuaries and wild windswept roads along peninsulas linked together by long bridges across the estuaries. We were fighting a headwind but made good progress, and by lunchtime had reached the border and entered the last state of our USA journey, Florida. *I was so close to the 'end of the World' now.*

31. The end of the road

The journey is the reward
- Chinese proverb

We spent that first afternoon in Florida riding along more beautiful white beaches on the Gulf of Mexico Coast. We had lunch on one of them then rode along a busy road to Pensacola and over a high and very windy bridge into a large nature reserve. We camped out on the sand of a perfect beach without the tents. During the night, a couple came down to the beach for half an hour or so. They sat down within about five metres of us and didn't notice us there. They were arguing about something then they ran off back to their car. We couldn't believe that they hadn't seen us.

In the morning we fought a headwind along the peninsula and sand was being blown across the road in drifts. The scenery was beautiful all day. The beaches turned into a forest full of deer and then lakes with more jumping fish. We passed non-descript Panama City, then crossed another bridge and saw a pod of dolphins. They were having a great time diving and jumping around. I could have watched them for hours. A long and boring straight road guided us to Port St Joe, where a storm was brewing. It started tipping it down when we got there. We sheltered in a Burger King; there wasn't much chance of finding anything other than a chain restaurant here unfortunately. Some American towns really have no character at all.

We asked around and purposefully looked miserable for over two hours but despite hinting heavily, nobody offered us a place to stay or suggested anywhere we might be able to camp. Resigned to getting soaked and having to carry on into the torrential rain to look for a wild camp site, we had a quick look around the town and found a hut leaning out over the sea. It was perfect; just a wooden platform with a roof but it was dry. I guess fishermen must use it during the daytime.

More beautiful coastline followed and nothing much happened until lunchtime the next day, when we walked out along a pier to eat. A woman stopped on the road and started shouting at us that it was private property, before driving off. I don't know if she owned it, but in any case there were no signs saying that it was private. After that, we cycled through a wood all afternoon and passed some beautiful rivers with yet more jumping fish. I stood there, trying to guess where they would leap out of the water next. We reached the small town of Sopchoppy in the middle of a wood and decided to camp there for the night. There was a free campsite at the town's park. The caretaker said that we were welcome to stay, but warned us that he had seen a bear there a week or two ago.

We ignored the warnings about the bear and cooked our dinner before pitching our tents. After we had eaten, I picked up our rubbish, and then carried it over to the bins. I was almost there when I saw the huge outline of an animal about five metres away. It was the bear and it was bloody massive! I retreated backwards slowly while watching it and threw the rubbish away, hoping that the bear would investigate the food supplies rather than me. It was the food it was after. When I got back to our tents I was buzzing and told Harry:

"I think I just saw a bear!"

We went back over with a bright bike light, had a good look at it, made loads of noise and it ran away and shot up a tree. It was so impressive to see something that big move so quickly. It went flying up the tree and stood on the large branches about half way up. We retreated backwards and made more noise, and then it came down and ran off to the back of the campsite. It was skulking around there later on but eventually it went away. We went back to the tents and tried to sleep. I didn't sleep well at all and thought that every noise outside was the bear coming back to attack us.

The next morning we had a great breakfast and discussed the bear. I thought that we had missed our chance to see one but was really glad we had done; seeing a bear was something that I really wanted to experience in America. We left Sopchoppy, and that day was spent cycling along a pleasant road in thick pine forest plantations. In the evening we met a homeless guy who was living on his bike. He had attached a cart to the back of it, in which he kept all of his possessions. He seemed happy and told us he just wandered around the countryside. It sounded like a comparatively pleasant existence for a homeless person. We warned him about the bear and to keep his food away from where he slept that night. Later that day, we saw a ridiculous pick-up truck that had been raised about two metres on springs.

In a supermarket that evening, I finally ran out of money. I would have to survive on almost nothing for the next few days. We found a lovely motel owner, who let us camp for free behind the building. They let us use their bathrooms and gave us five dollars to spend on dinner.

Our next friendly host was a guy called Rocky, who let us stay in his mobile home the next night. We walked the thirty metres or so from his door to the mobile home; Rocky drove the thirty metres in his Chevrolet Silverado Pick-up, opened the door for us then drove back to his house. He was a lovely, chatty guy, but it was unbelievable he had driven that distance. It took him more time than it had taken us to walk it. We had bacon butties for dinner.

Rocky came round at seven o'clock in the morning with two cooked breakfasts that he had bought from a petrol station. They were disgusting, but it was, again, a really nice thing to do. On the way out of the town, one of Rocky's employees gave us a battered Florida number plate to add to our collection. This was our penultimate day on the bikes. Nothing much happened, but my excitement at the thought of finishing was growing. I was really looking forward to seeing everyone at home again now, and it was nearly Christmas. We arrived at '*St John's Campground*' for the final evening on the road and I pitched my tent for the last time. We had a great dinner and a beer and talked about what to do next. It would be weird to be back in the real world, and I didn't know how quickly I would re-adjust to it.

We got up on the final morning, packed up quickly, and then got moving. We had arranged to meet a guy from *warmshowers.com*, Jerry Everetts, who had very kindly offered to put us up at his house for a couple of nights and then give us a lift to Orlando Airport. As we rode towards the Atlantic Ocean, we were approached by a journalist on the road. This was the first time that this had happened on the whole trip and it was the last day! She was really interested and told us that we would be in the Daytona Beach News Journal the following day. We cycled towards the coast all morning and I knew it was nearly over. The adventure was coming to an end. I was ready for the end but was also very emotional about finishing. I thought back to all the memories, good and bad, still not fully believing what I had done. In a sort of trance-like state, I climbed up the final bridge and could see the end of the world; Flagler Beach. From the top of the bridge we sprinted down the hill and cycled as fast as possible to the end of the road, which stopped at the beach; *my road had come to an end*. I cycled down onto the beach and ran out into the sea. My amazing bike had made it. It was a bit tired, the gears were skipping, the bottom bracket was wobbling all over the place, but on the whole it had been perfect.

It was a wonderful, emotional feeling to have made it, but also a bit of an anti-climax. I felt lost; what an earth would I do with myself next? The routine of waking up, eating, packing up, cycling seventy miles, searching for a place to sleep, setting up camp, eating, then sleeping had become my life. It was an easy way to live, a very simple life, and it had brought the most amazing experiences to me. I was sad that it was over. If I didn't have anything to go back to, I would have quite happily turned around and cycled on. *Would I go north to Canada or south to Mexico...?*

We still had a couple of days in Florida though and I wanted to make the most of them, so I stopped thinking about what would happen next. Harry and I put the bikes down on the beach and ran out into the sea. I put a piece of driftwood that I had picked up in San Francisco into the Atlantic Ocean. We took photos, and then went to a restaurant for a celebratory beer.

We managed to hitch a lift to Port Orange, where Jerry lived. We relaxed that afternoon, talked about American politics with Jerry and his wife Jenny, found some boxes to take the bikes home in and got an early night. The next day was great; Jerry took us shooting. We went with a group of Jerry's mates and fired a wide variety of guns: pistols, including a magnum which had a ridiculous recoil, a few .22 rifles, an assault rifle, a horrible little sawn-off shotgun which could have blasted a hole through a wall, and last of all a very valuable eighteenth century British rifle. It was great fun, but a little disconcerting to see a group of men whooping and cheering as they fired entire magazines from the pistols while drinking beer. We went to an absolutely rammed gun shop afterwards. People were buying ammo and there were some seriously horrible looking weapons in there. I definitely don't agree with the system where anybody from the street can go and buy a gun at any point. In my opinion, gun ownership is a massive problem in the USA.

On the way home, we went to a convenience store and bought the Daytona Beach Journal to read the report about us. It was rubbish and we had been completely misquoted, but it was good to be in the paper. As we were buying it, the following conversation took place:

"You guys have a great accent, where are you from?"

"England."

"I love England! So where did you learn to speak our language so well?"

...

We went back to Jerry's, got everything packed up for the flights, then watched a film. In the morning, Jerry very kindly drove us to Orlando Airport. We checked our bikes in; the American customs confiscated my stove because of a slight petrol odour, despite the fact that I had emptied it and cleaned it out. This really annoyed me; I had lost my round-the-world stove. However, I had made it round the world and completed my dream. We left America, and back in the UK my family and Nan greeted me at the airport. It was so great to see them. I said bye to Harry, was driven home to a waiting Laura, and that was that. The End!

....

Thank you to everyone who gave me support, to everyone who has so far sponsored my charity, SOS Children's Villages, and to everyone who sent me personal donations. Thanks to my amazing support team (Mum, Dad & Laura). A special thanks to Laura for waiting for me. She is now my wife and I couldn't be happier. Thanks to Harry and Phil for joining me and being such brilliant riding companions. Sorry for the times I was grumpy and made you cycle an extra ten miles at the end of the day.

Finally, and most of all, thank you to all the incredible people who helped me around the world. The farmers in Eastern Europe, the Orthodox Christians in Georgia, the Muslims in Tajikistan, the Tibetans in China and the Republicans in Texas, as well as all the other wonderful people who I met on the way. I had spent nights in people's houses all over the world, slept in Yurts, camped with nomads, eaten delicious food ranging from Tibetan stew to alligator meat, drunk homemade Georgian wine, been given clothes, got drunk with Kazakhs on the Caspian Sea ferry, seen photos of USSR soldiers in front of statues of Lenin, seen Stalin's house, cycled through massive hot deserts and over huge mountains, been treated for free by a Pamiri doctor, cycled with local people and old friends. Everyone who had helped me along the way made this trip possible. This is the end of my story, but I'll leave you with some final thoughts in the last chapter: "Lessons from my Adventure".

Lessons from my adventure

There is nothing like returning to a place that remains unchanged to find the ways in which you yourself have altered.
- Nelson Mandela

1. The world is good

All we ever hear about is how messed up the world is. We hear about suicide bombings, wars and disasters every day. What we don't hear about is how great the world is. How it's full of varied, beautiful and kind people. The world is a wonderful place and kindness is everywhere. Good people are much, much more common than bad people. If you put your trust in people, they will respond with kindness. Worrying about being harmed by people is harming our society.

2. Don't believe the press

Newspapers are full of rubbish! If you believe what you're told in the papers, everyone in places like Iran hate the West. It is absolutely ridiculous to say this. Everyone I met in Muslim countries were amazing and, having spoken to Iranians and Pakistanis and experienced the kindness of Muslim families, I can say for sure that 99.9% of them don't hate the West. They have similar problems with their press telling lies about Europe and America. For some reason, governments and newspapers seem to want to stir up tension and cause problems. It would be much better if everyone was allowed to get on!

3. Get out into the world

Too many people never experience nature. I am not saying go and cycle round the world, I am saying go into the countryside. Instead of watching the Coronation Street omnibus next Sunday, go on a walk or a bike ride. If you can afford it, travel. The world is amazing whether you're in Istanbul, the Pamir Mountains or the Peak District. Too many people don't experience it.

4. Society is important

In the West we have a great deal more money and personal possessions than most people in Asia. However, we have less socially. Supermarkets, online shopping, ease of getting what we need and improved technology have evolved to the point where we can quite happily survive with almost no interaction with other people. This isn't a good state of affairs! Becoming cleverer is de-evolving us. I don't have a solution to this...

5. You can achieve amazing things if you want to

I'm nothing special, just a nutter who loves cycling and had the guts to set myself a big challenge and leave to pursue it. Next time you think *"I can't do that"*, question yourself and try.

Photographs of America

Camping in Henry Cowell State Park with Laura

Alcatraz Island

Leaving San Francisco with Harry (left)

Yosemite National Park

It was a long way to the horizon in Death Valley

Vegas Baby!

208

The Bellagio Casino fountain show

The Hoover Dam

Route 66

The Grand Canyon

Stupid pick-up

Road legal

The Very Large Array observatory

Cowboys in New Mexico

Louisiana swamp

Gators

Sunset over Dauphin Island

The end of the road

A few interesting extras

1. A short reflection, 3 years on

So what was it like to return to normal life after spending most of a year of my life drifting around with infinite freedom?

It was difficult to adjust at first, and getting straight back into a normal life wasn't easy. I didn't last long in my first job back and resigned after six months, because I was not enjoying the work. Afterwards, I settled into a PhD at the University of Sheffield, which is much more stimulating. After the trip, it was great to move in with Laura, and this helped me return to normality. We're now married and I can say for certain that if my adventure has changed our relationship at all, it has only been in a positive way.

Looking back on the trip, it was the most valuable thing that I have ever done. The experiences I got from it and the lessons I learnt are invaluable, and I wouldn't change anything about it. I have changed slightly; I'm more restless and constantly need a "project". The latest challenges have been two Ironman triathlons and a bike tour through the Himalaya (photo book coming soon). I'm currently doing up an old tandem, which I have big plans for and building a fat bike (a go-anywhere off-road mountain bike with giant tyres). They will undoubtedly be more adventures in the future, but I doubt I will ever do anything of this magnitude again. The trip has changed me; but for the better. I have absolutely no regrets.

2. Statistics from the ride

- Total distance: 14,439 miles
- Total time: 280 days
- Number of countries visited: 20
- Longest day: 133 miles (UK)
- Shortest day: 7 miles (China)
- Longest climb: 156 miles (Wakhan Valley, Tajikistan)
- Longest descent: 78.8 miles (Kyrgyzstan)
- Living costs: £5 per day
- Average day: 68.7 miles (not including days off)
- Highest point: 4,655 m (Tajikistan)
- Lowest point: -150 m (China)
- Longest time without a shower: 18 days (Kazakhstan/Uzbekistan)
- Number of punctures: 36
- Longest time without paying for a hotel room: 41 days (USA)
- Heaviest total weight of bike and kit: 97 kg
- Hottest temperature: 45 °C (Uzbekistan and Krygyzstan)
- Coldest temperature: -10 °C (China)
- Calories required per day: 6,000 – 7,000

3.   Phil's 'Incident' in his own words...

Here is an email that Phil sent to his family from Pingyao, China, describing some of the last days of his trip. All I would say is that Phil has a unique writing style:

SUBJECT: China and the Deathly Hallows.

Hello there family,

Not sure when the last update was but we're in a hostel in some ancient town called Pingyao. It's quite nice but we were a bit tired from cycling so we wandered around a bit to eat and them came back to play pool.

Anyway the last few days from the Terracotta Army have been a bit of a blur for me. Yes I stared death in the face and it was diarrhoea shaped. We left Xi'an and some person gave me a kebab stick for free as they were too full to eat it so obviously I took it. It was spicy squid so I knew I'd be lucky to get away Scott free but I wasn't ready for that night....

We left the town fine and found somewhere quiet to camp a bit away from the road under a railway bridge in some bushes. That night I woke up with my guts in a twist feeling sick and went to find a suitable sick pole. Luckily I was in prime territory and was sick all down a telephone pole then to top it off my arse gave way and I dropped some yellow devastation all over the bridge support behind me (dump number three of that day!). It clocked up about a number two on the scale; very limited solids for those who don't know... and so the night continued... no this isn't just a story about me with D and V, those stories are ten a penny, this one has a clincher...

So eventually the sun came up after about six trips to my various poles. I was feeling like death so we decided to hole up for a while and probably write the day off. Then some guy walks over for no reason even though we were hidden and starts chatting and sees I'm ill. He goes away and comes back an hour later with two coppers. They obviously don't like us being there and kept 'trying to help us' by trying to move us on. We give in after a bit and as it's twelve o'clock and there isn't much left inside of me, I'd been spewing out clear water from my gob and pure yellow?? from my arse at that point so we decided to pack up. I'd gotten dressed and packed my bike up and knelt down to do my shoe up when I farted....

Instantly I knew I hadn't farted. I'd done much more than that... I jumped through the turtle head stage, passed the 'one is touching cloth stage' and straight into the 'Tom I've shit my pants' stage.

He said, "What literally?"

I said "I'm going to need some new nappy pants".

It was funny though so we cracked up and made all the funnier because the policeman was standing right behind me all this time. Tom threw me some boxers and off I went to clean myself up. Strolling back in my boxers and shoes with my literal nappy pants dangling in the breeze the policeman demanded our passports. So we got back on the road and I just about made it to the next town where I collapsed in the first hotel for the next 24 hours. Pretty messy but luckily there was a western toilet so I had the classic plastic bowl on my knees and was losing from both ends as they say. I couldn't even keep liquid down so that was a bit annoying.

Anyway the next morning we got back on the bikes and I had a few delirious days where luckily I can't really remember it. Managed a good sixty miles though on a few biscuits and sweets. Can't remember when that was now probably about five days ago, today I'm feeling pretty much back to normal. I almost had to have a day off and train it to catch up because I couldn't recover whilst riding so what should have been an easy ride to Beijing was probably the most horrific food poisoning I've ever had and then four days of riding on top. It's a bit further to the coast than we thought so we are going to have to do some bigger days to get there in time to see Beijing. Planning to get to the coast on the 14th then train to Beijing and a few days off before flying. I'm back on the 18th and Tom goes to San Francisco on the 17th. We're both ready to leave China though it's not the most relaxing place.

One time we asked to stay in a petrol station and they said yes because they all have meeting rooms here. Then the manager comes along just as I'm about to get into bed and says we can't stay. He was nice about it but very annoying, he said it was too dangerous even though the staff stays there overnight and they put a camp bed out for us so we had to pack everything up and cycle 10k down the road at night to a hotel which he did pay for in fairness but it's not what you want to do when you've brushed your teeth and in your PJ's and your recovering from a killer squid kebab. It's also a bit dull scenery at the end. We cycled through some coal power stations for a day. They were massive and everything was covered in coal dust. I still haven't gotten it out of my arms and we just looked like coal miners for about four days. I've never seen anything so messy or stinking and people live right near it. Retrospectively I can see that that was a bad day to wear a white T-shirt, I don't think it will ever be the same again.

When we stopped in a petrol station a few days ago this nice lady didn't speak much English but she managed a perfect, "you smell". Anyway so other than me pooing my pants not much has happened. It's Tom's birthday on the 11th but we've got to get cycling so hopefully we'll find some nice food to celebrate

4.   Crossing America – Harry's Story

It had been a standard summer on the farm, spending most of my time counting sheep and driving a tractor up and down, then up and down a field. If I wasn't doing that I was naturally catching up on the latest edition of Farmers Weekly, but if I wasn't doing that then I was catching up on Tom's epic adventure online and very much wishing that I could be part of it. Not that farming isn't totally captivating, but I decided it was an opportunity that couldn't be missed and booked some flights to San Francisco. Having seen him off from Cheshire six months earlier it was incredible to think that he had travelled all the way to China.

As I flew out I really had no idea what to expect. My research prior to leaving had consisted of three people telling me I was going to die if I tried to cross Death Valley, and a friend's dad asking if I was excited to be crossing the Sierra Nevada mountains, the night before I left. To which I responded, "Absolutely. Sorry, the sierra 'what' mountain range?" Then proceeding to drive home and pack an extra jumper into my pannier bags. Preparation or planning have never been distinguishing characteristics of mine, but luckily enthusiasm is, and I couldn't wait to get started.

I met Tom in San Francisco the next day and was glad to see he knew about the same amount as me about our intended route. We had a look at his map of the USA and I was relieved to see that it really didn't look that far, only about fifteen centimetres on the paper in fact. I wondered whether we should take a few detours and maybe go to New York on our way to Florida, but strangely Tom seemed to think he had a bit more experience at this cycling thing and thought we wouldn't have quite as much spare time as I did.

Fast forward three weeks to day nineteen of the trip and my journal reads; 'Removed my socks for the first time in six days this evening, have worn them day and night for a while. Certainly smelled like it too. Had one shower in the last eighteen days, though that doesn't include a wash in a river and one in a hot spring we found, so I can't complain.' I was writing this on one of the most glamorous nights of the trip, as we set up camp in the back of the pick-up truck we had hired to make a visit to the Grand Canyon. The evening had been a standard one, as we ate about one kilogram of pesto pasta each with some suspect looking bacon in it, whilst listening to an episode of Blackadder on my speakers, to finish off by lying back under an open sky, studying the vast array of stars on display. As my bike computer neared one thousand miles completed, it felt a million miles away from the life I had postponed in the UK.

We could quote most of any Blackadder episode by now, and had confused many an Arizonian by addressing each other as Ploppy or screaming "He's only got one arm!!" at the top of our voices as we descended a mountain pass (episode 3 series 2). It is these stupid moments that I remember as vividly as the stunning views along the road, and some of my favourite times were spent in the foyers of supermarkets as we both tucked into a ready cooked chicken and some cheesy puffs after a long day's riding, resembling a couple of homeless men. We'd strike up conversations with anyone who was willing, which being in America, was quite easy. Getting their head around why we had decided to cross their country by bicycle was harder at times. I remember one girl feeling very sorry for us and asking if there really was no other way we could get to Florida, and whether we would like her to do some research into trains for us. Cycling through Texas took people by surprise the most. We never had to worry about our bikes being stolen because no one would have known how to start them, or where to insert the gas.

If we return to the back of the Silverado pick-up truck, we were parked next to one of the seven natural wonders of the world, after arriving via several sites that would definitely challenge for a place on the list. California had been incredible, with everyday topping the one before. Yosemite was possibly my favourite part of the trip, and our campsite overlooking much of the park was stunning, with no one around for miles. It's amusing to look back at that night, as we spent about half an hour trying to hoist our food bag up into a tree to stop bears stealing it, only to realise about a month later that climbing trees is pretty much what bears are designed to do.

Tom had been plotting each campsite on the map of the USA that he was carrying, and after three weeks' riding we had still only made a small dent into the overall distance. While the riding was varied and scenic it was all fun and easy to motivate yourself, but the real tests for me came later when we hit the straight flat roads in Texas. I found cycling on the flat far harder than in the mountains, and with about three weeks of headwind from Texas to Florida it became as much a mental challenge as a physical one. Gone were any glamorous views or high speed descents, and your mind wandered to such interesting things as what you might eat for dinner, or maybe counting the outrageous number of dead deer on the roadside.

This is where Tom came in, and I can confidently say that without him I wouldn't have made it across America. He just keeps going no matter what and was unfazed by any obstacle. I have to thank him for his patience when I constantly wanted to take detours, and if he hadn't kept us pointing east and moving I would probably be still cycling somewhere in Alaska now. His determination to keep going when things got tough or boring was impressive and he must have needed it to make it across so many deserts and barren stretches on his own.

I would have loved to have been there for the other parts of Tom's trip, but I'm sure he's fairly thankful that I wasn't. I imagine he would have probably finally strangled me for wanting to light one fire too many or for yet again taking a horrendously long time to pack away my stuff in the morning.

Bike touring is such a free way to travel, and puts a lot of things in perspective. You soon lose any concern over your image (or smell) and only get on with the things that are important. Life is simple on a bike; any flat piece of land is an ideal place to camp and any flat piece of packaging rubbed clean with some grass is an ideal plate to eat off. My best plate that I used was probably my map of New Mexico for some particularly runny spaghetti Bolognese, with the only problem being that we were still in the centre of New Mexico, making navigation slightly harder beyond that point.

Every Inch of the Way

Our favourite campsites soon became the drainage tunnels below the larger roads, until one night our drainage tunnel performed its function beautifully and washed us out into the rain during a heavy storm. Luckily, the following night we were treated to a night in the Hilton and were able to dry all our stuff - thanks Dave! Another night I don't remember quite so well was the one when I took a midnight stroll over a bridge to go to the toilet and then found myself lying headfirst three metres below a few seconds later. I still have the scars to show it and don't know what happened. Maybe I was too excited about the prospect of taking on Sin City the next day. How was I to know that we would walk away so casually with a cool $6 dollars in our pocket? We were able to use it on the motel we stayed in, the only night of the trip that we paid for accommodation.

Las Vegas provided such a contrast to the unbelievable scenery that we had seen on the way. For all its glitz and glamour it only highlighted to me that when we try and create a paradise of our own we fall seriously short of the beauty that already exists within creation, and it was hard to see old ladies glued to the slot machines. Maybe it is because I have grown up in the countryside, but it was one of the only places that I didn't feel at home in when in America.

We soon found that if we were hoping to be invited in somewhere then we would have the most luck in the smallest towns, where people were much more open and there was far more of a community. It saddened me to see large slogans proclaiming, 'Jesus is Lord,' then look past them to see a house with a locked gate and guard dogs outside. Hardly practising what they preach. However, in every state we met countless friendly people who were willing to share their houses and time with us, challenging us to do the same when we returned.

As we neared the finish we must have looked fairly amusing. Tom's bike had developed some pretty funky noises as his bottom bracket was falling to pieces after 14,000 miles on the road, and my pannier rack was being held together by some bits of bamboo and cable ties. You really can fix anything with cable ties. I probably got more strange looks for my interesting attempt at a beard, which was as patchy as most American's geographical knowledge. One guy seriously asked us in a café if we were intending to cycle on to the UK once we reached Florida...

Another thing that seemed to attract attention was our impressive collection of license plates that we found en route. Despite trying to save every gram of weight elsewhere on our bikes, we ended up each carrying about five kilograms of license plates. Each one had a story to it and we refused to ditch them even if it meant missing our flight home for Christmas.

We managed to keep up enough pace, despite the extra weight, and two months after we started the East coast rolled into view. For me it was the end of an unbelievable trip, but I couldn't imagine how it felt for Tom after nine months on the road. I feel totally honoured to have been able to share a small part of his trip with him and catch his excitement for adventure and his desire to make the most out of any opportunity.

America is a country of contrasts. One day you are cycling along through a deserted swamp and the next you count fifteen McDonalds before nine o' clock in the morning. Other than a desire to avoid peanut butter for a while, I left Florida with several valuable lessons. One of these is never to leave burning toilet paper unsupervised in a forest after a wild poo. And on a more serious note, never under any circumstances ever walk a cat on a lead.

My last journal entry reads, 'We'll never make it!! We made it. Unbelievable scenes....going to sleep for about twelve hours then apparently go shoot some guns tomorrow. Only in America! Staying with a lovely couple called Jerry and Jenny, only problem is that they are... vegetarians! Anyone want to buy any lamb?'.

5. Kit list

1 amazing bike	1 pair of prescription sunglasses
5 panniers	1 pair of glasses
1 Vango helium tent	1 pair of cycling shoes
1 foam mat	1 pair of flip flops
1 sleeping bag	0 – 5 books
1 survival bag	4 diaries
1 toolkit	15 maps
2 pumps	1 radio
2 front lights	2 phones
3 rear lights	1 waterproof phone case
1 wind up torch	1 camera and 3 SD cards
1 spare tyre	1 Dazer dog deterrent
1 bag of spare disc brake parts	Some chargers and adapters
1 bag of spare gear cables	1 pocket knife
0 – 4 spare inner tubes	½ a fork
Loads of spare spokes	1 small spoon
Loads of puncture repair stuff	1 petrol stove
1 bag of spare nuts and bolts	2 saucepans
3 water bottles	1 frying pan
1 pair of boxers	1 wooden spoon
2 pairs of lycra shorts	1 first aid kit
2 pairs of cycling shorts	1 solar charger
3 T– shirts	Lots of spare batteries
1 fleece	1 Garmin Legend GPS
1 hoody (ditched in China)	1 Cateye Adventure speedo
1 pair of trousers	1 hipflask (full and then not)
1 pair of swimming shorts	1 set of earphones
1 set of thermals	1 real wallet
2 pairs of socks	1 fake wallet with old cards
1 pair of warm socks	1 passport
1 waterproof jacket	1 compass
1 pair of waterproof trousers	2 pens
1 knee support	Photos of people from home
1 buff	A helmet
1 hat	

6. The Bike

For any cycling geeks (like me) out there, here's Sandy's full setup:

- Frame: Sanderson Breath (kindly donated by Sanderson Bikes)
- Gearing: Rohloff internal gearhub (donated by Rohloff, thanks very much!)
- Front wheel: Hope Pro 2 Hub and Mavic 719 rim
- Rear wheel: Rohloff Speedhub and Rigida Andra 30 rim
- Brakes: Shimano SLX hydraulic disc
- Handlebar/Stem/Seatpost: Halfords Bikehut
- Cranks: Shimano Saint
- Pedals: Shimano Deore SPD
- Front Fork: Salsa CroMoto rigid fork
- Saddle: Specialized Body Geometry
- Rear Pannier Rack: Tubus Disco
- Front Pannier Rack: Tubus Smarti
- Tyres: Schwalbe Marathon Plus Tour

7. A note from the frame builder

Being of an age when all bicycle frames were made from steel, all of my bikes as a youngster were as such. The first I fell in love with though was hung in the window of my local shop in Tamworth. I drooled over it for several months before being drawn inside to find that it would cost the princely sum of £40. That Bob Jackson is still hung on the wall of my garage today.

Many years later I sat down with Steve Weir to design the first Sanderson frame. I knew what I wanted and Steve knew how to do it, so it seemed that we might be in with a chance of getting somewhere with the project.

Three months later and the first sample was built. I loved it so much that I must almost have worn a groove around the Wyre Forest. You can't describe the emotion of riding Mayhem, Brecon Beast, or whatever on a bike that is really your own.

Since then we have sold frames to riders in numerous countries all over the world. I never tire of hearing or reading their stories or seeing photographs of their bikes.

One day out of the blue Tom rang. He told me he was going to ride round the world on his own and wondered if we had a Sanderson frame that was either bumped or scratched as his budget was limited.

On a personal note, I hope that everyone who reads this book will be struck by the generosity shown to you during your journey, particularly by those with the least who would shelter and feed you so willingly.

Congratulations Tom, It made me proud to read in this book that you completed your epic journey riding Sandy, surely the ultimate road test.

-Tony Wilkinson (Sanderson)

Other books

Available from **www.tombrucecycling.com**:

Every Inch of the Way: ebook version. The same as this but an electronic copy.

Early 2015 – Biking to the roof of the world. My next big adventure was in the Indian Himalayas in October 2014 with Harry, during which we cycled over the highest road in the world. Photo book and ebook coming soon.

Late 2015 – Mini Cycling Adventures. A book of smaller adventures from the past couple of years, which will hopefully act as inspiration for more realistic and achievable trips for most adventure minded people. It will include trips in France, China, India, Scotland and many other places